THE CUSTODY AND COURTSHIP OF EXPERIENCE

To Rosemarie

Pádraig Hogan

The Custody and Courtship of Experience

WESTERN EDUCATION IN PHILOSOPHICAL PERSPECTIVE

the columba press

First edition, 1995, published by
the columba press
93 The Rise, Mount Merrion, Blackrock, Co Dublin

Cover by Bill Bolger
Origination by The Columba Press
Printed in Ireland by Colour Books, Dublin

ISBN 1 85607 153 7

Acknowledgements

I am deeply grateful to the following people, who have read all or portions of the text and offered valuable observations, insights and criticisms: John Coolahan, Michael Drumm, Joseph Dunne and Rosemarie Hogan. Earlier versions of the first four chapters were also discussed in seminars with graduate students on the M.Ed. course in the Maynooth College during the academic year 1994-95. I am also grateful to these students for their comments, questions and criticisms. I remain solely responsible however for the opinions expressed in the book.

An earlier, and somewhat different version of Chapter Five appeared in *Partnership and the Benefits of Learning: A Symposium on Philosophical Issues in Educational Policy*, which was published by the Educational Studies Association of Ireland (Maynooth: 1995)

Finally, I owe a special debt of gratitude to my wife Rosemarie, whose encouragement and support in so many ways ensured that this project was brought to completion in time for inclusion in the Maynooth Bicentenary Series.

Contents

Introduction

There are four main currents of argument advanced in this book. The first of these is that the traditions of learning which became the dominant ones in Western civilisation arose from a major cultural shift in Classical Greek conceptions of education: namely, the eclipse of a Socratic heritage, in its emergent stages, by the central doctrines of Platonism. The first current goes on to argue that the consequences of this eclipse became associated at a crucial time with a conception of learning as a custodianship of heart and mind, enforced by the spiritual and temporal authorities of Christendom. The second current of argument is that the demise of this custodial conception, occasioned by the Enlightenment and its legacy, made way not for a restoration of learning as a pursuit which was to enjoy sovereignty from now on, but for new and conflicting varieties of custodianship itself. Recognising the disparities and disabilities to which this has given rise in the educational discourse of our own day, the third current attempts to reclaim and elucidate insights of singular merit and promise which custodial conceptions of learning largely obscured from both historical memory and cultural tradition in Western civilisation. The unavoidable play of influence which attends teaching and learning is explored here as a courtship, as distinct from a custodianship, of experience. It is argued that this is a courtship which happens in any case, whether recognised or overlooked, whether in a dominating or emancipating way; in essence, a courtship of sensibility. The fourth current then explores how this reclaimed conception of learning – as a sovereign pursuit – fares against possible objections, from both radical and avant garde standpoints, and aims to show also that it provides a robust, coherent and defensible rationale for educational policy – its making and its implementation. An educational rationale with these three characteristics is especially important at a time when the conduct of education internationally is vulnerable in a recurrent way to the designs of powerful interests.

The book has three main divisions. Part One, which contains

four chapters, pursues the first two currents of argument – namely the eclipse of the Socratic in the Western heritage and the shortcomings of the Enlightenment – and concentrates on landmarks of particular significance in the historical review of Western educational traditions it undertakes. Part Two contains three chapters and these explore the key issues of the third current of argument, namely the reclamation and elucidation of what the custodial heritage eclipsed. Part Three, which also contains three chapters, carries out a similar task in relation to the fourth current of argument: the further elaboration and practical defence of an educational orientation which is not only rich in possibilities for teachers and learners but also for educational policy-making in our own day.

The achievements of numerous major figures in Western philosophy are encountered in pursuing these four currents, and to some readers (particularly those with a background in philosophy), it may seem that I take an unusual perspective on many of these achievements. For instance, it may be claimed that I tend to see Plato in a restricted light, that I am selective in my reading of Aristotle, that I focus more on shortcomings than on merits in Augustine or Aquinas. It is important from the start then to alert the reader to the kinds of expectations which the book sets out to meet, and those that it doesn't.

It would not be possible to undertake in a book of even twice this length an inclusive survey of what all the major thinkers of Western philosophy wrote on education. A survey of this kind is not the purpose of the book. Such a project would be mainly informative in purpose. Even then, however, it would still involve personal selection and judgement on its author's part. If such a project were to be a work containing a sustained line of argument however, further judgements would have to be made on what parts of the informative contents of the larger work were pertinent to the argument. That is to say, a work containing an argument or series of arguments would necessarily be shorter on information than one whose primary purpose was informative. But there is a more important feature which distinguishes a work of argument from one of information. This feature is the taking up of a basic standpoint, which seeks to give the argument its direction and force; for example, a Marxist, or a Christian, or a liberal-individualist, or a pragmatist, or a positivist standpoint. This standpoint might be overtly avowed or might remain largely implicit, but either way it would influence *whose* works would feature more prominently than others, *which* works of the selected authors would feature more prominently than others, and *how* the arguments identified for review would be handled.

Of course this would also give to the book in question the character of a *thesis*; that is, an argument or series of arguments which seeks to be insightful and coherent, consistent and convincing. The four currents of argument put forward in this book are, accordingly, four contributions to a larger thesis. This thesis has not been a familiar one in the history of Western philosophy, including Western philosophy of education, and this is why the 'philosophical perspective' of the book's sub-title might seem strange to some readers, particularly where the two currents of Part One are concerned. It should not, however, seem strange to those whose thoughts and outlooks are regularly occupied with practices of teaching and learning. If the taking up of an *educational* perspective requires philosophy to accomplish a lateral shift of thought, and to carry out its appraisals of some major figures from a different standpoint, then this should be counted as an advance for educational thought and an enrichment for philosophy.

But is there such a thing as an *educational* standpoint as such? The familiar wisdom which Western philosophy itself has popularised, and which I am keen to question in the following pages, would suggest that there is not: that any educational standpoint must take its purposes and orientations from some substantive doctrine, or ideology. Thus we commonly hear references to a 'Marxist educational ideology', or a 'Christian education system', or more recently, a 'market philosophy of education'. So deeply rooted are conceptions such as these in our outlooks that we can hardly fail to be taken by surprise, or even taken aback, by the suggestion that they are all variants of the same conception. Yet this is one of the main the suggestions I am keen to make and to defend. In each case here, education is prevailed upon to serve the interests and do the bidding of the currently ruling party. If the philosopher's surprise is the greatest of all at this suggestion, then this serves to show how deeply implicated philosophy has been in denying to education – to the actual conduct of teaching and learning – any effective integrity of purpose as a practice in its own right, i.e. as a practice entitled to certain rights which are inviolable, but also accountable.

Yet it is a conception of this latter kind which inspired the work of one of the most illustrious figures of Western education, namely, Socrates of Athens. The crucial thing to understand about the Socratic educational practice is that is was not so much about a method – even less about a doctrine – as about a unique kind of *con-*

viction. This conviction is the issue explored by the opening pages of the first chapter. Its distinctive characteristics, which are identified in these early pages, remain central for all the arguments that follow. The first chapter also notes what is perhaps the greatest irony of Western educational history. Plato, to whom we owe more than to anyone else for our understanding of Socrates, furnished Western learning with a conception of education which became so influential that it obscured what was *educationally* most essential in the example of Socrates. The chapter goes on to argue that this eclipse of the integrity of education was not identified as such, mainly because of the majestic scope and splendour of the metaphysics that Plato installed in its place. Aristotle's criticisms of Plato and his affinities with him are then considered, and the case is made that these contributions to Western thinking on education, despite their own singular merits, added further to the eclipse of the Socratic, as did the Romanising of this heritage through Cicero and Quintillian.

This is not to disparage the efforts of any of Plato's successors. Rather it is to see the wealth of insight in the observation by Alfred North Whitehead that Western philosophy is a series of footnotes to Plato. Nothing could be further from a dismissive remark. But if it could have been said instead that Western philosophy was a series of footnotes to Socrates, then the dominant traditions of Western education would look very different, and this book would be very differently conceived, if at all.

The second chapter examines the embrace of an ascetic Platonist metaphysics by some of the most influential figures in Christianity, particularly St Augustine. We see here moreover how this embrace was paralleled by Augustine's attraction to the more deeply pessimistic aspects of St Paul's theology. Platonism was content to regard its educational task as releasing human beings from an enslavement to the world of the senses; a release which trained the eye of the human soul to fix itself on the changeless, eternal Good of the world of spirit. For Augustine, not only did this concentration on the 'higher' world become a central theme. The world of the senses for him was not merely a form of bondage, but one in which human nature languished in a *depraved* state. Thus the chief features of the religion which became predominant in the shaping of Christendom was not so much the Christianity exemplified in the teachings and example of Jesus Christ, but rather an austere and Platonised Christianity. Some notable efforts to break apart this austerity by leading figures in Medieval learning are then considered, particularly those of Peter Abelard. The second chapter concludes with an appraisal of Thomas Aquinas' unprecedented achievements in the cause of learning, but notes also the closed character of his system of thought and the unhappy educational consequences of the long era of scholasticism which followed in his wake.

Erasmus' artful attacks on scholasticism introduce the third chapter. Acutely conscious of the fetters which the dominant traditions of learning imposed on the enquiring spirit, Erasmus playfully praised the 'folly' of learning and identified in such 'folly' a refinement of sensibility and of spirituality inspired by classical and Christian texts, and unmatched by anything in the existing traditions of learning. But Martin Luther's revolt, in which he sought to enlist the support of Erasmus, darkened again the dawn of a new age of humane scholarship. The consequences of the Reformation meant that ecclesiastical constraints on learning now became denominational in character and also became more severe. This became especially evident in the Vatican's attitude to scientists who attempted to build on the advances of the Renaissance, as for instance in the burning of Giordano Bruno in 1600 and the humiliation of Galileo at the hands of the Inquisition. England, however, where crown and ecclesiastical authorities had broken with Rome, became the vibrant home for a new orientation in learning. This home was provided especially by the Royal Society, which supplied an enormous impetus for scientific endeavours of a practical character. In some Continental European countries, emerging scientific societies and institutes provided a similar impetus. Descartes' influence was especially significant in France and gave to French science a rationalist emphasis, as compared to the experimental emphasis characteristic of England. The third chapter explores the special significance of this rationalism in undermining ecclesiastical power in the field of learning and in paving the way for the Enlightenment. The chapter concludes with a review of Rousseau's passionate revolt against the new rationalism; a revolt which was all the more alarming for church authorities because its also attacked church authority directly and championed a new cluster of claims: those of childhood, romance, and especially conscience.

Chapter Four investigates the spread of cultural disparity in the age of modernity (that is, the era inaugurated by the Enlightenment) and it notes the State's increasing efforts during this age to influence and control schooling. Four particular themes are chosen and reviewed to identify some of the implications of these developments for education. The first of these is John Henry Newman's restatement of Christian ideals of learning, in the face of competing utilitarian ideals. The second theme is the more radical ideal of liberal learning championed by Germans like Humboldt and Schleiermacher, but influenced also by the energetic nationalism of Fichte. The third theme concerns the outlook of an anti-modern standpoint – a standpoint which retains an allegiance to ideals of authority and coherence in 'pre-liberal' conceptions of learning and which views the Enlightenment and its legacy as a calamity for culture and education. The final theme explores some features of one of the most recent cultural developments in the age of modernity, namely, the 'postmodern'. It notes that 'postmodern' standpoints imply a rejection of anything resembling 'a search for truth', regardless of whether such a search is inspired by classical, medieval, modern-rational, or any other tradition of learning. Focusing in particular on the work of Jean François Lyotard, but also anticipating the standpoints of other 'postmodern' writers in the later chapters, Chapter Four offers two conclusions which mark the passage to the second part of the book. Firstly, it concludes that despite its flamboyant gestures in throwing off the shackles of tradition, 'postmodernism' may represent the most complete and unprecedented captivity of the spirit of learning. Secondly, it adds that to appreciate this point fully, we need to make explicit the roots of 'postmodernism', both acknowledged and unacknowledged, in Nietzsche's theses on power.

Part Two undertakes a close examination of educational experience itself, or more specifically, it seeks to describe what happens to us in any case, as understanding (or mis-understanding) takes place in our experience. Proceeding from this, it then seeks to describe what might most appropriately and most defensibly happen to us as deliberate intentions of teaching and learning are brought into play. Chapter Five carries out a critique of Nietzsche's 'will-to-power' philosophy, partly to reveal the undisclosed prominence of power motives in many educational outlooks and practices which enjoy widespread acceptance at present. It also credits Nietzsche, however, with illustrating that no acts of human understanding can escape the limits of perspective and partiality. This insight is pursued further in the chapter, not to advance power-seeking or partisanship of any kind, but to show that its refinement in different ways by some leading twentieth century thinkers – Heidegger, Gadamer, Popper, Ricoeur – brings the insight itself fruitfully back into harmony with its Socratic origins. Thus the chapter concludes that the most promising and most defensible orientation for learning is that of a *discipline* of dialogue, which distinguishes a commitment to teaching and learning from the patterns of influence that are the more common ones in most contemporary walks of life. This point is underlined then by outlining the distinctive features of the discipline of dialogue itself, as a particular kind of commitment.

The educational significance of these arguments is examined in some detail in Chapter Six. Taking up the point that teaching and learning always involve an interplay with tradition in one or other of its embodiments, the emergence of personal identity which unfolds through this interplay is considered under three contrasting headings. The first of these is 'identity-as-imposed', and the connections between this and conceptions of learning which are chiefly custodial in character are investigated. Such imposition would of course be rejected by the Enlightenment tradition of individual rational autonomy. But the argument here seeks to show that 'prejudiced' classical conceptions of identity, particularly those which embodied a *telos* (aim, end) which citizens were happy to embrace and to honour, may yet be less prejudiced than the Enlightenment tradition's own claims for the autonomy of reason. The second heading, 'identity as chosen', takes up Richard Rorty's 'postmodern' ideal of freedom, which goes something as follows. Firstly, one's attitude towards tradition remains one of scepticism, or incredulity, or irony, because the truth claims of different traditions are 'incommensurable'. Secondly, one chooses and rechooses one's own identity not by reference to the truth value of any tradition, but according as one finds oneself in different circumstances – historical, social or cultural. Thirdly, the new, the avant garde, and the aesthetic more generally, receive here the place reserved for 'truth' in more traditional conceptions of learning – whether 'truth' as an objective certainty to be acknowledged or 'truth' as the elusive *telos* of a self-critical search. Recognising the doctrinaire characteristics of the first heading and the incoherencies of the second, the third heading considers the emergence of identity as a matter of epiphany, or more precisely, as the epiphanies of the everyday, when the everyday is taken into the discipline of dialogue which acknowledges authenticity and difference in the potentials and promise of each person. Arising from these arguments, teaching is then characterised as a special kind of cultural and communicative art, which seeks to get the epiphanies of learning under way and to sustain them in practice. Such practice constitutes the sovereignty of learning, just as it realises insights of philosophers of human understanding from Socrates to Gadamer, and makes fully transparent the universality of its claims to defensibility.

The art of teaching and the experience of learning are examined at closer range in Chapter Seven. The importance of the playful, not only in childhood experience but also in the educational encounter between the learner and tradition, receives fresh attention here. The contributions of 'child-centred' authors, particularly Rousseau and Dewey, are highlighted, but in acknowledging their insights, the point is also made that an air of controversy still attends many of these insights, not least because the playful did not receive its due place in the structure of human understanding itself in their writings. The middle section of the chapter – 'Uncovering the Presence of the Playful' – seeks to correct this omission by drawing together some of the more remarkable claims for the playful in the 'child-centred' tradition with what Chapter Five uncovered as primary, inherent and vital features of human understanding itself. The last section of Chapter Seven represents the final and most important step in presenting the case for the sovereignty of learning. It does so by viewing the experience of teaching and learning not merely as a cultural interplay, but more crucially as a courtship of sensibility. It provides an illustration of this courtship in action, not as a theoretical possibility, but as a practical event, including the experience of the courtship foundering and getting under way again on a different basis. A number of key 'virtues' of teaching and learning are identified in the course of this illustration. These arise from the imperatives of practice itself, if practice takes seriously the discipline of dialogue considered in Chapter Five.

But despite the effort to make the case for sovereignty as robust and as practical as possible, objections might still be brought against it. Part Three addresses what might be the most significant of such objections and, in dealing with these, also puts the book's argument to a number of tests in the public arena of educational discourse and decision-making. Chapter Eight begins by considering the constructive character of this argument against one of the most radical and widely-cited critiques of educational effort in Western countries, *Reproduction in Education, Society and Culture* (1977), by Pierre Bourdieu and Jean Claude Passeron. That schooling reproduces the unequal relations of capitalist society is a familiar theme of Marxist critiques, but it receives extensive and forceful elaboration by Bourdieu and Passeron. They give a special emphasis to the 'cultural capital' and 'linguistic capital' accumulated by schools' more successful products, and to the arbitrariness of what schooling imposes ('cultural arbitrary') on those who are already dispossessed where such 'capital' is concerned. The Bourdieu-Passeron thesis is considered in some detail and I argue that in regarding education primarily as a social, economic and cultural force, its incisive insights still miss something more significant. In overlooks the primary point that teaching and learning constitute a distinct *human practice* and that it is in this practice, rather than in any battle of social forces, that the integrity of education and its claims to sovereignty reside. To recognise this moreover is to recognise a responsibility which is also overlooked by Bourdieu and Passeron: the responsibility of putting forward constructive improvements which may well have their birth in critique but which respect and advance the integrity of the practice itself. One might evade this responsibility by claiming that the social critic's concern is with schooling as a social force, which is different from a concern with education in a more pure sense. The fact remains however that public resources allocated to education in most democratic societies are overwhelmingly granted to schooling, including that provided in institutions of higher learning. And this allocation grows rather than lessens in significance yearly. Schooling therefore remains the primary arena where the question of education must be engaged. There are, however, other Marxist-inspired critiques which acknowledge this responsibility to a lesser or greater degree and a number of these are then reviewed. The chapter concludes by drawing attention briefly to one of the most striking of them. This is the work of Jürgen Habermas, which was never undertaken as a critique of education itself, but which has nevertheless provided some of the most constructive and self-critical explorations of the practices of human communication to be furnished by contemporary philosophy. The virtues identified in my own account of teaching and learning parallel in some respects the requirements of 'communicative action' proposed by Habermas. Consideration of these similarities is postponed until the end of the following chapter, however, because a further objection, which applies to both, must first be addressed.

This objection comes from a further variant of 'postmodernism' and arguably its most influential to date, namely the 'deconstruction' movement associated with Jacques Derrida. Chapter Nine notes not only the widespread influence of this movement in the humanities in recent decades, but also the equally widespread controversy it has given rise to in very many of the Western world's centres of higher learning. Derrida's work seeks to dismantle, or to 'de-construct' some of the central assumptions of Western philosophy, and of Western learning more generally. In particular, he wishes to set aside the assumption – which underlies most traditions of learning – *that there is truth to be discovered*. Deconstruction's apparent similarity with nihilism and with radical cultural anarchy has drawn hostile fire from its critics. One of the most notable of these is the literary critic George Steiner, whose forceful attack on deconstruction is considered in the early part of Chapter Ten. Steiner is particularly severe on what he sees as deconconstruction's irresponsibility: its depiction of humankind as 'homo ludens' – a carefree, innocent species, free to frolic without meaning, truth, or other burdensome care amid the world's earnest concerns with learning. Such a criticism invites precisely the opposite connotations of the spirit of the 'playful' which Chapter Seven identified as one of the wellsprings of culture itself. Derrida has rejected both nihilistic readings and 'irresponsible' manifestations of his enterprise, claiming that his is a *rational* undertaking, the main purpose of which is to undermine the self-assurance of those traditions of learning which have seen themselves as preservers of truth; particularly that 'truth' which excludes or marginalises those whom they cannot accommodate, or whose sense of their own identity is radically other than what such truth enshrines. On this view (which is a modification of his earlier efforts) Derrida's work would be a plea not altogether unlike the argument of this book, and Habermas, to whom we return in the final section of the chapter, recognises something of this kind. He criticises Derrida, however, for his failure to provide anything recognisably constructive in place of what his own efforts have deconstructed. The constructive features of Habermas' own later work are then taken up in the final part of the chapter and these are compared, and contrasted, with my own arguments on the sovereignty of educational practice. The main purpose of this comparison is to establish the precedence of practice over theory; a precedence which is ambiguously present in Habermas' theories of communicative action and discourse ethics, but whose non-theoretical (or Socratic) character I am keen to emphasise more clearly.

The final chapter addresses the concerns of educational policy in a more direct manner. It opens by addressing the question of quality in education. This question has been much to the fore in the discourse of policy-makers within the last decade and has been treated mainly as an issue of effectiveness and management in the growing body of recent literature in educational research. One of the more prominent of these texts, *Total Quality Management and the School*, by Stephen Murgatroyd and Colin Morgan (1993), is representative of a new genre, and mainly because it *misrepresents* the question of quality in education as being primarily about market expectations, as distinct from the quality of *practice* experienced by pupils and teachers. The criticism of market conceptions of quality in this chapter does not, however, dismiss the claims of commerce, industry or other vocational pursuits from the conduct of teaching and learning. The educational merits of these pursuits are examined under the heading 'The Affirmations of Ordinary Life' and this is followed by a reconsideration of the ideal of liberal education, which seeks to connect, or more precisely to *re*-connect the question of vocational pursuits with that of personal potentials, aptitudes and identity. This is explored as a practical question, with important consequences for what is understood not only by liberal education, but also by balance in the curriculum through which such an education is to be experienced, and in the assessment arrangements by which its benefits are to be evaluated.

The Epilogue makes reference to a recent major international survey of empirical studies of policy changes and innovations in education – Michael Fullan's & Suzanne Stiegelbauer's *The New Meaning of Educational Change* (1991) – and brings together a few of its key findings with the essentials of the sovereignty argument. Calling on the insights which have thus been brought together it reviews in summary eight important concerns of policy in education at present: the purposes of learning itself, the control and management of schooling, the conduct of teaching and learning, the education of teachers, equity and balance in the experience of the curriculum, the educational purposes of assessment and certification, the claims of economy and society, and finally the integrity of higher education.

PART I

Education as Guardianship – A story of ascendancy and decline

CHAPTER ONE

The Classical Pattern Of Western Education

Introduction

In a time when the fruits of technology continue to unshape and reshape the worlds of commerce and culture, of work and leisure, schooling becomes increasingly looked to not so much as the bearer of a cultural heritage, but as an agent for accomplishing change. The array of lifestyles which nowadays canvasses the outlooks and sensibilities of youth and age alike frequently carries the cultural message that the present is all-important, that the future is a source of alternative possibilities and that the past, by comparison, is just the past. In such a time it is all too easy to forget that traditions of learning in Western civilisations have been shaped in a much more enduring sense by the intimate connection the Ancient Greeks forged between formal education and a cultivated sense of identity. More importantly, it is also all too easy to overlook the fact that some of the institutional outlooks and practices which took root in this event still remain defining characteristics of modern educational systems, notwithstanding the changes these systems are called on to accommodate or promote. Some of these long-standing characteristics have become such a matter of habitual practice that their actual character and consequences are hardly noticed.

Of course it is still accepted by most adults that a formal education should contribute something decisive and abiding to one's identity and outlooks. But what is declared authoritatively as the aims of formal education may be quite different from what that education achieves in practice. Indeed many of the institutionalised habits of daily practice may – in an overlooked way – even pull in a contrary direction to what the aims envisage. Sooner or later, however, as the historical evidence shows, this generally leads to widescale disillusionment with the educational authority which articulated the aims, or even to a disregard of the tradition whose virtues and beliefs the aims sought to embody. Thus the neglect of educational practice can do more than a little injustice to the most worthy of traditions. And the neglect itself can become an institutionalised feature of even the most influential of traditions. In this opening chapter I hope to show that some of the most deeply-rooted traditions and practices of Western education – despite many splendid achievements of learning – involve such a neglect of educational practice. I will argue that this institutionalised neglect in Western education had its beginnings in what I call below an eclipse of the Socratic by the central tenets of Platonism. I will also seek to show here that some important themes from Aristotle's *Politics* contributed to this eclipse, as did the Romanising of Greek educational influences associated with Cicero and Quintillian.

The Essence of the Socratic

Scholars have long recorded the central importance given to education by the three leading Greek philosophers Socrates, Plato and Aristotle, and continue to debate the distinctive contributions of each of the three. Insofar as it deals with the question of education, however, most of this scholarly debate has been concerned with the educational aims and provisions in the *writings* of Plato and Aristotle rather than with the dynamics of teaching and learning in the educational *activities* of Socrates (who left no written accounts of his own work). In other words, emphasis is placed on the strategic concerns of policy-making authorities when education is debated in public rather than on what *actually befalls experience whenever teaching and learning are attempted*. The consequences of this one-sided emphasis can still be discerned. The shaping of the learner's sense of identity is assumed to be properly determined by the *capacity* of an educational authority to frame aims and by its *power* to implement provisions. This kind of assumption – the preoccupation with decision-making power to the neglect of the dynamics of educational experience – has probably been the most common assumption in Western philosophy of education, including many philosophies of revolutionary and Marxist ancestry. It grants most significance to issues like control of schooling and contents of curricula, as distinct from issues of experience and practice. But assumptions like this, because they view the learner's identity largely as a property of the powers of an educational authority or management, allow this identity little in the way of sovereignty, or individuality. It is as if the emergent characteristics of personal and collective identity could properly be viewed as raw material to be moulded to the pattern envisaged by that authority or management.

Plato's educational arguments in his *Republic* and his *Laws*, but also Aristotle's arguments in his *Politics*, provided a powerful impetus to the kind of assumption described in the previous paragraph. In doing so, not only did they give decisive shape to the conceptions of education which were to become predominant in Western civilisations; they also eclipsed an incisive conception of the manner in which the learner's identity is actually engaged during any practical instance of teaching and learning – a conception which Socrates seems to have understood with great subtlety of insight, and which also seems to underlie most of his work in a tacit but crucial way. The two-fold import of what I shall call 'the Platonic assumption' can thus be summarised as follows:

(a) the taking for granted that a person's identity can, and should, be moulded to a pattern contained in the philosophical aims and curricular contents of an educational authority which has the power to implement its own provisions;

(b) the eclipse – generally contained in this assumption – of the dynamics of teaching and learning and of the subtleties of the play of influence in actual instances of teaching and learning.

In this opening chapter, the origins of the classical pattern which became seminal for Western education will be examined, but with an emphasis on what was lost as well as what was achieved in this accomplishment. This emphasis on the progressive loss, or eclipse, of insights which had a singular *educational* promise, is being undertaken not for any controversial or iconoclastic reasons. Nor can it go under the name of 'deconstruction' of any kind. Far from any dismissiveness, the opening arguments, and indeed the arguments throughout the book, will seek to engage a number of authors – mostly dead ones – in a living and lively conversation. As the example of Socrates shows, while a conversation remains living it also remains unfinished. No one therefore has the last word. Neither does this mean, however, that nothing of decisive significance can be discovered along the way. In the four themes of the first chapter I hope to advance arguments which might not only modify our perspectives on the traditions of learning which have been the more influential ones in the West; I hope also to prepare the ground for a more promising way of viewing and of influencing our educational prospects at a time when Western traditions of learning themselves seem to be in some disarray.

It is all too commonly assumed in educational circles that the chief importance of Socrates for teaching and learning lies in something called 'the Socratic method'. Thus 'Socratic' or 'dialogical' methods are contrasted with 'didactic' or 'traditional' ones. Even more misleadingly, Socrates' own declaration that he had 'never taught or professed to teach anything' (*Apology*, 33) may be cited by some advocates of 'Socratic methods' to support a view that the teacher should shy away from active, purposeful teaching and allow 'discussion' or 'facilitation' to take pride of place in the pupils' encounters with what they are studying.[1] This kind of misappropriation of the teaching work of Socrates can readily get anything Socratic a bad name, particularly among those whose inclinations lean towards preserving the existing order of things. It is worth recalling here that the caricatures furnished about Socrates and his work in his own day played no small part in leading to his trial and conviction.

It is important then to emphasise from the start that the significance of Socrates' work for education lies essentially *not in any method*, but rather in a *particular kind of conviction*. The kinds of methods Socrates used were characteristically ironic, rather than direct; so their application in any kind of human intercourse remains dubious, indeed rootless, unless one grasps the nature of the conviction they were designed to serve. But the nature of this conviction seems persistently elusive, particularly to anyone in search of definite and positive doctrines. Although Socrates makes occasional reference to principles which have guided his actions, it is very difficult to pin down in the recorded instances of his educational work any explicit body of positive teachings, any clearly formulated precepts, either on religion or morality or indeed on any aspect of human learning.[2] This may lead many to conclude that he can be studied not as a source of educational aims, but rather as an inspired strategist, or as an argumentative tactician of exemplary stature. The consequences of these latter kinds of approach, however, are that the methods employed by Socrates are now torn from the contexts in which they are properly coherent, and are called on in a distorted form to do duty for educational aims derived from established doctrines of religious, secular, commercial or other origin. It is worth noting that these latter sometimes include, in our own day, the doctrines of 'non-directive' approaches drawn from modern psychology and counselling.

But these arguments seem to lead to an impasse. For if, on the one hand, it is a serious distortion to use Socratic methods for advancing aims based on one or other body of doctrines from elsewhere; if, on the other, the Socratic practice seems to supply no unambiguous doctrines itself, from which educational aims might be drawn; how can the example of Socrates then have any coherent, or authoritative significance for education? I would like to argue in response to this question not only that it can, but more crucially that it *has*. But to uncover such significance requires us to probe with a keen educational eye, as well as a philosophical alertness, those contexts in which the teaching and learning episodes in the life of Socrates might reveal their full coherence. Those contexts are recorded most notably in the early Dialogues of Plato, particularly the following: *Protagoras*, *Gorgias*, *Euthyphro*, *Apology*, *Crito*, Book 1 of the *Republic*, and possibly *Meno*, as a marginal case. In these Dialogues Socrates can be seen to speak with a different voice (most likely that of the actual Socrates) than that which Plato attributes to him from the second book of the *Republic* onwards and in all of the later Dialogues. This distinction between the historical and the Platonic Socrates will be crucial in the following arguments. The distinction is of course noted in most of the literature which deals with Plato's educational philosophy but its import is rarely pursued. As a consequence, what is distinctly Socratic remains largely undifferentiated from what is Platonic.[3] Only when the early Dialogues are read with an eye to their *educational import*, and not merely a critical eye to their philosophical conclusions (or lack of conclusions), do they begin to reveal the distinctive nature and tenor of Socrates' educational commitment.

Much is written about Socrates' recurring criticisms of the professional teachers of his own day, the sophists. Plato and Aristotle, for their part, were quite explicit in arguing that control of schooling should be taken out of private hands (of the sophists) and made a responsibility of the state. Socrates' criticisms were concerned not with any lack of attention by the sophists to their students' sense of their own accomplishment. Rather his criticisms invariably sought to expose that the kinds of accomplishment being nurtured were largely dubious, frequently substituting an articulate blend of presumptuousness and credulity for a disciplined self-criticism in the pursuit of knowledge. Socrates held – most notably in the *Apology* – not only that the sophists' claims to teach the arts of public morality were counterfeit but also that they were destructive of the communal solidarity by which any public morality could itself be sustained.

The reference to communal solidarity here provides us with a clue to what was essential in the educational work of Socrates. The community in question was the Greek *polis*, or city state, in this case Athens. The *polis* differed in key respects from what we now recognise as a nation state, or even a municipality or a metropolis. The chief characteristics of the *polis* included:

(a) A shared understanding of being governed by some publicly recognised virtues (e.g. courage, truthfulness, pride);

(b) a shared sense of disdain for some publicly recognised vices (e.g. cowardice, underhandedness, humility);

(c) a shared avowal of the forceful but ambivalent hand of the divinities in human affairs;

(d) complete sovereignty over its own affairs – military, civic, cultural, mercantile;

(e) the intimate scale of the *polis* as a city state.

Citizenship of a *polis* then clearly conferred a strong sense of community identity, associated with notable traditions of public virtue, with courageous military exploits and, particularly in the case of Athens, with distinctive artistic accomplishments. Socrates' famous defence of his life's work during his trial underlines not only the communal nature of life in the *polis*. It also shows his own belief that what sustained this communal sense was now in a serious state of decline :

> Athenians, I honour and love you; but I shall obey God rather than you, and while I have life and strength I shall never cease from the practice and teaching of philosophy, exhorting any one whom I meet and saying to him after my manner: You, my friend – a citizen of the great and mighty and wise city of Athens – are you not ashamed of heaping up the greatest amount of money and honour and reputation, and caring so little about wisdom and truth and the greatest improvement of the soul, which you never regard or heed at all? And I shall repeat the same words to every one whom I meet, young and old, citizen and alien, but especially to the citizens, inasmuch as they are my brethren. (*Apology*, 29-30)

In this and other passages of the *Apology*, Socrates makes clear the singleminded vision and appeal which remain implicit – i.e. presupposed by his *actions* – in virtually all of his other recorded Dialogues. For Socrates it is a vision of life's essential *telos:* its aim or end. It is an appeal to that for the sake of which life is lived, or *ought to be* lived. We learn that the inspiration of his work was a 'divine sign', which came not through any approval by the incumbents of high office, but from the oracle which spoke the mind of the god at Delphi – for the Greeks a supreme and 'an unimpeachable authority'. Had Socrates responded to the god's declaration that he was 'the wisest of men' by setting up an academy which proclaimed bold doctrines and charged high fees, it is likely that he would have been regarded as being of first rank among the sophists; controversial indeed, but no threat to the existing political and moral order. By setting out to dis-prove the oracle, however, Socrates gave life to a kind of teaching and learning which were strikingly different from anything practised in the schools of the sophists. This he did by seeking out those with the highest reputation for wisdom and questioning them on those matters on which their reputations were particularly based. During the early stages of this work Socrates was progressively taken aback to discover that those distinguished figures, one after another, soon became confounded when engaged in any searching debate about their teachings and their hitherto unquestioned assumptions. He eventually concluded – in contrast to the prevailing conceptions of knowledge and learning – that:

> real wisdom is the property of God, and this oracle is his way of telling us that human wisdom has little or no value. It seems to me that he is not referring literally to Socrates, but has merely taken my name as an example, as if he would say to us 'The wisest of you is he who has realised, like Socrates, that in respect of wisdom he is really worthless'. (*Apology*, 23)

It is likely that Socrates could still have escaped the court's eventual judgement if he could reassure the jury – of 501 fellow citizens – that he would henceforth hold this radical view merely as a private opinion. At the heart of his life's work, however, lay the conviction that precisely this radical principle should govern the entire approach to teaching and learning in the *polis*. By enunciating it clearly in court now, he was providing an unambiguous context – for anyone who still needed it – within which his educational work in the streets and public places of Athens could be viewed. He was now making clear *why* his approach so often gave priority to question over answer, *why* irony and double irony frequently had to take priority over literal directness, *why* he could not claim the title 'teacher', although his work was unfailingly concerned with bringing about a crucial kind of learning. If the majority of Socrates' hearers were incensed to hear the rebuke of commonly accepted malpractices contained in the defendant's words, their fury could only have been increased to learn that this defendant now frankly submitted that his life's efforts had been in the service of a religious imperative, had never been pursued for personal gain, but had ever been engaged in for the benefit of the *polis* and its citizens. And Socrates even added that he understood the reason for the resentment he aroused. To the more elevated and flattered personages of the *polis*, it was intolerable to have 'to confess the truth: that their pretence of knowledge has been detected'.(*Apology* 23)

These brief explorations help to uncover what is distinctive in a Socratic conception of teaching and learning, properly so called. I shall now try to capture the essentials of this conception by listing its more notable features. The following points are misunderstood from the start, however, if they are taken as theoretical educational aims based on the 'teachings' of Socrates. On the contrary, they attempt to recover faithfully the distinctiveness of Socratic educational practice. That this practice had an aim in view is beyond doubt, but the nature and the scope of this aim can be understood only as the distinctiveness of the practice itself is appreciated, or better still, actually experienced.

1. The apparent absence of doctrine in Socratic teaching and learning arises from Socrates' belief that what is most important for humans to learn – how we *ought* to live – cannot be classed as the kind of knowledge that can properly be taught by instruction. He continually submitted this belief to the test of refutation. (*Protagoras, Meno*)

2. Education in how we ought to live is nevertheless the most important concern of humankind. This education is, in each person's case, more a matter of search than one of conformity. It becomes truly promising, moreover, only when we can submit to scrutiny those beliefs and outlooks we have appropriated in our experience hitherto, whether through instruction or otherwise. (*Apology*)

3. There is an unyielding reluctance among some, and an ardent eagerness among others, to submit to a searching questioning those beliefs and outlooks – about justice, morality, religion, politics, etc. – which have become the prevailing order of a particular *polis*, or community. The reluctance is to be found mainly among those whose sense of identity has already conformed to an established pattern and who see their best interests in preserving existing arrangements. The eagerness to question, on the other hand, is mainly associated with the idealism and emergent identity of many of the more youthful members of the community. (*Republic* Bk. I)

4. There are discerning insights and subtle skills involved in getting this questioning under way in a disciplined manner. These constitute the 'true political art' of teaching. (*Gorgias* 521) It is an *art* precisely because the insights, skills and judgement called for here are in themselves distinctive human accomplishments. It is a *political* art because it is concerned with identifying the individual's best relation to the *polis* and proper conduct in the *polis*.

5. This 'true political art' should cultivate respect for the best traditions of the *polis*. But this would be an informed and a questioning respect, inspired by those principles which are ones of universal justice. (*Crito* 51) Socrates makes explicit here two 'teachings' which serve as examples of universally defensible contents of a moral tradition: that agreements freely entered into must be honoured and that it is wrong to repay injustice with injustice. Yet the 'true political art' of education provides the best service to the *polis* by leaving politics itself alone. (*Apology* 31-32) Its office is primarily that of self-knowledge, in the context of what the voices of tradition address to the personal in human experience.

6. The outlooks called into question in the most notable instances of Socrates' educational work are invariably treated with respect and are offered a generous, but critical hearing. (*Gorgias* 482c-486c; *Protagoras* 320d-328d; *Euthyphro* 4a-6d; *Crito* 44b-46b) Irony, mock flattery, baiting, and other rhetorical devices are employed by Socrates only where the conceit, or petulance, or blustering of the other party to a debate is interfering with the effort to follow an *unhindered* search for truth.

7. The pursuit of an unhindered search for truth would also view established doctrines as possible hindrances, though not *necessarily* as hindrances. The latter would be the case only where the declared status of a doctrine as the 'final truth' precluded any further search and commanded assent to its own precepts. The key Socratic point to recall here is that any such thing as a final truth would be beyond the grasp of human knowledge – i.e. as knowledge, it would be the preserve of a divinity. (*Apology*)

8. When the pursuit of truth gets under way, it involves an interplay of ventured standpoints, each willing to give generous but critical ear to others which are prepared to observe a similar discipline. This interplay is possible in all branches of learning, but, for Socrates, its key import is for that kind of learning which pursues the question of how we *ought to live*. (*Apology, Gorgias, Protagoras, Crito*)

9. Far from any spontaneous assertiveness, the kind of discipline involved here calls in the first place for an attentive deference towards cultural and religious tradition, together with a commitment to high standards of fluency. These qualities enable questioning to become pertinent, criticism to become informed. (*Euthyphro, Apology, Crito*) In each case this discipline matures with the learner's own practice of it. That is to say it has varying, but complementary implications for how teaching and learning are carried on from childhood onwards.

10. The practice of such a discipline in a systematic or formal manner (e.g in a setting such as a school) requires the alert presence of a mature person (teacher) who is prepared to initiate the venturing, to sustain it, and defend it from falling prey to this or that certainty; who is therefore thoroughly versed in the moral traditions of the community; who is a circumspect student of the spirit and details of moral teachings and doctrines; who has a perceptive eye for the integrities and the duplicities of customary practices in interpersonal dealings and public affairs; who understands, above all else, the educational import of the claim that, in relation to any final truth about how life ought to be lived, humankind has never arrived at certainty, but is ever *on the way* to truth.

It becomes clear from these ten points that a certain kind of solidarity, a keen sense of collective purpose, pervades the Socratic practice of teaching and learning. This solidarity emerges from the experience of teaching and learning itself, from habituation in an *ethos* where the characteristics described above are the ones which actually constitute the practice. Solidarity is itself a matter of mutual trust and belief, a faith in one another which is nurtured by a keen awareness of uncertainty and contingency of all human undertakings; a faith which is often tacit, but everywhere vulnerable to conquest by doctrines which answer to another human characteristic – the desire to overcome uncertainty and contingency, to embrace certainty and security. This last suggestion brings us to the second of our four themes in this chapter.

The Platonic Aspiration

The sentencing to death of Socrates by a large jury representative of the *polis* convinced Plato that the solidarity exemplified in the work of Socrates was already undermined in Athens by an ethic of self-seeking and corruption; an ethic which attired itself in fine rhetoric and mistook its own public observances for a more genuine piety. It is not surprising then that Plato included more than the sophists in his famous critique of Greek education in the *Republic*. The censorship proposed in the *Republic* of the works of the most celebrated figures of Greek cultural tradition (Homer and Hesiod) rested on Plato's belief that these works misrepresented the divine order and nurtured a thoroughly sensual and worldly sensibility. Such a sensibility was for Plato a dark prison from which the human soul must be released in order to experience the radiant vision of the Good, unsullied by anything sensual. Education would be the key instrument in bringing about a society where the rulers were philosophers committed to public service and immune to seductions, where sensuality was mastered and where affairs were ordered and conducted in the light of the Good. It should be emphasised at this point that the idea (*idea*) of the Good was for Plato the supreme but otherworldly source of knowledge and truth:

> It (the Good) is the cause of knowledge and truth, and you will be right in thinking of it as being itself known, and yet as being something other than, and even more splendid than, knowledge and truth, splendid as they are. (*Republic* 509e)

The un-Socratic nature of Plato's opening arguments on education – in Book II of the *Republic* – is indicated in the words which he now boldly places in the mouth of Socrates: 'Then it seems that our first business is to supervise the production of stories, and choose only those we think suitable, and reject the rest'. (*Republic* 377c) This abrupt departure from anything Socratic is somehow masked, however, by the fact that Plato presents his own view here as if it were something which recommended itself quite reasonably to a small group during the course of a collective enquiry. The continual use of the first person plural – 'our first business', 'those we think suitable', 'nor can we permit', 'shall we therefore allow' – conveys an impression of the joint efforts of a mature teacher (Socrates), with two eager students (Glaucon and Adeimantus). It is of course possible to envisage Socrates, or indeed *any* mature teacher, engaged in just such a joint enquiry, granted that his idiom and tone would be quite different from those used here by Plato. What marks the break with the Socratic, rather, is that this new departure in Book II of the *Republic* is the first of a succession of *prescriptions and prohibitions* concerning how education is to be ordered and conducted. Secondly, the kinds of decisions being arrived at here, ostensibly by a teacher in dialogue with senior students, are in fact decisions which Plato's own argument decisively removes from the hands of teachers and concentrates instead in those of specially chosen 'philosopher rulers'.

The autobiographical fragment contained in Plato's *Seventh Letter* presents us with a context in which the chief purpose of his educational writings becomes clear, and also provides clues as to why his educational thinking differs sharply from that of Socrates. In that *Letter*, Plato explains that as a young man he aspired to a political career. When he discovered how corrupt the government of the *polis* had become under the reign of an oligarchy known as the Thirty Tyrants, he became disillusioned and 'withdrew from the prevailing wickedness'. After a revolution restored a democratic government in Athens, he again felt the desire, though more cautiously this time, to take an active part in public life. He was greatly distressed, however, to witness the indictment, conviction and execution of Socrates under the democratic regime and to discover that corruption now seemed to have an irrevocable grasp on those with political power and influence. His reflections on the unhealthy state of politics in Athens were broadened to include the condition of other states, which he found to be similarly grim. Eventually his desire to participate in politics gave way to another, more far-reaching kind of desire:

> Finally I came to the conclusion that the constitution of all existing states is bad ... and I was driven to assert, in praise of true philosophy, that nothing else can enable one to see what is right for states and for individuals, and that the troubles of mankind will never cease, until either true and genuine philosophers attain political power or the rulers of states by some dispensation of providence become genuine philosophers. (*Seventh Letter* 326a-b)

The *Republic* is the main fruit of this more far-reaching desire. The book begins as an enquiry into the nature of justice, but Plato soon has the participants in this contrived dialogue discover that justice in the state is the counterpart of justice in the individual, and that neither is possible unless the most intellectually promising of the youth in the *polis* – both male and female and regardless of social rank – are carefully selected and given a lengthy and rigorous education. The chief aim of this education is to produce a corps of philosopher rulers in whose hands the supreme power over the affairs of the *polis* would be placed. Plato's later work *Laws*, adds that the most important office among the philosopher rulers would be that of 'minister of the education of youth, male and female'. (*Laws* 765d-e) It is clear then that Plato *shared* with Socrates a deep concern that education should enable people to recognise and overcome obstacles to the kind of life humans ought to live and also a concern that the benefits of education should be evident in the conduct of public affairs. For Socrates, however, such benefits were invariably the outcome of a personal quest which remained sceptical of both obedience to authority and conformity to custom, while for Plato, obedience to the prescriptions of the philosopher rulers must be insisted upon if learners (and their teachers) were ever to overcome enslavement to popular opinion and to attain an unblemished vision of the Good.[4]

Socrates' reluctance to give explicit instruction in ethics arose from his conviction that such instruction invited the danger of sophistry: that it tackled questions about how life should be lived not with a self-critical personal search but rather answered them with definite propositions which could be taught and mastered. Now Plato was no more a sophist than Socrates himself, but his *Republic* abounds nevertheless with the most decisive of moral and religious prescriptions. What Socrates viewed as an ethical quest which never arrives at a final certainty, Plato recast as an accomplished metaphysics: a grand doctrine which included theories about the human soul, the nature and purpose of the arts, the non-worldly origins of goodness (i.e. the separately existing 'Form of the Good'), the requirements of authority and obedience, the regulation and control of public affairs, including education. In other words, Plato not only introduced an entire body of teachable contents concerning how humans are to understand themselves and conduct their lives. Equally significant, these teachable contents were now inseparable from an approach to teaching and learning which emphasised orthodoxy rather than criticism, obedience rather than questioning, finality rather than an unfinishing search.

A custodial attitude towards the experience of learning becomes increasingly manifest as the *Republic* proceeds. By the middle of Book III, where some of the most notable artistic accomplishments of Greek civilisation have already been subjected to severe censorship, Plato has Socrates declare to his companions: 'We have, without noticing it, been purging our state of the luxury from which we said it suffered'. (399e) This purging is but the preliminary step in turning the eye of the soul – alternatively called the eye of the mind – away from the pleasures, gratifications and honours of the physical and sensual world. Such pleasures and prizes are for Plato the source of recurring discord and corruption and he insists that the world which proclaims and pursues them is *less real* than the contemplative world, unseen by most, where enduring truth can be attained and changeless good has its origins.(508e) By means of three famous similes – those of the sun, the divided line and the cave – the *Republic* seeks to establish the case that the Good, 'once seen, is inferred to be responsible for whatever is right and valuable in anything'. (517e) This seeing, moreover, would not be an implanting of sight, but a recollection by the human being of its more heavenly existence prior to its birth. In striking contrast to Socrates, Plato is here advancing a metaphysics which claims that a world of ultimate truth is not only attainable by humankind but also that it constitutes the *highest form of knowledge*. (505a, 519c) The contrast becomes even more striking when we now see how Plato conceives the most important purpose of teaching:

> Then this turning around of the mind itself might be made the subject of a professional skill (*techne*) which would effect the conversion as easily and effectively as possible. It would not be concerned to implant sight, but to ensure that someone who had it already was not either turned in the wrong direction or looking the wrong way. (518d)

Unlike the self-assured conjectures of the sophists, Plato's metaphysics sought to provide a coherent and fully adequate account of the nature of human being, of knowledge, of justice, of politics, of art, of religion and, not least, of education. This metaphysics, in a series of successive modifications and institutionalised forms, came to have the most authoritative place in the history of Western learning. In doing so, it overshadowed the Socratic conception, the main characteristics of which I have attempted to recover in the previous section. And here we are anticipating some arguments to be explored a little later. But a few features of this cultural shift from the Socratic to the Platonist are worth noting before proceeding to our third theme in the present chapter.

Firstly, where Socrates gave priority to collective enquiry and committed personal action in teaching and learning, Plato emphasised contemplation of final truths, which he saw as superior to, but also necessary for, public action. But the priority which Socrates gave to reflective action Plato now gives to metaphysical *theoria*. Secondly, the kind of educational activity carried on by Socrates seems to have included the entire civic community of the *polis* within its scope. That prescribed by Plato accommodated only the most intellectually promising of the citizens of the *polis*. Thirdly, for Socrates, the essential purpose of education was to assist the learner in pursuing the search for his own identity through an ever renewed engagement with the cultural, moral and religious traditions of the *polis*. For Plato, by contrast, that identity was essentially defined in advance, in accordance with the Good, which was 'the highest form of knowledge'. Finally, the approach to teaching and learning practised by Socrates was not compatible with the approach required by Plato's metaphysics. Where Socrates recognised the ever vulnerable nature of the search for truth, Plato aspired to make education the vehicle for overcoming such vulnerability; to secure what Martha Nussbaum has recently described as 'a life of goodness without fragility'. (*The Fragility of Goodness*, p.138)

In summary, the educational doctrines of what I shall describe from here on as 'Platonism' include, most notably, the following three features: firstly, the hierarchical division of knowledge into a higher *intellectual and spiritual* world and a lower *sensual* world, each with its own sub-divisions; secondly, the claim that the higher of the two worlds was one of changeless truths while the lower was one where illusions and unworthy arts featured largely among the accepted cultural pursuits; thirdly the claim that the higher truths whose source was the changeless *idea of the Good* were attainable only by the strictly disciplined and properly tutored 'eye of the soul', and that educational effort must dedicate itself wholeheartedly to such tutoring.

Aristotle and the Practical

In the opening book of his *Nicomachean Ethics* (*EN*) Aristotle criticised Plato's idea of the Good as being too remote and unspecific to guide the concerns of practice: 'Even if there is some one Good existing apart, alone and by itself, it is plain that it will not be one that man can attain to or possess, and that (the latter) is the sort of good we are looking for now'. (*EN* 1 vi) By way of example, Aristotle declares that it is difficult to see how a shoemaker's or a carpenter's trade could be bettered, or how the work of a doctor or a military general could be improved, by contemplation of Plato's idea of the Good. Although Aristotle could in turn be readily challenged on this from Plato's standpoint, the real thrust of Aristotle's insight should not be missed. This can roughly be summarised as follows. Activities which aim at anything considered a human good risk losing sight of what is most essential to their own nature as *practical* activities unless the good they seek is grasped in clear and specific terms; terms as clear, that is, as the nature of the practice in question allows. (*EN* 1 iii) 'Practical' for Aristotle always concerns what *ought* to be done. This applies equally to such different spheres as military strategy, ethical conduct, political activity and, not least, to education.

For Aristotle, therefore, good practice proceeds not from a theory, whether of the Good or of knowledge, but from a reflection on the characteristics of practice itself. This kind of reflection enables Aristotle to highlight something which is virtually overlooked by Plato, namely the crucial significance of circumstance, and more particularly of *ethos*, in any practical engagement. Indeed there seems to be some recovery of a Socratic kind of insight in Aristotle's comments on being educated in the two specific kinds of goodness which Aristotle himself distinguishes, goodness of intellect and goodness of character:

> intellectual goodness is both produced and maintained mainly by teaching, and therefore experience and time are required for it. Goodness of character, on the other hand, is the outcome of habit, and accordingly the word *'éthos'*, character, is derived from *'êthos'*, habit, by a slight modification in the quantity of the vowel. (*EN* II i)

This connection between the unfolding moral identity of the learner on the one hand, and, on the other, the beliefs, attitudes and practices *to which the learner has become habituated* in a particular educational setting, identifies a vital point which is all too often forgotten in modern educational discourse. That point is that an educational ethos is much more a matter of emergent practice and experience than something which can be prescribed or laid down from above by educational authorities. That to which a person becomes habituated in an everyday way could, of course, be conformist and unreflective, rather than critically alert. In other words an educational ethos could be such that those who are chiefly affected by it largely become creatures of habit. If Aristotle is aware of this possibility he chooses not to explore it. In fact, as we shall see in a moment, there is evidence to show that where the education of youth is concerned, Aristotle prized conformity higher than moral autonomy. For Socrates, by contrast, the possibility of becoming a creature of habit is precisely that where lurks the danger of an unexamined life. Only where the raising of critical questions had itself become habitual, where innovation and continual venturing had become part of an accepted way of proceeding, could this danger be averted.

Much has been written in recent years about Aristotle's penetrating accounts – in Book VI of his *Nicomachean Ethics* – of the kind of knowledge which is most appropriate to civic decision making and practical action. This particular kind of knowledge, described as *phronesis* and usually left untranslated, is concerned in a special way with the uncertainties of human circumstance – with what Aristotle calls 'the variable', to distinguish it from the 'invariable' with which science (*episteme*) deals. We shall be returning later to the significance of *phronesis* for education in our own day, but it must be pointed out here that this kind of knowledge, which allowed very considerable scope for discretion and freedom in the conduct of the chief practices of the *polis*, was circumscribed by strict limits where education was concerned. Indeed Aristotle's remarks on education in Book VIII of his *Politics* seem to align him much more closely with Plato than with Socrates. The following extract is quoted at some length as it brings together these points where Aristotle's attitude contrasts most sharply with that of Socrates:

> And since the *polis* as a whole has but a single aim, it is plain that the education of all must be one and the same, and that the supervision of this education must be public and not private, as it is in the present system, under which everyone looks after his own children privately and gives them any private instruction he thinks proper. Public training is wanted in all things that are of public interest. Besides, it is wrong for any citizen to think that he belongs to himself. All must be considered as belonging to the *polis*: for each man is a part of the *polis*, and the treatment of the part is necessarily determined by the treatment of the whole. (*Politics* VIII, i)

The final sentence here may sound a note of alarm in many modern ears, for it seems to champion a totalitarian principle: that individuals are the property of the state and that the state's interests must take priority over any uncovering of individuality or any engagement of personal identity through education. It seems that scarcely anything could be less Socratic than the assertive finality in this bold declaration by Aristotle. It must be recalled however that for Aristotle, the 'one aim' for the state as a whole is the happiness of its citizens and that this happiness is not anything passive or acquiescent, but rather a conscious *activity of the soul* in accordance with goodness. (*EN* 1, vii & *Politics* VII, xii) When we recall moreover the rather intimate scale of the *polis* as a city state, 'belonging to' the *polis* loses much of the anonymous starkness of being owned by the state. Thus, on a more sympathetic interpretation of Aristotle, it could be rephrased as: identifying strongly with one's own civic community; or alternatively, being identified as a person belonging to a community with a strong sense of its collective identity.

A further pertinent point must be added here concerning the importance of leisure in Aristotle's conception of education. The cultivated ability of 'being at leisure in the right way', or of 'using leisure aright', was for Aristotle the distinguishing mark of the educated citizen. This was precisely the practical end he had in mind as the happiness which consisted in an activity of the soul in accordance with goodness. (*Politics* VIII, iii) Leisure was thus to be distinguished from play, or recreation, which was merely a way of resting from work, and therefore subservient to the requirements of work. Leisure, in contrast with work, was to be pursued and chosen 'for its own sake', not as a means to some other end. From this Aristotle concluded that there were hierarchical divisions in the schooling to be followed by the youth of the *polis*.

> Thus it becomes clear that, in order to spend leisure in civilised pursuits, we require a certain amount of learning and education, and that these branches of education and these subjects studied must have their own intrinsic purpose, as distinct from those necessary occupational subjects which are studied for reasons beyond themselves. (*Politics* VIII, iii)

In enlarging on this requirement, Aristotle added that there were certain things which the young citizens of the *polis* should *not* learn, such as those skills called mechanical, 'which have a deleterious effect on the body's condition' and are unworthy of the dignity of a citizen of the *polis*. Thus, despite his concern with 'the practical', there were kinds of practical knowledge - such as crafts and trades – to which Aristotle gave a low standing among the things an educated and leisured citizen should learn.[5]

Here again, a comparison with Socrates proves instructive. While the kind of educational activity pursued by Socrates in the streets and houses of Athens often begins amid the bustle of everyday life, it seems nevertheless that most of the participants recorded in the early Dialogues not only have ample time for, but are also keen to pursue, the kind of activity Socrates invariably seeks to get under way. In other words the use of leisure for the pursuit of truth has itself become here a distinctive cultural accomplishment, and in the most informal, unforced way. Yet the hierarchical distinctions between different kinds of knowledge which feature prominently in Aristotle's work, and even more strongly in Plato's, have little or no place in this Socratic accomplishment. For Socrates, the only distinction in knowledge that made a crucial difference was that between the kind of knowledge which gave a better insight into our own beliefs, attitudes and actions, and that which failed to do so.

While care must be taken not to overestimate the contrasts between Socrates' and Aristotle's standpoints on education, some crucial differences nevertheless remain. Three of these are of particular significance for us. Firstly, Socrates' essential concern was for educational activity, understood as a personal and critical engagement with the moral, cultural and religious traditions of the *polis*. Aristotle's concerns were much wider – including science, metaphysics, ethics and politics. Education for him was far less a personal moral quest than a branch of politics which must be legislated for by the lawgivers of the *polis*. Secondly, Socrates continually behaved as if the enterprise of teaching and learning, when undertaken as a self-critical pursuit of truth, was entitled to a certain freedom of conscience, or a qualified measure of sovereignty ('Athenians, I honour and love you but I shall obey God rather than you'). For Aristotle, no such sovereignty was envisaged for education. Aristotle in fact seems no less definite than Plato in regarding education as a strategic instrument, to be controlled in all key respects by the rulers of the *polis*. The third difference concerns practice itself – as *described* by Aristotle and as *experienced* by Socrates. Aristotle is nowadays widely acclaimed as the philosopher who attained an unsurpassed understanding of the subtleties of practical decision-making and whose insights and authority can be called on when the discretion of professional groups looks threatened by the technocratic rationalism of economics and technology. Aristotle himself seemed to deny this discretion, however, to a practice such as education, apparently because of its subservient status to politics in his scheme. In this denial he contrasts most completely with what was distinctive in the actual practice of Socrates. At least where education is concerned, Aristotle supplied more a *theory* that constrained acceptable practice than an account of practice itself, including critical reflections on its own conduct.

Institutionalising the Visionary – the Greco-Roman Confluence

Both Plato's and Aristotle's arguments on education granted supremacy to political and institutional considerations over the essentially personal considerations championed by Socrates. The influence of Plato's and Aristotle's works on the subsequent history of Western civilisation, and particularly Western learning, is incalculable. As we shall explore in some detail in the next chapter, Platonist themes were systematically incorporated into Christendom through the writings of authors such as Plotinus, Porphyry and Saint Augustine. Aristotle was similarly served, and more completely so, by the work of Thomas Aquinas.

But the eclipse of the Socratic occasioned by these decisive cultural shifts also had another important contributory source, namely the writings of Cicero and Quintillian, which marked the distinctive Roman current in the history of Western education. There is a revealing, but generally overlooked remark in Cicero's *Tusculan Disputations* where he describes his own 'method' as following closely that of Socrates:

> it allows me to refrain from expressing a personal opinion of my own, while I am at liberty to correct other people's mistakes and

> make my own search for the most probable solution, whatever subject might be involved. (*Tusculan Disputations* 3-4).

Notwithstanding his supreme accomplishment in making Latin a language of ideas and of literary discourse, Cicero fails to grasp the unique character of Socratic practice and this misrepresentation is strengthened by Cicero's own frequent use of the dialogue form in his writings. His description of Socratic practice just quoted is quite misleading, and is so in at least three respects. Firstly, the self-assurance in the tone misses entirely the *self-critical* character of Socrates' work. Socrates' reluctance to express an opinion, far from being a liberty which enabled him 'to correct other people's mistakes', was born of his own previous experience of the limitations of human intellect. His continual efforts to find answers to the most important of life's questions had brought him a long way in correcting his own assumptions but had still fallen far short of definite answers, and his questions to others, insofar as they can be described as corrections, were invariably designed to allow them to share a similar chastening. Cicero suggests, secondly, that he is laying hold of a Socratic 'method' and thirdly, that this method could be applied to any number of topics: to 'whatever subject might be involved'. For Socrates himself, the subject at issue was much nearer to hand and was essentially one, not many or any. As we have seen, moreover, his method was an *intrinsic* feature which united his vision of the issue to be pursued and the unfailing commitment with which he pursued it.

Critically viewed then, the frequency with which Cicero does *not* refrain from expressing his own opinions in his written dialogues presents us with both a gain and a loss. On the one hand, his writings are an eloquent testimony to his sense of civic justice, which trancended the bounds of any *polis* (*civitas*) to include all of humanity. On the other, insofar as they claim congruence with the practice of Socrates, they represent a recurring distortion of that practice. Unlike the later writings of Plato, where the distortion of anything Socratic is clearly evident in the boldness of Plato's own metaphysics, the urbane richness of Cicero's prose and the *humanitas* which pervades it invariably elicit an approving response in the reader. But this is a response to something which is now memorably, but wrongly, represented as a Socratic approach in action. When we consider that Socrates himself left no writings to posterity and that the writings of Plato and Cicero became central to Western conceptions of civilised life, the true magnitude of the eclipse of the Socratic begins to strike us.

Quintillian's major work, *Institutio Oratoria* (*The Education of an Orator*) provides rare insights into educational practice in Roman schools in the first century AD and also reveals how important Greek cultural influences had become in Roman education by the early period of the Empire. Quintillian himself recommended Greek as the language which Roman pupils should learn first, while Latin would later accompany it. The 'Grammar' which became the central feature of Quintillian's public education included not only a detailed study of correct speaking and writing, but also a study of poetic and literary works, particularly Homer and Virgil. He was keen moreover that pupils should draw personal satisfaction from their studies and that teaching should cultivate a love of learning among pupils. Deeply concerned at the characteristic harshness of Roman schools and the bondage which schooling all too often meant for pupils, Quintillian sought to infuse teaching and learning with the humanity which he so earnestly respected in Cicero.

Quintillian's writings show, however, that his educational concerns, like those of Plato, Aristotle and Cicero, were more political than personal. In this, all of the four differed essentially from Socrates. In the writings of all four, the Socratic concern with the quality of each individual's experience of teaching and learning is superseded by considerations of an institutional nature. Where Plato emphasised the legislative provisions he saw as necessary for the education of the philosopher as ruler, Aristotle emphasised those which he viewed as central to the schooling of the loyal and happy citizen of the *polis*. Both Cicero and Quintillian were concerned with the cultivation of the orator: the person of high reputation who would be well read in both Greek and Roman literature, who would appreciate the merits of philosophy, but who would be chiefly occupied with conducting the affairs of public office in a state which was no longer a *polis*, but rather the home of an empire. It is difficult to conceive a more sharp contrast to this fourfold confluence of institutional voices than the following bold declaration by Socrates at his trial, which reveals a striking disavowal of institutional power: 'The true champion of justice, if he intends to survive even for a short time, must necessarily confine himself to private life and leave politics alone'. (*Apology* 32) Yet, paradoxically, the entire thrust of Socrates' work – as we have seen a little earlier – was in practising what he himself called the 'true political art' of education.

The difference here between Socrates and the other four is not merely a difference in emphasis; nor can the paradox just mentioned be explained by such a suggestion. Indeed the subsequent history of Western education shows that it was not the Socratic practice, but rather the concentration of educational influence in powerful institutional hands, whether of Empire or Church, secular or ecclesiastical, that became the predominant pattern. The difference lies rather in the nature Socrates' vision of *what constituted* the true political task; namely, that of attempting to involve the citizens of the *polis* in a shared effort to give self-criticism a special importance, to submit acquiescent tendencies to renewed questioning, in their understanding of themselves, their culture and traditions. Apart from this difference with the major Greek and Roman authors on education, the distinctiveness of the Socratic lies more particularly in Socrates' wholehearted reliance on the earnestness of personal presence in the interplay of influence between older and younger generations. It lies further in his suspicion of institutional provisions which would give a privileged standing from the start to standpoints which sought more to wield influence than enter into the to-and-fro of its disciplined play, more to secure compliance to established authority and received wisdom than to get discerning questioning under way.

Conclusion

The four themes of this chapter have attempted to uncover the origins of what I have called the eclipse of the Socratic. In the course of these investigations the distinctive features of Socratic educational practice were identified and their contrast with the tone and tenor of the major educational writings of Greek and Roman authors of the classical period was emphasised. Chief among these Socratic features, as far as the conduct of the educational enterprise is concerned, is the requirement that the practice of teaching and learning – as a quest for truth undertaken in a participatory ethos of self-criticism and sincere study – should enjoy a measure of independence, or sovereignty, from the strategic and tactical concerns of institutional political life. In the following chapters the major consequences of the eclipse of the Socratic for the history of Western education will be explored. The first of these consequences to concern us is the denial of sovereignty to the conduct of education, or perhaps more accurately, the widespread absence of an awareness that education as a cultural undertaking should be entitled to any sovereignty. Let us now consider this absence at closer range, beginning with the period when the institutional foundations of Western religion and politics were being laid and secured. Our attention will focus in particular on the harnessing of educational endeavour to the purposes of an ascendant political and religious orthodoxy in Europe – that of Christendom.

Notes:

1. In the late nineteen eighties in the Republic of Ireland, campaigns were carried out by conservative Catholic activists against programmes of 'health education', 'values clarification' and 'lifeskills'. These programmes normally included 'facilitation of learning', or 'non-directive' approaches to teaching. A trenchant collection of articles attacking these approaches was issued by D. Manly, V. Cox, L. Brown & N. Lowry, and published under the title *The Facilitators* (Dublin: Brandsma books, 1987). Other Western countries have experienced similar campaigns.

2. Even in the *Apology*, which contains some of Socrates' most explicit declarations, one finds not so much a body of doctrines as an attitude of deferential regard for inherited moral and religious tradition, and the conviction to live life by the most challenging standards of such tradition (e.g. justice, consistency, self-control, courage). Hand in hand with this deference, indeed part of the moral conviction of Socrates himself, is a questioning stance which subjects to further critical inquiry even the highest standards which he has already provisionally, but earnestly, accepted. The other early Dialogues show the unfinishing character of such further enquiry.

3. A major contribution to this literature has been made in recent years by Gregory Vlastos in his book *Socrates – Ironist and Moral Philosopher* (Cambridge: Cambridge University Press, 1991). Vlastos explores here in detail the differences between the historical Socrates and Plato's 'metaphysical' Socrates. These differences are pertinent to my own arguments, but my main concern, unlike that of Vlastos, is to focus on what is *educationally* distinctive in the work of the historical Socrates.

4. The presentation of Plato's views here as *prescriptions* sits perhaps too comfortably with the argument, championed for instance by Karl Popper, that Plato's provisions are a philosophical design for dictatorship. If, on the other hand, the *Republic* is read allegorically rather than literally – if it is understood not as a series of prescriptions but as an incisive and detailed fable – the emphasis on things dictatorial recedes considerably and its remarkable imaginative conceptions are cast more strongly to the foreground. This latter kind of reading is championed by Hans-Georg Gadamer. Unfortunately, the institutional history of Western education provides more evidence in support of the literal-prescriptive influence of Plato on educational authorities than of any abiding inspiration of such authorities by Plato's more emancipatory themes. See Karl Popper's *The Open Society and its Enemies: Volume 1 – The Spell of Plato* (London: Routledge and Kegan Paul, 1950, 1980) and also Hans-Georg Gadamer's *The Idea of the Good in Platonic-Aristotelian Philosophy*, translated with an Introduction by P. Christopher Smith (New Haven: Yale University Press, 1986).

5. In a recent study Paddy Walsh notes that the disparagement of the physical, the bodily and the material in Plato's metaphysics found an unsurpassed, yet incomplete, series of counter perspectives in Aristotle's work. Walsh suggests that it was Aristotles's social position, rather than anything of philosophical principle, that prevented him from appreciating the merits of craft and technical activities. Walsh also argues that if an Aristotelian influence had gained the ascendancy which Platonism gained in the crucial centuries of the institutionalising of Christianity, this Chrisianity would have been more authentic to its biblical roots. See Walsh's *Education and Meaning – Philosophy in Practice* (London: Cassell, 1993) p.167.

CHAPTER TWO

Christendom and the Custodianship of Learning

Introduction

Roman persecutions of Christians ended early in the fourth century and the remainder of that century was to witness dramatic changes in the fortunes and the public character of Christianity itself. Edicts issued by Emperors Galerius in 311 AD and Constantine I in 313 AD gave all religions equal rights, and this enabled Christians to worship openly and to engage in missionary work. Thus the way was opened for Christianity to become the predominant religion of the Roman Empire, a development which received additional impetus from a declaration by Emperor Theodosius I in 381 AD making Christianity the state religion and forbidding pagan rites. This transformation gave a new importance to the pursuit of learning by Christians, who could now aspire to high public office, but it also rendered more problematic the standing among Christians of the philosophical and literary heritage of the pagan Classical era in Greek and Roman civilisation.

Towards the end of the second century the Christian preacher Tertullian had denounced the pagan learning of Greece and Rome as folly, and as superfluous for Christians. The Sacred Scriptures, he insisted, contained all that a Christian needed to know. Clement of Alexandria, a contemporary of Tertullian, argued that Christian faith did not require philosophical learning but he also claimed that the Greek learning, despite its many idolatries, provided insights which could enrich and deepen the understanding of a Christian. Clement's successor as head of the School of Alexandria, Origen, pushed this idea further early in the third century by urging that Greek philosophy should be viewed as the 'handmaiden' of Christianity. Views remained divided on the proper attitude of Christians to the classical learning until the prolific writings of Augustine (354-430 AD) set forth a radical solution, namely a philosophy which was no longer a mere handmaiden but one which was itself a Christian theology of intellectual sophistication and compelling force. Augustine's christianised adaptation of Greek ethical and political philosophy also contained significant new elements and was to become a major source of authoritative arguments in the church's efforts to expand and consolidate its institutional power. More specifically, Augustine's work set the design for some of the most important developments in Western learning. In this chapter we shall be exploring how these developments were themselves part of the shaping of Christendom – namely the thousand year era from the coronation of Charlemangne to the revolutions of the late eighteenth century, during which ecclesiastical power and influence dominated not merely the religious but also the educational and political life of Western civilisation.

The Augustinian Precedent

Prior to his conversion to Christianity Augustine had been deeply influenced by the writings of Cicero, which he first studied as a student in Carthage, and by the Platonist tracts of Plotinus and Porphyry, which he encountered while a professor of Rhetoric in Milan. In Cicero's texts Augustine discovered not only a model of literary grace, but also the inspiring idea of an ordered civic community (*civitas*) not in thrall to indulgent pleasures but rather governed by reason, justice (*iusticia*) and law (*ius*). In the writings of Plotinus and Porphyry he found a wholehearted renunciation of sensuality, by which a purification of desire and an unclouding of vision might be achieved. To Augustine, who declares in his *Confessions* that he was continually troubled by the force of his sexual appetite, the ascetic emphasis in Platonism offered the possibility of emancipation into a higher happiness and more serene existence. His attraction by this possibility became more pronounced as he practised meditation along Platonist lines, listened to the sermons of St Ambrose in Milan, read the Letters of St Paul and studied accounts of the lives of Christian hermits – like Antony of Egypt – and of ascetic Christian communities. It is not surprising then that his conversion to Christianity was accompanied by a decision to become celibate. More striking are the nature and the intensity of the conviction underlying Augustine's Christianity: that the human soul is inescapably abandoned to corruption and that human will is perverse, without the all-saving, undeserved and *all-controlling* grace of God. This conviction, as we shall see, was crucial to Augustine's views on learning and on authority and obedience.

The Greek ideal of civic community, the *polis* of the writings of Plato and Aristotle, became latinised to *civitas* in Cicero's works. Here, however, the scope of the *civitas* attains a new significance, as being the hub of an empire. A further and decisive transformation takes place with Augustine. In his book *De Civitate Dei* Augustine now put forward a spiritual counterpart of the *polis* or *civitas*, namely a 'city of God'. To this he attributed many of the characteristics of a civic community, particularly those concerning justice, law, duty and obedience. In keeping with the Platonist dualism of a higher, unseen world of truth and good on the one hand, and the everyday world of the senses and their gratification on the other, Augustine sought to distinguish a 'heavenly' from an 'earthly' city. In the first of these, human aspiration and action were guided by a love of God, in the latter by a wilful love of self. The earthly city was in each instance contained by physical boundaries, which it frequently sought to expand by invading other cities and which led to recurring strife and bloodshed. In Augustine's view, all earthly cities, including the most powerful city of Rome, must sooner or later crumble through internal struggles, or fall prey to conquest. The city of God, by contrast, was universal and eternal. Its members included God's elect from all races, in whom the vice of pride, or self-glorification, had yielded to the virtue of humility, or submissive will, in the face of God's omnipotent love and justice and his promise of eternal salvation.

Injustice, for Augustine, results then not merely from an enslavement of human vision by sensuality, as Plato had taught, but also from a perversion of will; a perversion moreover which remains humankind's essential condition unless redeemed by the all-powerful *gift* of God's grace. Augustine's depiction of divine grace as a gift sought to point out that humankind had done nothing, or could do nothing, to deserve it, although individuals could re-direct and discipline their wills as a consequence of having received the gift of grace. Augustine's grim view of human nature – as being essentially and helplessly corrupted since Adam's fall – introduces a pessimistic note which goes decisively further than the accounts of human shortcomings contained in the moral philosophies of Plato, Aristotle and Cicero. In each of these philosophies the quality of an individual's own efforts, including the moral insights and civic benefits achieved through these efforts, was given a substantial part to play in enabling humans to achieve a share in happiness. On the Augustinian account, however, the civic purposes of education, as envisaged for *polis* or *civitas*, now became worthless, or even worse, unless the human will which underlay these purposes had first been redeemed by the saving power of divine grace and re-directed by the commandments of God.

In accordance with these views, Augustine claimed that the entire enterprise of education must be oriented towards an acknowledgement of God's saving grace. His book *De Magistro* (The Teacher) emphasises that learning must be dedicated to the pursuit of truth. It also makes the apparently Socratic point that it is a mistake to construe the teacher as a transmitter of truth. Rather Augustine sees the teacher as one who assists learners to discover the truth by their own insights. In this way the learner would hold to the truth more strongly than if it had merely been taken on the teacher's command.

So how, in the light of all of this, would things stand with the Socratic conception of education, which, as we saw in the last chapter, the educational writings of the classical authors effectively eclipsed? Recall that Socrates himself declared at his trial that all of his educational activities proceeded from his willing obedience to a divine, not a human command. On the face of it, there are grounds for claiming that the course taken by Augustine's appropriation of classical philosophy might open the way for some kind of renaissance of Socratic educational practice – albeit a Christianised one. The ascetic tendencies in Socrates' own lifestyle, and his conviction that the majority of humankind inclined towards worldly goals rather than self-knowledge, lend weight to such grounds. And these grounds still remain worthy of exploration.

But the possibility of such a renaissance was never conceived by Augustine himself, nor by the successive generations of leaders of church and state on whom his doctrines were to have a pervasive influence. Augustine's unyielding insistence on humankind's inherent perversity and on the worthlessness of moral action unless redeemed and re-oriented by divine grace, (an insistence evidenced in his controversy with Pelagius) gave birth to theological conceptions of authority and obedience which were quite at odds with Socrates. The truth which the teacher in Augustine's *De Magistro* (*DM*) was to help his pupils to appropriate for themselves was, in Augustine's words, one disclosed by 'the enlightening action of God from within'. (*DM* section 40) But for Augustine this was a *certainty* already established in the teacher's mind – 'God, Who is Truth itself'. (*DM* section 21) The teacher's actions were to establish this sense of certainty in the pupil's mind also – the sense that all essential questions and all doubts have already been answered – as can be gathered from the closing paragraph of *De Magistro,* which is spoken by the teacher's pupil.

You have not neglected a single question that had caused me to

> doubt, or which has not been answered for me by that inner oracle exactly as you had expressed it in words. I am grateful, however, that your remarks have continued without interruption, particularly because they have anticipated and answered all the objections I was prepared to raise. (*DM* section 46)

We have seen that a comprehensive censorship of literary works and a close custodial control of the learner's sensibility were among the most un-Socratic of the speculations in Plato's *Republic*. Features such as these now achieved a *practical reality*, however, and an enduring institutional form, through the application of Augustinian theology to ecclesiastical, political and educational affairs. These developments, as we shall shortly consider, took place in the early centuries of Christendom and ensured that the ideals of Socratic educational practice were consigned to forgotteness during the long ascendancy of Christendom in Western civilisation.

Pope Gregory I (Gregory the Great) had come from an aristocratic Roman family and despite his advocacy of a monastic way of life, he advanced the powers of the papacy very considerably during the late sixth century by cultivating the regard of leading Roman political figures. By the end of the eighth century the political power of the Christian church had advanced to such a degree that Pope Leo III was able to take the boldest and most significant of initiatives. In an unprecedented departure during Mass on Christmas day in the year 800, he crowned the Frankish king Charlemagne as 'Charles Augustus, Emperor of the Romans'. By setting himself up as the bestower of the title, Pope Leo was assuming the superior position. In receiving the crown from papal hands, Charlemagne acquiesced in placing the Emperor's powers under the authority of the pope. Leo's action also carried the implication that the papacy had the power to withdraw what it had bestowed, and thus to unseat kings and emperors. The practice of monarchs being blessed by ecclesiastical figures at their inauguration had already become widespread in Europe. The idea behind the practice was that kingly authority derived from God. The significance of Charlemagne's coronation however was that this authority was now properly to be conferred – and withdrawn – by *the church*, which had its earthly seat in Rome.

In this growth of the church's dominion in public affairs the theology of Augustine played a crucial part. This came about in particular through the major reforms of Gregory VII (Pope from 1073-85, formerly Hildebrand, Archdeacon of Rome). Gregory's appropriation of Augustinian theology, together with its significance for Medieval civilisation, has been presented in an illuminating way to contemporary readers by Alasdair MacIntyre in chapter 9 of his book *Whose Justice? Which Rationality?* (1988). MacIntyre identifies four strategic aims in Gregory's papacy. Firstly, he set about an internal reform of the church, through such measures as the enforcement of clerical celibacy, a prohibition on the purchasing of ecclesiastical office, the systematic application of Canon law and the upholding of papal authority over all other bishops. Secondly, Gregory sought to end the power of kings and princes to appoint people to ecclesiastical office in their dominions. In this he attempted to emphasise the duties of European monarchs as champions of the church and to take from them a liberty which he regarded as belonging to the church. Closely associated with this effort was Gregory's third task, namely the detailed formulation of Christian principles of universal justice and of the Church's claim to freedom – its *libertas* – to proclaim and implement these principles. Fourthly, Gregory undertook the codification of principles of justice into the law of the church, a task which was to become a continuing one in the history of the papacy.

MacIntyre traces the Augustinian rationale in Gregory's pursuit of these tasks. Central to this rationale is the concept of the 'city of God'. The supremacy which Augustine claimed for this over any earthly city now becomes a moral supremacy of the papacy over the regal and feudal dominions of Europe. As MacIntyre explains it: 'God reigns as king of a city with sovereignty over the entire universe and the pope is God's viceroy'. (p.159) Inherent in this rationale is the transformation of the concept of *polis* or *civitas* into a Christian theocracy, or more precisely perhaps, into a province of a higher theocracy which claims universal dominion. The institutions, laws and public offices of such a society cannot be described as secular, but receive their purpose and character from a hierarchy in which the papacy is the highest earthly authority. MacIntyre provides a revealing instance of this in the following passage, which shows that Gregory's claims for the papacy were not circumscribed by the geographical limits of Europe: 'Gregory wrote to Toirdealbhach Ua Briain, king of Munster and claimant to the high-kingship of Ireland, that the whole world must obey and revere the Roman Church, and he re-iterates similar claims to other princes'. (p.161)

For Gregory, as for Augustine, true justice could not be a secular concept, any more than it could be a concept of any of the classical pagan religions. Nor could it even be a rational concept, unless reason had first acknowledged that its own proper exercise was made possible only by a submission of human will in obedience to God's commandments. Humility thus becomes the principal religious virtue and the classical virtues of pride and the pursuit of honour are recast as vices of the earthly city. But the importance given to humility in Augustinian philosophy bears almost exclusively on its relation to obedience to God and his earthly representatives rather than on its relation to the other major Christian imperative of loving one's neighbour. It seems that the hierarchies of Platonism retained such a strong hold on Augustine's mind that, for him, the quality of relations with human neighbours was of comparatively minor importance to that of the sublime and mystical quality of relations with God. This point has many implications for education, which we will return to a little later. Here, however, it is necessary to make explicit the consequences of Augustine's – and Gregory's – hierarchical Christianity for how the church came to an abiding position of supremacy in the era of Christendom.

The fusion of the theological with the political in Augustine's philosophy, which enabled the church to achieve this supremacy through the actions of Gregory VII and his more notable successors, is neatly paraphrased in MacIntyre's account:

> The order of *iusticia* (justice) is an order embodied in the universal church, an order in which each human being has his or her own allotted place and his or her own allotted duties. To occupy that place and to perform that function well is to be just. To refuse to occupy that place or to discharge its duties badly or to rebel against the order defining that place is to fail in respect of justice. . . Injustice is *inobedientia*. The vice to which disobedience gives expression is *superbia*, pride. The virtue underlying and required for justice is humility. (p.160)

Gregory's reforms sought everywhere to translate the principles of *iusticia* into codes of *ius* (law); that is, into binding rules of conduct for the various levels of office and 'allotted places' of the *societas christiana*. MacIntyre's account of the Gregorian enterprise concludes that it constituted the highest achievement of the Augustinian tradition until the synthesis between Aristotelian philosophy and Augustinian theology achieved by Thomas Aquinas in the thirteenth century. MacIntyre's account is written, however, from the standpoint of an 'Augustinian Christian' (p.10) and contains little that is critical of Augustine's theology or Gregory's application of it. The merits of the Augustinian-Gregorian achievement are cast in a more sombre light, however, when the consequences of this achievement for education are considered, together with the long shadows it cast over the conduct of teaching and learning in Europe. In the following pages we shall examine the Pauline character Augustinian Christianity and contrast this with a Christianity which is based on the life and teachings of Jesus Christ, as these are revealed in the New Testament Gospels. My purpose in this effort is nothing nostalgic, but rather the reclamation of the practical ideal of education as an unfinished and unfinishing human seeking; a seeking which allows an essential measure of sovereignty to the teachers and learners who engage in it.

Learning as Acquiescence

We have already noted that the Christianity which became institutionalised in European Christendom was strongly influenced by the doctrines of Platonism, the Letters of St Paul and the writings of Augustine. Let us recall, in summary, the contributions of the first and last of these before considering the educational significance of St Paul. The ingredients contributed by Platonism included three chief features: firstly, the hierachical division of knowledge into a higher intellectual-spiritual and a lower sensual realm, each with its own sub-divisions; secondly, the claim that the higher of the two main realms was a world of changeless truths; thirdly the claim that these higher truths were attainable only by the strictly disciplined and properly tutored 'eye of the soul'. To this metaphysical framework Augustine added three further ingredients: firstly the twofold doctrine of a City of God, presided over by a loving Father, in contrast to an earthly city in thrall to sensual lusts of all kinds; secondly, his belief in the essential perversity of human will, prior to its penitent submission to God's all-redeeming grace; thirdly his claim that the God proclaimed by his own theology was the final truth and that all teaching must proceed in such a way that learners are brought to accept this in a voluntary manner.[1]

Plato's claim that the upper world was one of changeless truths found a strong echo in the teachings of St Paul, as did his custodial views on the contents of teaching and learning. It is by no means clear however if Paul was acquainted with Plato's writings. From an educational viewpoint, what is most striking about Paul's Christianity is its paucity of pedagogical insight and its preoccupation with the passing on of an orthodox body of doctrine. In these two respects it contrasts sharply with the reported teaching episodes in the life of Jesus Christ. Paul identified Christian 'faith' more with an obedience to the doctrines contained in his own Letters rather than with a *trusting and questioning belief* which was primarily a personal response to the invitation contained in the words of Jesus Christ. Some of these Pauline doctrines are curiously – even notoriously – at odds with what the four New Testament Gospels report of the actual teachings of Jesus. For instance, in his Letter to the Romans, Paul initially places himself in the Gospel tradition by affirming Christ's teaching that God will reward all according to their good works. (Rom 2:6; also Gal 6:7-8) A little later however, he declares that the substance of Christianity lies not in moral acts but rather in justification *only* through 'faith':

> For we conclude that a man is put right with God only through faith, and not by doing what the [Jewish] Law commands. (Rom 3:28)

Also:

> But the man who has faith, not works, who believes in the God who declares the guilty to be innocent, it is his faith that God takes into account in order to put him right with himself. (Rom 4:5)

The displacement of good works by Pauline 'faith' is associated with another distinctive note in Paul's Letters, namely the conviction that the impulses of the sensual, and particularly the sexual, are essentially evil. This conviction prefigures the Augustinian doctrine that human nature is claimed by corruption and can only be saved by a penitent acknowledgement of its own wickedness in the face of the wholly undeserved grace of God. The condemnation of the 'flesh', that is, of human nature itself, builds up in the early chapters of the Letter to the Romans and by the seventh and eighth chapters it receives an emphasis which amounts to an onslaught:

> I know that good does not live in me – that is, in my human nature. (Rom 7:16)
>
> This, then, is my condition: by myself I can serve God's law only with my mind, while my human nature serves the law of sin. (Rom 7:25)
>
> To have your mind controlled by human nature results in death: to have your mind controlled by the Spirit results in life and peace. (Rom 8:6)

Paul hastened to claim that what he was offering through such pronouncements was not a personal opinion or interpretation, but rather that his teachings accurately represented the Gospel of Jesus Christ, Divinely inspired Son of God, and that any contesting interpretations should be shunned. (Rom 2:8, 16:17; 1 Cor 11:2, 15:1-3). The presumption underlying these claims is that Christianity is a fixed body of doctrines, as now elaborated by the Pauline Letters, which must be accepted unquestioningly and *in toto*. This presumption however overlooks a number of points which mark a decisive contrast between Paul's authorship on the one hand, and, on the other, the contents of the four Gospels of the New Testament. Chief among these points are the following:

* that Paul's judgements on some important Christian teachings might be coloured by regretful recollections of excesses of his own past and that there may be human natures which might be different from Paul's own, at least in some respects and in some degree;

* that the teachings of Jesus Christ were *primarily* a call to the reign of God; a reign which gave to a two-fold call to love (God and neighbours) the primacy which existing religious practices tended to give to fulfilling the letter of the Law;

* that the moral teachings of Christianity included many condemnations of human selfish inclinations, but not a fatalistic judgement on human nature as such;

* that the social teachings of Christianity – the practical virtues and good works called for in attempting to love one's neighbour – had an imperative status which the less social Christian practices, such as mysticism, asceticism, celibacy, did not have;

* that in communicating his message Jesus Christ always anticipated his audiences judiciously: for instance, to groups which included non-believers, sceptics or potential believers (i.e. 'multitudes' as distinct from 'disciples') he never spoke in the didactic tone or literal idiom characteristically adopted by Paul, but rather in parables only ('and without parables *he did not speak to them*' Mt 13:34; Mk 4:34);

* that pedagogical devices such as parables – by granting the hearer *the dignity and privacy to interpret*, and either to apply the point of the parable to his or her own life and circumstances or to discard it – largely got around the difficulty of forcing religious and ethical teachings on those who recoiled from being lectured on religion and ethics;

* that parables have an additional merit of prompting the hearer to further reflection – namely a questioning of his or her own existing outlooks and conduct and, arising from this, to a further exploration and questioning of those teachings to which parable first drew the hearer's unforced attention.

The last three of these seven points are primarily educational in character and are strongly reminiscent of the Socratic educational practice described in the previous chapter. The main difference lies in the fact that whereas the religious traditions which became the contents of Socrates' efforts had an ambiguous ancestry and an often uncertain character, the ancestry of the Christian teachings was clearly evident, and the particulars of these teachings received their essential character from the central two-fold commandment of love. Both the Socratic morality of spiritual aspiration and the teachings proclaimed by Christ showed the reality (not merely the possibility) of an approach to teaching and learning which could be defended on universal rather than on sectional grounds. Yet, a Pauline reading of Christianity, with its neglect of the kind of pedagogy which allowed generous play to questioning and was particularly conducive to a religious gospel of love, became the predominant pattern in the schools and colleges of Christian Europe.[2] Recalling the central part played by Augustine's theology in the shaping of Christendom, we can now see the effects of Pauline themes in his grand synthesis. This synthesis, and its subsequent adoption by church authorities, made it almost inevitable that education in Christendom would be under an ecclesiastical control which was invariably authoritarian in character and that the conduct of teaching and learning would have to acquiesce in this event.

And thus, for the most part, it turned out. But this institutional custody of learning had to endure recurring tensions, which continued to threaten the established orthodoxy with the prospect of a different kind of engagement of imagination, sensibility and commitment. In the educational history of Christendom these tensions were marked by periodic skirmishes and attempted reconciliations until eventually Luther's sustained revolt in the sixteenth century precipitated the violent events of the Reformation. These upheavals, however, strengthened rather than weakened church determination to control learning and it was not until the European Enlightenment and its revolutionary aftermath that more questioning conceptions of teaching and learning began to make effective headway once more. These latter developments are now well known through our widespread acquaintance with the tradition which can be traced from the writings of Rousseau the later part of the eighteenth century, to the works of Dewey in our own century. In this tradition of the modern historical era, however, (which is reviewed in Chapter Seven) the play of questioning never quite achieves the primacy explicitly given to it in the educational practice of Socrates and equally evident in the teaching activities of Christ. In fact, as we shall see a little later, to give it this status would require a view of human experience as being fulfilled more by a questioning search than by an uncritical acquiescence in received doctrines, and, equally significant, as being stirred by questions of a personal, recurrent character.

To establish this more clearly, we need to look briefly now at how the frequent play of question and answer gave a vital quality to the teaching activities of Christ and at how this vitality, despite recurring efforts to rekindle it, was displaced by something much more restrictive in the educational practice of Medieval and later Christendom.

The Educational Distinctiveness of Christianity

The discernment shown by Christ in employing parables for the multitudes and a more literal style of address for those who were already keen to give eager attention to his words provides an initial insight into his entire approach to teaching and learning. The more dramatic exchanges in the New Testament Gospels show moreover how the teaching approach changes depending on the audience present at the time. In addition to the parables for the undifferentiated multitudes – which could include disciples as well as the sceptic and the hostile – a number of other key approaches can be identified. With his disciples his teaching was generally direct and thought-provoking (as in the sermon on the mount), and frequently illustrated with imaginative similes. For the most part the purpose of these similes, unlike the parables, was clearly stated from the start: the kingdom of heaven is like a treasure hidden in a field, or like a merchant seeking good pearls, or like a net cast for fishes. With the questions earnestly put to him by individuals he was invariably frank and earnest in his responses, as with Nicodemus (Jn 3), or the rich man who asked what he must do to merit eternal life.(Mt 19:16ff; Lk 18:18ff) Yet, in other instances he left his disciples in some troubled an thoughtful suspense, as when he spoke obliquely about his forthcoming capture and execution. (Mk 9:31; Lk 9:45) The educational significance of this suspense lies in its contrast with religious complacency on the one hand, and with a dogmatism born of religious certainty on the other.

But perhaps the most striking aspect of Christ's teaching approach was his handling of the orchestrated attempts of many members of the established ecclesiastical order to ensnare him. The fury aroused by Christ's teachings and activities among many of the Sadducees, Pharisees, lawyers and scribes who represented this order is reminiscent of that aroused among the more powerful Athenians by the activities of Socrates just over four centuries previously. Where Socrates, however, was content to bring those who challenged him to face up to their own ignorance and pretentiousness, Christ went considerably farther. In passage after passage of the New Testament gospels he exposed and condemned the hypocrisy of those who made a virtue of public piety, yet bore no compassion in their hearts. From an educational viewpoint a number of things can be noted about Christ's approach in these encounters.

Firstly, the resentment of the scribes and Pharisees was provoked by the effectiveness of Christ's efforts in getting followers of the Jewish law to question the quality of their own religious commitments.[3] Secondly, the unity of belief and practice evident in Christ's teaching activity exposed the pretentiousness and inhumanity of many of the ritual observances of the established religion. Thirdly, this palpable integrity of belief and action embodied a new message of categorical love; a message which relegated the significance of Jewish law and its enforcement and presented instead a direct personal challenge to the spiritual aspirations of each person. Fourthly, the superior appeal of the new message was publicly demonstrated through its teacher's manifest success in anticipating his opponent's objections, and in turning both ensnaring questions and ill-willed murmurings to exemplary effect in his replies. Indeed many of the chief features of the new religion of Christianity were revealed in such replies. For instance, the two-fold imperative to love God and neighbour wholeheartedly, together with the primacy of this imperative amongst the rest of the Christian teachings, was made clearly explicit by Christ in response to one of the many questions from Pharisee lawyers which were designed to incriminate him in the presence of hosts of witnesses. (Mt 22:34-40; Lk 10:25-37) Finally, Christ's teaching style took insightful account of the *interplay* of reason and feeling in human experience as it unfolds. In this it contrasted to all pedagogy – then and since – which presumed proprietorial rights on the learner's commitments, and which sought to implant fixed doctrines in an unyielding way, to such an extent that the learner as adult could view alternative doctrines only with resistance, or even vehement rejection.

These distinctive educational features of the new religion scarcely survived the confluence of influences – Platonist, Pauline, Augustinian – which marked the institutionalising of Christianity as the established religion of a European empire. The *libertas* claimed by the medieval Church to preach carried, as its corollary, systematic restrictions on the freedom of intellect to question the Church's doctrines. These restrictions had already become comprehensive by the time of Charlemagne's coronation in the year 800. They were most pronounced in the detailed Rules of the various monastic orders, some of which were particularly hostile to classical learning.[4] But the general rule of censorial supervision – of texts, of students and of teachers – was scarcely less strict in the Cathedral and Grammar schools, which were under episcopal rather than monastic control. The writings of earlier authors, whose reading of Christianity leaned more towards ascetic sanctity than towards neighbourly love, had secured a decisive emphasis in the early centuries of the church as an institution. Some of the more important of these, including St Augustine, St Ambrose, St Jerome and St Gregory the Great were not only included in the group referred to as Church Fathers, but were also accorded the more formal distinction 'Doctors of the Church'.[5]

Accordingly, where the main prescribed texts of Medieval learning were concerned, the writings of the Fathers ranked next in importance to the New Testament Scriptures, followed by glosses and commentaries on both these Scriptures and the writings of the Fathers themselves. In keeping with this restrictive canon an early encyclopaedia, the twenty-book *Etymologiae*, compiled by Isidore of Seville (570-636), was in key respects the product of the kind of detailed censorship of pagan learning recommended by Plato in his *Republic*. The important difference, however, was that Isidore's selection was now carried out on a grand scale in practice, and from the standpoint of church orthodoxy, as distinct from the merely speculative pre-Christian theology of Plato. Isidore's *Etymologia* also proved decisive for the organisation of curricula. It added further weight to the earlier division of knowledge by the Christian Cassiodorus into seven 'liberal arts': the *Trivium* of Grammar, Rhetoric and Dialectic and the *Quadrivium* of Arithmetic, Geometry, Astronomy and Music. This hierarchical classification was meant as a preliminary curriculum to the study of theology. Together with Isidore's compendium, it remained a standard feature of teaching and learning during the Middle Ages.

The Fortunes of the Questioning Spirit

With these observations we have set the scene to review some of the tensions which attended teaching and learning as the early centuries of Christendom were succeeded by Christendom's own period of greatest power – the Middle Ages. We have seen how Augustine's synthesis of Platonism and Pauline Christianity were embraced by the papacy and set the pattern for the contents of learning and the supervision of teaching in monasteries and episcopal schools throughout Europe. By the early twelfth century the *Trivium* and *Quadrivium* were well established and served as introductory studies for the higher branches of learning, namely theology, law and medicine. One of the subjects of the *Trivium*, namely dialectic (or philosophy), had, since Augustine's time, become closely associated with theology, and featured ever more prominently in the courses of studies of the universities which became established from the thirteenth century onwards. Theology was now composed mainly of study of Scripture and of orthodox commentaries and 'glossess' by Church Fathers. Philosophy was once again theology's handmaiden, although it still included the study of such pagan classics as were available – mainly the Platonist works of Plotinus and Porphyry and sections of Aristotle's logical writings which had been translated into Latin by Boethius. The relationship of philosophy to theology underwent a significant change, however, during the twelfth century – a change which was to resurrect something of the challenge and appeal of the Socratic and first Christian example, before eventually leading to a new institutionalisation in the form of scholasticism. The person chiefly responsible for initiating this change was a French scholar and teacher Peter Abelard.

A native of Brittany, Abelard was in his early twenties when he arrived in Paris around the year 1100 to study philosophy in the Cathedral school of Notre Dame, whose master was William of Champeaux. Abelard's gifted intellect, together with his contentious and assertive temperament, soon found him in heated debates with his master. The lecture format, rather than the formal disputation (*disputatio*), was still the main method of teaching at this time and Abelard felt that it allowed second-rate teachers to cultivate presumptuous ideas about their own wisdom, while at the same time inducing students into a spirit of unquestioning conformity and intellectual mediocrity. Before long Abelard had set up his own school, giving prominence to the disputation in his approach to teaching. Abelard's ease in the unpredictable play of the disputation, together with the lively appeal which ardent argument had to questioning and spectator students alike, soon greatly increased his reputation at the expense of William's, but ill health then forced him to retire to Brittany for some six years. Shortly after his return to Paris Abelard became involved in an intense debate with William on the philosophical standing of universals.[6] This ended in a humiliating defeat for William and in increased enrollments at Abelard's own school at Mont Ste Genevieve, from which the

University of Paris was later to grow. Family matters again summoned him to Brittany, however, but on his return to Paris on this occasion he departed once more, this time to study theology under the renowned Anselm of Laon. Whether Abelard had become keen to extend his prowess to further fields of study or whether his mother had persuaded him to turn his studies more towards his eternal salvation remains unclear.

But disappointment and impatience again met Abelard's expectations. Anselm's conservative approach to both theology and teaching meant that he did not entertain questions from his students, so Abelard began to compose theological commentaries of his own, to show that Anselm had neglected to focus on what was most worthy of questioning, but also to show the other students that he could outclass Anselm at his own profession. News of these events, and of Abelard's superior esteem among the student body, was brought to Anselm by two of his closest students, with the result that Abelard was forbidden to teach at Laon. But Abelard's reputation for scholarship *and for teaching* in theology now matched his eminence in both of these in philosophy and he was soon appointed master of the cathedral school of Notre Dame. William of Champeaux had gone to great lengths to prevent Abelard from succeeding himself in this post. Abelard was now at the height of his fame. His poor estimation of existing approaches to learning and to teaching, indeed of the most renowned teachers of his day, is revealingly, if audaciously, summed up in this extract from his autobiography, where he speaks of his experience in Laon:

> Anselm could win the admiration of an audience, but was useless when put to the question. He had a remarkable command of words but their meaning was worthless and devoid of all sense. The fire he kindled filled his house with smoke but did not light it up; he was a tree in full leaf which could be seen from afar, but on close and more careful inspection proved to be barren. (*Historia Calamitatum*, p.62).

But misfortune was soon to befall Abelard. As master of the school at Notre Dame he was a Canon, though not necessarily a priest. Another of the Canons, Fulbert, appointed Abelard as personal tutor to his seventeen-year-old niece Heloise, and the celebrated love affair which followed eventually brought about Abelard's castration at the hands of Fulbert's servants.[7] The rage which Abelard initially felt at his mutilation gave way, however, to an acceptance of his misfortune as God's punishment for his former sinful excesses. His reflections henceforth reveal a devout turn to the spiritual, yet in some respects an uncharacteristic acquiescence in the more pessimistic of Pauline and Augustinian themes. But his fame as a teacher spread throughout the Christian dominions of Europe. In particular, his questioning approach to the teaching of theology was a departure from the restrictive practice of the monasteries and the predictable routines of the cathedral schools. Abelard's most famous work, *Sic et Non*, was a collection of 158 questions of Christian doctrine, on which there were conflicting or ambiguous authorities. He assembled pertinent quotations and arguments from opposing authors on these questions but, with perceptive ingenuity, left the resolution of the question in each case to the to-and-fro of debate among students and their teachers. That Abelard's purpose here recalls something of genuine Socratic practice is clear from the following extract from the Preface to the book:

> We thought it good to collect the diverse statements of the Holy Fathers, as they have come to our memory, containing some problem which they seem to raise because of their lack of agreement, so that it may stimulate youthful readers to greater energy in the enquiry after truth and make them more acute in their pursuit of it. For the first key to wisdom is called questioning, diligent and unceasing.[8]

Of course Abelard's aim was more definite and more doctrinal than that of Socrates; yet his recognition of the fact that questions of religious doctrine cannot escape the conflicts of human interpretation contained two educational insights of first importance: firstly, that propositions which are candidates for people's beliefs and loyalties deserve to be examined in the light of conflicting propositions; secondly, that an acceptance of neither should be uncritical but should result, rather, from a disciplined consideration of both. In addition, his decision not to foreclose the questions with his own answers reveals a subtle understanding of the scope for freedom which any experience of educational consequence or merit calls for.

Abelard's approach drew sustained fire, however, from his theological adversaries, chief among whom was Bernard, abbot of a famous Cistercian abbey at Clairvaux. Bernard was an ascetic and mystic by temperament, for whom the mysteries of faith were certainties, thus incomparably beyond the powers of human reason to explore. Bernard viewed Abelard's efforts as a scandal. He campaigned vigorously to have Abelard's writings condemned as heresy and his letters to the Pope and the Roman cardinals reveal the uncontrolled depths of his indignation: 'The mysteries of God are forced open, the deepest things bandied about in discussion without reverence'.[9] Despite Bernard's success in orchestrating a victory over Abelard at the Council of Sens in 1140, Abelard's work was to have abiding effects. The papal condemnation which followed the Council was soon lifted, mainly through the intercession of Peter the Venerable, abbot of the Benedictine abbey of Cluny, but also because of a rapid acknowledgement of the merits and appeal of Abelard's work among leading theologians and Canon Lawyers.

Among the former was Peter the Lombard, author of *The Books of Sentences*, and among the latter was Gratian of Bologna, author of *The Concord of Discordant Canons*, more commonly known as the *Decree* of Gratian. Both books showed influences from Abelard's approach, in presenting passages and viewpoints from contrary authorities on major questions - of theology in one case and law in the other. Unlike *Sic et Non*, however, Peter's *Sentences* supplied answers to the questions considered, and thus tried to reconcile questioning with orthodoxy. Similarly, Gratian's *Decree* set forth authoritative principles from an adjudication of the various sources it cited and greatly enhanced the standing of Canon Law within the church. This approach became one of the chief characteristics of the scholastic learning of the Middle Ages. Indeed both books became central texts in the medieval universities and added substantially to the prevalence of the *disputatio* as a method of teaching and learning. It is clear, however, that with the methodical provision of answers to the questions raised, doctrinal orthodoxy was re-asserting its supremacy in the conduct of education. The qualified release of the questioning spirit which Abelard's efforts sought to accomplish was once more being subjected to tighter rein by ecclesiastical authority. In the course of this development the most remarkable philosophical achievement of Christendom, namely the prolific authorship of Thomas Aquinas, was to play a crucial part.

The Educational Character of Scholasticism

Shortly after Abelard's death (1142) Latin translations of Aristotle's writings, together with commentaries on them, became available in European centres of learning. Many of these were the fruits of non-Christian scholarship – most notably that of a Spanish Muslim, Ibn-Ruschd (known in Latin as Averroes) – and their study brought forth a series of condemnations by the church. Two leading Dominican scholars however, Albertus Magnus and his student Thomas Aquinas, were keen that Aristotelian studies would be made respectable within the church. To this end they sought successfully to have the papal denunciations lifted and they also undertook scholarly efforts of daunting proportions. Albertus set out to produce an encyclopaedia of the new learning in such a way that it would be brought into conformity with orthodox Christian doctrine. Although he never completed this task, he supplied during the course of it commentaries on Aristotle which became widely used in the universities. The task of bringing the works of Aristotle within a new Christian-classical synthesis was carried out by Thomas, whose labours were greatly assisted by new translations of Aristotle's writings by his fellow Dominican, William of Moerbeke and by Robert Grosseteste of Oxford.

Thomas' synthesis was considerably more ambitious in scope than that of Augustine. It sought to establish theology not merely as a science, but as supreme among sciences. The crowning achievement of his work was the *Summa Theologica*, which attempted not only to draw on all sources of philosophical and religious learning to date, but also to accomplish its own synthesis in the manner of a *disputatio*, or more precisely, a *series* of disputations. The *Summa Theologica* is what Thomas himself called a 'magisterial disputation', but in a written form, containing no less than 631 questions (*quaestiones*). The *quaestiones* are themselves divided into a number of 'articles', or sub-questions, and each is answered with an initial assertion, which is then backed up with primary and often secondary arguments. This is followed by the formal presentation of contrary arguments, which is in turn followed by Thomas' own adjudication between the arguments and his own authoritative answers to the question, or sub-question, at issue. The *Summa* was designed primarily for use with students of theology and Thomas, like Abelard before him, considered that the pursuit of questions was a far more fruitful approach to teaching than was the exposition of texts and commentaries. Mindful however of the accusations of heresy that the raising of questions could provoke among conservative theologians, he was careful to give an explicit rationale for his approach:

> One form of disputation is magisterial disputation, which is conducted in front of students not in order to dispel incorrect conceptions but in order to guide the listeners to realizing themselves the truth of the thesis proposed. In such cases one should use arguments which encourage the truth to grow, to show what is being said is true. If the master is content merely to present the solution to the question in the form of bald statements from the authorities, the listener will admittedly learn what the truth is,

> but his scholarship and his understanding will have gained nothing and he will leave the disputation empty.[10]

One of the chief pedagogical merits of the approach adopted in the *Summa Theologica* (*ST*) is that it introduced the student to a range of weighty arguments which was incomparably wider than what the student was otherwise likely to encounter. According to one estimate, the number of standpoints advanced in the entire text is roughly ten thousand.[11] In addition, the sobriety evident in its consideration of argument and counter-argument provided exemplary instances of the advances in understanding which could take place when, for the purposes of teaching and learning, one's passionate commitment to a particular standpoint can yield pride of place to the more dispassionate discipline that *disputatio* requires. The conclusions reached by Thomas to each of his questions provided, moreover, a fresh body of unambiguous principles. Although these were initially framed by Thomas for acceptance by theology students, their importance in the longer term is that they, in turn, became questions for the critical consideration of later generations of philosophers and theologians. The following example should help to illustrate the educational significance of this point.

Thomas' consideration of the question 'Is theology a science?', having examined the arguments for and against the proposition, concluded that it *was* a science, but that there were two kinds of science: one which proceeded from propositions of reason alone, such as arithmetic and geometry, and another which proceeds from 'principles revealed in the light of a higher knowledge, in other words the knowledge possessed by God and the blessed.' (*ST* Ia, q.1, a.2). Thomas' conclusion that theology is a science of the second kind would be acceptable to those whose belief in Revelation enabled them to regard key passages from Christian scriptures as basic principles for the study of theology. This group would have been taken to include virtually all of the teachers and scholars of Christendom. On the other hand, philosophers and scientists for whom scriptures were not acceptable, or not acceptable in this way, had for their part ample and clearly formulated *material for critique* in this, and in other of Thomas' conclusions. Scholars of this latter kind were not, however, to become a dominant force in European intellectual life for some centuries after Thomas.

Thomas' achievements therefore expanded the scope of philosophy by giving Aristotle's writing a central place. They also enriched the discipline of theology by balancing the prevailing pessimism of Augustinian themes with more promising Aristotelian ones. Thirdly, and not least, they improved the quality of teaching and learning by promoting and consolidating the scholastic practice of disputation. These achievements also loosened somewhat the constraints of church orthodoxy on learning. But in the final analysis, it must be acknowledged that Thomas' enterprise was conceived from the start *within* such constraints. To put this another way, and recalling a distinction made in the previous chapter, the disputations of the *Summa Theologica* are akin more to the *later* than to the earlier Dialogues of Plato, and indeed to the contrived dialogue in Augustine's *De Magistro*. In each of these cases the dialogue form no longer describes the interplay of a live event but rather serves to secure a more effective acceptance in the reader of the conclusion the author has already reached. In this respect, Abelard's *Sic et Non* shows a keener insight into the subtleties of educational experience, though it may indeed be the case that Thomas was not blind to Abelard's insights, but deliberately chose a different kind of pedagogy.

In any case, the range of sources assembled by Thomas for the purpose of presenting objections rarely enough gave prominence to ones which were sceptical or atheistic. Such sources may have been scarce, of course, but Thomas' famous 'proofs of the existence of God' show that he was nevertheless aware that a case could conceivably be made against God's existence. (*ST* Ia, q.2, a1). More significantly, it becomes clear during the course of Thomas' consideration of the relative merits of faith and reason in theological argument that faith is not only accorded a superior standing, but also that it proceeds from an unchallengeable certainty:

> As our faith is founded on infallible truth it is impossible to use any truth to prove anything that contradicts our faith. For this reason 'evidence' adduced against the faith must be invalid evidence, arguments which can be dismissed. (*ST* Ia, q.1, a8).

This bold conclusion of Thomas' may of course be sustainable in a particular sense if it is taken to apply only to theology – as a field of study where the highest scientific status is granted from the start to principles taken from sacred scriptures. But if it is applied to any field of study which must take a critical stance towards its own first principles, such as philosophy and the natural sciences, then it represents an imposition of the most restrictive kind. The role in which Thomas cast philosophy in the course of his investigations made it subordinate to theology. Where Plato produced a metaphysics which wedded philosophy to a purified Greek theology, Thomas Aquinas produced a metaphysics which Christianised some of

Aristotle's more significant themes. Perhaps the most striking instances of this can be seen in the use Thomas made of some of the most distinctive concepts of Aristotle's *Nicomachean Ethics*. For example, Aristotle's Greek term *episteme*, which meant knowledge of that which necessarily *is*, became *scientia* in Thomas' Latin translation but, as we have seen above, theology, based on principles of revelation rather than those of a questioning reason, became the supreme *scientia*. More particularly, Aristotle's *phronesis*, which identified the virtue of judicious deliberation over alternatives with a view to practical action in the *polis*, became the theological concept of *prudentia*, which was the virtue of bringing human policy-making into accordance with divine law. (*ST* IIa-IIae, q.47)

In conclusion, we can see that Thomas' efforts aimed at a consecration of all human learning and teaching. Although some aspects of his work provoked controversy in the short term, his canonisation in 1323, just forty-nine years after his death, gave his metaphysics an unparalleled standing, though not an exclusive one, in the schools and centres of learning throughout Christendom. From an educational viewpoint, however, this consecration could more critically be seen as a conquest of the spirit of questioning and a foreclosure of that freedom which, for Socrates, was crucial to education as an unfinished search and, as far as humans were concerned, an unfinish*ing* search for truth. In the course of time, the formal routines, the predictability, and the essentially closed character of scholastic approaches to study, tended increasingly to carry out thinking on the student's behalf, thus depriving learning of its much of its vitality. This prevailing custodianship suffered no serious challenge until the spirit of learning gained new energies and directions in the late fifteenth century, an event which is universally known as the Renaissance.

Notes:

1. In another of the volumes in this Maynooth Bicentenary Series, Gerard Watson explores in illuminating detail the seminal influence of Platonism – and more specifically the neo-Platonism of Augustine and others – on the Christianity which became institutionalised in Europe, including, significantly, the preservation of Platonism in the work of Thomas Aquinas. Watson's study is titled *Greek Philosophy and the Christian Notion of God* (Dublin: Columba Press, 1994)

2. It is possible to object that the reading of Paul presented here does less than justice to the *totality* of his works. And in some respects the objection may well be justified. What I am arguing however is that this is the kind of

reading of Paul which became the predominant one in the history of learning in Western civilisation.

3. Of course the reports of the miracles worked by Jesus would have aroused deep suspicions among the Pharisees, which led in time to allegations that he was possessed by the devil. (Jn 8:48-59)

4. The original Rule of St Benedict is the clearest illustration of this point. Under this Rule, there was little provision for study, no monk was to be allowed a book or pen of his own and reading took second place to daily manual work. William Boyd points out that Pope Gregory I ('Gregory the Great' 540-604) sought to impose the strictest form of the Benedictine Rule on the monasteries of Europe. The Irish monasteries of the seventh and eighth centuries provide a notable contrast to this Rule. There, the study of Latin and Greek classics and Irish literature seems to have been pursued harmoniously with that of sacred scriptures. (William Boyd, *The History of Western Education,* revised by E.J. King, London: Adam & Charles Black. Chapter IV).

5. There were other Fathers of the church, figures like Irenaeus and Justin Martyr, who seem to have had a more embracing vision of Christianity. They also seem to have been less influential however than those like the Doctors I have mentioned in the text.

6. This debate recalls something of Plato's distinction between manifestation of goodness in the physical-sensual world, and the idea of the Good as something independent of such manifestations, i.e. something universal rather than something merely present in particular manifestations.

7. Abelard recalls in his autobiographical work, *Historia Calamitatum,* that this appointment as tutor to Heloise was the consequence of his own artful work, as he had sexual designs on the girl for some time. He now availed of the opportunity to abandon himself to these designs with a truly remarkable intensity. Heloise, who was an educated, alert and exceptionally sincere girl, seems to have trusted and loved Abelard with a generosity which was the very opposite of the baseness of his original motives. In any case, their lovemaking was discovered and Abelard removed her secretly to Brittany when she became pregnant. He tried to assuage Fulbert's rage with a promise that he would marry Heloise in a secret ceremony. A public wedding would jeopardise Abelard's career as a leading teacher and philosopher. Heloise argued strenuously against any wedding but Abelard's will prevailed. After the birth of the child he removed Heloise to the Abbey of Argenteuil for her safety. His own safety was in greater danger, however, and one night while he slept, servants of Fulbert entered his room and brutally castrated him. After his initial shame and indignation, Abelard seems to have accepted this catastrophe as a punishment from God, for he now saw his life in a much different light and urged Heloise to take the nun's veil in the abbey, which she eventually did, not for any religious reasons but in her frustrated and now hopeless love for Abelard. The later correspondence between Abelard and Heloise provides numerous insights into their outlooks and human qualities and into the transformations which took place in their relationship in the months and years following Abelard's mutilation. See *The Letters of Abelard and Heloise,* translated with an Introduction by Betty Radice (Penguin Classics 1974).

8. An edition of *Sic et Non* (in Latin), edited by Blanche Boyer and Richard Mc Keon, was published by University of Chicago Press in 1977. The passage from the Preface quoted here is taken from *A Short History of Educational Ideas*, by S.J. Curtis & M.E.A.Boultwood (Slough: University Tutorial Press 1953/1977) p.101.

9. From Bernard's Letter No 238, quoted by Betty Radice in her Introduction to *The Letters of Abelard and Heloise*, p.36.

10. Thomas Aquinas, *Quaestiones Quodlibetales* 4, 18. Quoted by Anders Piltz in his book, *The World of Medieval Learning* translated by David Jones (Oxford: Basil Blackwell, 1981) p.186.

11. ibid.

CHAPTER THREE

From Good Letters to Modernity

Introduction

The humanism which history associates with the Renaissance was not so much a development of secularist origin but rather one of a religious and educational inspiration: its guiding ideal was to make learning the pathway to a new and civilising union between the classical literature of Greece and Rome and the spirit of early Christianity. The writings of Vergerius (1349-1420) and the practical example of Vittorino da Feltre (1378-1446) mark the Italian beginnings of this inspiration. But its flowering as an inspiration of European proportions is associated chiefly with Erasmus of Rotterdam (1466-1536), and with his English friends John Colet (1467-1515) and Thomas More (1478-1535). What was most distinctive in this inspiration was not just its religious character, but more particularly the *nature* of its religious character: firstly, its optimistic view of humankind and its prospects and secondly, its low regard for the prevailing scholastic theology. The first of these features marks a break with the doctrine of the depravity of humanity, a doctrine which, as we have seen, gained a central place in Christendom – chiefly through the importance given to St Paul's more grim themes in the seminal writings of St Augustine. The second feature expresses a distaste for the preoccupations and orthodoxies of scholastic learning and champions an aspiration for a climate of scholarship where piety would be served more faithfully by originality and practical application than by conformity to doctrinal accretions. The European humanists of the fifteenth and sixteenth centuries saw their work as a movement for enlightenment; a movement whose weapons were themselves educational ones such as erudition, eloquence and wit, and which relied on the promise of reform rather than on the prospect of revolt. Their efforts to win some freedom for the pursuit of learning were eventually defeated by the rush to denominational orthodoxies occasioned by the Reformation. Yet they remain an inspiration for any concern with learning which seeks to establish an authoritative and defensible case for sovereignty.

The 'Folly' of Learning

Erasmus was constantly accused by his enemies of lacking one of the deeper attributes of Christian consciousness: an awareness of the depraved character of humanity. Some scholars have also criticised him for an absence of depth in his spiritual analysis, or for indulging in the comparative safety of satire when a commitment of a more passionate and singleminded character was called for.[1] More recent study, by contrast, finds in the writings of Erasmus the most perceptive and remarkable of spiritual insights.[2] These insights are frequently clothed in a bantering irony or satire, which may have seemed – and may still seem – unacceptably trivial to the more puritan variants of scholarly discipline. This bantering style however is itself a device designed not only to ruffle the pretensions of puritanism but, more importantly, to loosen its manacles on spiritual loyalties and to allow human experience a more expansive share in the deeper play of religious address and response. The Socratic note here is unmistakable. Although Erasmus's loyalty to the institutions of Christendom was never in question, his criticism was withering of some of its highest office holders (including 'Supreme Pontiffs'), no less than it was of many of Christendom's most accepted practices and of the doctrinal preoccupations in some of its more famous seats of learning.

As in the case of Socrates, the work of Erasmus sought to call attention to a more worthy kind of commitment than that manifested in most of contemporary religious and educational practice. Socrates had been concerned with the individual's search for self-understanding in the context of the communal solidarity of the *polis*. Erasmus' concern with the individual's self-understanding was no less central, but the context of Erasmus' enquiries and aspirations now included most of Europe, and his questions and arguments invariably took written, not merely oral form. Like Socrates, he declined to take an active hand in the power politics of the day and devoted himself instead to a determined effort to advance a compelling vision of personal and practical life, a life where religious and civic virtues were informed by the most edifying of classical and Christian sources. Despite his many references to Socrates, however, it is clear that Erasmus did not distinguish between the early and later Socrates in Plato's writings. Indeed he seems to have been deeply influenced by the Platonist tradition which eclipsed the earlier Socrates and also by the ascetic writings of the early Church Fathers, particularly Origen, Ambrose, Jerome and even Augustine.

It is all the more remarkable then that Erasmus' reading of Christian and classical sources was such that it reveals both a disposition and commitment which in key respects strongly resemble the Socratic. We have already noted above the use of irony and satire, guided by a religious inspiration, which was incisive in character and emancipatory in purpose. Coupled with this was Erasmus' strong distrust of scholastic philosophy and theology and his plea for a kind of learning which, in contrast to the intellectual 'majesty' of scholasticism, nurtured an educated awareness of the meagreness of any merely human knowledge. These characteristics feature continually in his most famous work, *Praise of Folly* (*PF*), published in 1511 and 1515 and dedicated to Thomas More as *Moriae Ecomium*. Adopting the persona of a talkative, mercurial female - 'Folly' – Erasmus invites the reader who feels challenged or ridiculed by Folly's declamations to take initial refuge in the comforting attribution of foolishness to the author of these ceaseless barbs. As the book nears its end, however, the dignity afforded by such refuge becomes increasingly ambiguous, until finally it becomes a double ridicule: an awareness of having been seduced, and then confounded, by Folly's striking erudition and 'her' artful lowering of the mask at key points. For instance, that scholastic philosophy and theology had become something of a monstrosity is suggested in satirical tones by Folly in the following passages:

> There are any amount of 'quibbles' ... about concepts, formalities, quiddities, ecceities, which no one could possibly perceive unless like Lynceus he could see through the blackest darkness things which don't exist.

Closely followed by:

> better to let the whole world perish down to the last crumb and stitch, as they say, than to tell a tiny insignificant lie. These subtle refinements of subtleties are made still more subtle by all the different lines of scholastic argument, so that you'd extricate yourself faster from a labyrinth than from the tortuous obscurities of realists, nominalists, Thomists, Albertists, Ockhamists and Scotists – and I've not mentioned all the sects, only the main ones. (*PF* 155-156)

Although the charges contained in these and many similar passages could perhaps be laughed off by scholastic philosophers and theologians as the foolish utterings of a wag, or dilettante, there remains, from the scholastic's own standpoint, something of disturbing authority in the effortless deployment of classical allusions in Folly's sparkling prose and in the ubiquity of finely honed wit amidst 'her' outpourings. This unsettling note becomes an indictment of the entire scholastic enterprise a little later, in those passages where Folly drops the mask sufficiently to allow Erasmus to praise a foolishness which is now decidedly more disturbing to the scholastic temperament:

> All this surely points to the same thing: that all mortals are fools, even the pious. Christ too, though he is the wisdom of the Father, was made something of a fool himself in order to help the folly of mankind ... Nor did he wish them to be redeemed in any other way save by the folly of the cross and through his simple, ignorant apostles, to whom he unfailingly preached folly. (*PF* 199)

It now becomes clear – happily or distressingly, depending on how Erasmus's reader is disposed to acknowledge the point – that Folly was all along a priceless kind of *insight*, whose antics of self-mockery cost 'herself' nothing; yet they furnished the means of disclosing to the upholders of scholastic routines and distinctions the pretentiousness which frequently prevailed amid the European centres of higher learning. But this kind of insight also had a positive character – as distinct, that is, from its more negative merits in disrobing scholasticism of its dignity. Perhaps the most significant – though also the most overlooked – of these positive merits concerns the question of 'depth' in Erasmus's analysis. This issue therefore calls for a few brief comments here.

Firstly, passages such as those quoted enable us to see that criticisms of Erasmus for an 'absence of depth' in his spiritual insights betray a singularly scholastic type of prejudice: namely that depth in such insight must be associated with intellectual complexity and with the more abstract reaches of academic learning. The prejudices of scholasticism assumed that depth of spiritual insight must be foreign to anyone who is not well versed in, or who tends to make light of, such learning. It should hardly surprise us then that, despite the recurring Platonist echo in the writings of Erasmus, his entire appropriation of this tradition is focused not on metaphysics (or any other *scientia*) but on the many similies, narratives and myths which can be readily presented as imaginative stories and allegories; presentations, that is, which are addressed more to conscience and religious sensibility than to self-regarding intellectual prowess. Secondly, and quite remarkably, the established theological tendency to pursue the more grim themes in St Paul and St Augustine is happily declined by Erasmus, in favour of a copius appropriation of these and the ascetic authors of early Christianity into a *new genre*; a genre which has no pretensions to the *gravitas* of *scientia* but which seeks instead to inspire human learning with the twin ideals of practical piety and religious *humanity*.

In his essays 'On the Right Method of Instruction' and 'On The Liberal Education of Children', both of these ideals are to the fore. In an age noted for the insensitivity and cruelty of its schools, Erasmus called attention to the quality of the child's educational experience – as Montaigne did some decades afterwards and as Rousseau was to do more dramatically two centuries later – pointing out that this experience was to be understood in its own way; that children were not adults in miniature. He emphasised the need to ensure that the pupil should at each stage be able to follow what was being taught and, through a judicious habituation, should be enabled to associate study with satisfaction and a cultivation of personal interest and effort.[3] By such means Erasmus sought to promote the independence of mind, combined with refinement of sensibility and character, which he valued so highly and which were exemplified in his own work and writings. Accordingly, it is in his views on the merits and conduct of human learning, and in the exemplary significance he gives to a venturing, questioning stance in the pursuit of study, that Erasmus adds authority to the case for learning to enjoy an essential measure of sovereignty in the face of institutional authorities, most notably those of church and state.

The Triumph of Acrimony

If Erasmus championed the critical spirit of learning in a manner which was variously engaging or satirical, yet characteristically urbane and humane, his contemporary Martin Luther came to embody that spirit in the mode of passionate indignation. Where Erasmus criticised the pomp and worldly lifestyle of popes and ecclesiastics by means of a jesting ridicule, Luther's attack on abuses in the church was also an attack on theological doctrines – such as indulgences – which he saw as part of the decadence he witnessed everywhere in ecclesiastical life. Prior to his challenge to the church in 1517 – when he posted his famous ninety-five theses against indulgences onto the door of the church in Wittenberg – Luther was an admirer of Erasmus' work. Indeed Erasmus sent copies of the ninety-five theses to his friends John Colet and Thomas More in England with a note of approval, but he was also becoming uneasy that Luther's hotheadedness would eventually bring ruin on the cause of the new humanism, the *bonae literae*, which he was so keen to advance in place of scholastic orthodoxies. In 1519, while he was resident in the University of Louvain, Erasmus expressed these fears in a reply to a letter from Luther (whom he had still never met), which had sought Erasmus' support for Luther's refusal to recant.

> I could never find words to express what commotions your books have brought about here [among the Louvain theologians]. They cannot even now eradicate from their minds the most false suspicions that your works were composed with my aid, and that I am the standard-bearer of this party, as they call it. These men cannot by any means be disabused of the suspicion that your works are written by my aid ... I declared that you were quite unknown to me, that I had not yet read your books, and accordingly neither approved nor disapproved of anything ... As for me, I keep myself as far as possible neutral, the better to assist the new flowering of good learning; and it seems to me that more can be done by unassuming courteousness than by violence. ('Letters of Erasmus' in Huizinga, pp.229-30)

But the hopes of Erasmus for a new, enlightened era in European learning were being rapidly overtaken by the growing fanaticism of Luther on one hand and by an uncompromising bigotry among monks and ecclesiastics on the other. This bigotry became steadily more determined not only to defeat Luther but also to smother the spirit of reform of learning. Luther's vehement embrace of the doctrine of the inherent perversity of human will was deeply distasteful to Erasmus, and clearly showed that Luther's earlier avowals of the new humanism were superficial. In addition, the increasing prominence of German nationalism in Luther's standpoint revealed that he was never seriously committed to humanistic learning as a *European* ideal.

Erasmus had translated the bible into Greek, thus challenging the authority of the Latin Vulgate version, which had been the church's officially sanctioned scripture since its publication by St Jerome in the fourth century. Erasmus had perceived many unreliable renderings in the Vulgate and his intention in producing a Greek version was to supply an accurate scriptural base for theology and religious studies. Such studies would include a critical discipline and would therefore be in marked contrast to the authoritarian traditions of learning which had grown up around the Vulgate and the many commentaries on it. Luther's challenge was more bold however, and also less scholarly. In translating the bible into German, he sought to provide the means whereby scripture could be read in the vernacular by lay people, as distinct from having it interpreted and presented to them by church authorities. Lest anyone should mistake the radical nature of Luther's motives, he declared them forcefully as follows:

> I wish to be free. I do not wish to become the slave of any authority, whether that of a council or any other power, or of the University or the Pope. For I shall proclaim with confidence what I believe to be true, whether it is advanced by a Catholic or a heretic, whether it is authorised or not by I care not what authority.[4]

Luther's apparent championship of the freedom of conscience in this striking declaration was soon put to the test however and was shown to be less than wholehearted. He had allied himself with the German princes and when the peasants rose in revolt against the princes in 1525 they were led by 'anabaptists', who had not only followed Luther in rejecting papal authority, they had gone further in dispensing with the need of scriptures as well, in favour of direct revelation from the Holy Spirit. Against the peasants' hopes Luther declared emphatically that 'the only rights you can legitimately demand are those that pertain to your spiritual life'. He showed himself in this event to have little or nothing of the spirit of humanism and when the revolt became more violent he wrote a vitriolic pamphlet counselling the princes to exterminate the peasants. When the revolt was finally crushed the following year, over 100,000 peasants had been slain.

But despite his own anti-humanism, the radical nature of Luther's cry 'I want to be free', and the challenge it contained for traditional custodial conceptions of learning, had sown the seeds of systematic dissent in the intellectual climate of Europe. These revolutionary seeds would come to fruition however only in the following century – and in ways quite contrary to Luther's designs. In the more immediate aftermath of the Reformation, the establishment of universities and schools in German and other states whose leaders adopted the reformed religion gave impetus to new traditions in learning and culture. In the German states, these developments were mainly associated with Philip Melancthon, who attempted to combine humanism with Protestantism and who supervised the establishment of many school systems and organised new Protestant universities. Melancthon's friend John Sturm became headmaster of a very influential school in Strasbourg, which emphasised both Protestant doctrines and the learning of Latin by rote. Although Sturm's pedagogy seems to have been successful in the case of his own school, its doctrinaire character embodied the very opposite of the educational ideals cherished by Erasmus. Its widespread influence in Europe moreover meant that the mature and urbane reflections of Cicero – whose writings were the mainstay of Sturm's curriculum – became a lifeless ordeal for countless generations of the less mature. In Geneva, John Calvin organised an educational system in accordance with the strict tenets contained in his *Institutes of the Christian Religion*, first published in 1536, when Calvin was twenty-six years old. Because of its concern to promote bible reading among literate ordinary citizens, Calvin's educational system included the poor as well as the rich among its pupils, and despite its autocratic character, it was widely perceived to have many practical benefits. Like Sturm's system, on which it was partially based, Calvin's enjoyed widespread influence, not only in Geneva itself, but also among those communities which adopted the essentials of the Calvinist religion: the French Huguenots, the Puritans in England, the Presbyterian followers of John Knox in Scotland, the Reformed Church in Holland.

The determined educational undertakings of the Reformers were matched, however, and in many ways surpassed, by Roman Catholic efforts in the world of learning in the wake of the Reformation. These were chiefly associated with the activities of the Society of Jesus, founded by Ignatius Loyola, a Spanish military nobleman, in 1534 and receiving papal recognition in 1540. Although Ignatius' original intentions were concerned with improving the morals of Christians and with missionary work in lands not yet converted to Christianity, the chief interests of the Catholic church were at this time preoccupied with containing the advances of Protestantism and, if possible, reversing them. Thus the Jesuit system of education, which was focused mainly on schooling at secondary and university level, came to play a crucial part in the Catholic Counter-Reformation. Ignatius viewed the Society as the spiritual counterpart of a military regiment. Its leader was a to be a 'General' and very careful attention was to be given to the selection of recruits and to their training through 'spiritual exercises'. In response to a papal request in 1541, Ignatius set to work on the *Constitutions* of the Society. The requirements set forth in these recall in central respects Plato's requirements for his guardians and philosopher rulers and reveal a conception of learning which was, if anything, more regimented and more custodial than Plato's. Unlike the provisions of the *Republic*, however, those of the Jesuit Constitutions were unambiguously a set of directives for enforcement in practice.

The Jesuit plan of studies was more fully elaborated by a group working under Claudius Aquaviva, General of the Society from 1581 to 1615, and was issued in 1599 as the *Ratio Studiorum*. This meticulous scheme contained prescriptions for virtually every aspect of study, discipline and teaching in the Jesuit system. And it did so in a way which combined a substantial emphasis on classical learning and humanities with a vigilant and systematic supervision of what was studied and how this was taught. The practical success of the Jesuit system was remarkable. By the time of Ignatius' death in 1556, the Society had one hundred schools and colleges. By 1610 this number had risen to over three hundred, and the Society was henceforth to become one of the major forces in the educational history of the West.

In France, writers like Francois Rabelais (1495-1553) and Michel de Montaigne (1533-1592) embraced the humanist heritage of Erasmus rather than the divisive spirit of the Reformation. In his satirical writings *Gargantua* and *Pantagruel*, Rabelais employed an exuberant wit and double edged irony to ridicule both the relentless cramming of grammar into pupils and also the intellectual laziness which this approach occasioned. In contrast to the foolishness he lampooned in his writings, Rabelais' own conception of learning was that of something to be pursued without external rule or prescription, by committed communities who regarded their calling as one of honour.[5] Montaigne recognised that mere quantity of knowledge, whether in classics, humanities, or whatever, could frequently lead to pedantry rather than wisdom. Thus he focused in a particular way on the *quality* of the learner's experience. In this connection, among the seminal insights his *Essays* supplied were: that method in teaching must not be doctrinaire, but should vary in accordance with the nature of individual differences among learners; that learning should be availed of to cultivate discernment and judgement rather than a school-induced conformity; and perhaps most important, that the learner should be 'tempted' rather than threatened – that teaching and learning should be something of a courtship, or espousal, as distinct from a harsh custodianship.[6]

But the partisan fervour which characteristically attended the world of learning during the Reformation and its aftermath boded ill for the most cherished ideals of Renaissance humanism. While different versions of Protestantism became institutionalised in new educational systems, scholastic theology and philosophy continued to be studied in Catholic centres of learning. The Council of Trent (1545-1563) reasserted Catholic doctrines, confirmed papal authority and condemned Erasmus as an 'impious heretic'. It also instituted an Index of banned publications, on which *Praise of Folly* was promptly listed. The heritage of Christendom was thus constituted anew, not by any effort at reconciliation, but by rival and mutually antagonistic orthodoxies, each seeking to advance its sphere of influence by securing a more exact control of doctrine and a more exacting control of teaching and learning than had been possible during the illustrious but truncated era of Renaissance humanism.

The Rise of the Scientific Temperament

Renaissance learning had flourished not merely in the sphere of arts and letters but also in the field of scientific investigations. With Leonardo da Vinci (1452-1519), these took primarily an experimental form and, with Copernicus (1473-1543), a bold, theoretical form. Although the scientific fruits of neither's work were properly acknowledged during their lifetimes, their influence was nevertheless to prove crucial. Leonardo's concerns marked a very different kind of learning to that of the humanist retrieval of the classical past. They also gave a matter-of-fact importance to experimental evidence. This *technical* orientation was quite alien to the speculative assertions of scholastic learning and it also embodied, in a remarkable but unremarked way, a conception of scientific enquiry which was essentially separate from religion. Copernicus, for his part, understood that his astronomical theory would undermine the accepted Aristotelian physics, on which Christendom's scientific picture of the universe then rested. In particular, he was aware that his system included a radical conception of evidence; one which would in central respects contradict the untutored evidence of the senses. Equally significant, he sensed that this system would be regarded by the church as contrary to orthodox doctrine. Not until the year of his death did he allow his book *The Revolution of Heavenly Bodies* to be published.

The humiliation of Galileo at the hands of the Vatican almost a century later showed Copernicus' misgivings to be well-founded. The Copernican system was condemned by the Vatican in 1616, until 'corrected' by the Vatican's own authorities some four years later. This, and other persecutions of scientists – most notably the public burning of Giordano Bruno in Rome in 1600 – emphasised to the world of learning the church's insistence that all scientific explanations must be in accordance with the supreme *scientia* of theology. It was also made clear that all of the sciences, including the most supreme, must be subject to the authority and discipline of the Holy Office. Galileo's dissent from this view led to a historic clash between the established power of the church and the new spirit of scientific enquiry. He was forbidden in 1616 to advocate the system of Copernicus, but it is unclear if this prohibition was a total one. During the latter part of the next decade then, Galileo composed a lively 'dialogue' on the relative merits of the traditional theories of Ptolemy and those of the Copernican system. This enabled him to refrain from open advocacy of the Copernican view, while at the same time giving the struggle between the contrasting systems a dramatic and wide appeal. By placing the case for the Ptolemaic system in the mouth of the weakest participant in the dialogue, artfully named 'Simplicius', Galileo availed of rhetorical as well as logical means in presenting the more favourable case for the Copernican view. The *Dialogue on the Two Great World Systems* was published in 1632 but was soon suppressed and Galileo was summoned to Rome to face trial before the Inquisition. Threatened with torture, he was forced to recant. The *Dialogue* was placed on the church's Index, where it remained until 1835.

The burning of Bruno and the harshness inflicted on Galileo illustrate how little freedom the post-Reformation church was prepared to tolerate in the world of learning. This was true of the reformed religion no less than of Catholicism. The Index inaugurated by the Council of Trent and the vigorous revival of the Inquisition in Italy France and Spain marked the chief Catholic contributions to the demise of the educational ideals of humanism during this period. As regards the Protestant contributions, both Luther and Calvin had roundly condemned the Copernican theory as contrary to Scripture. Luther moreover was not prepared to accept any interpretation of Scripture which conflicted with his own. His actions during the peasants' revolt and afterwards manifested an outlook which was quite the reverse of his famous declaration on the freedom of conscience during the height of his own revolt against Rome. Calvin's *Institutes of the Christian Religion*, and particularly his doctrine of 'pre-destination', gave a more explicit and a more dogmatic form to Luther's grim interpretations of the writings of St Paul and St Augustine. Calvin instituted a theocracy of unyielding severity in Geneva, establishing a Consistory to supervise morality and investing the city council with the power to banish any deviating citizens. His treatment of the French doctor and scientist Servetus, whom he eventually had executed by burning, reveals that, like Luther, his emphasis on the primacy of conscience was curiously at odds with granting conscience the freedom to live by its *own* best efforts to enlighten itself.

But Galileo's discoveries could not be smothered. The stature of his work recommended itself on rational, rather than on authoritarian grounds and showed a kind of learning which was in marked contrast to that which imposed conformity by terror. In an intellectual climate where scholars were compelled to acquiesce in one or other rival version of Christianity on grounds other than rational ones, the example of Galileo was unique. It served as an inspiration to a generation of scientists which succeeded him – not in Italy, where papal power reigned supreme in matters of learning, but in England, where it did not. It was here, through the endeavours of a growing and vibrant scientific community whose most illustrious figure was to be Isaac Newton, that the various currents of scientific thought which had been strengthening since the Renaissance – those associated with Copernicus, Kepler, Galileo, Descartes – produced a remarkable intellectual harvest. The Scientific Revolution, as this event came to be called, not only discredited the pretensions of the church to judge the claims to truth of scientific enquiries which proceeded from sources other than Christian Scriptures. Equally significant, it validated the claims to independent status, and thus to intellectual liberty, of both empirical science and mathematical method. This new concern for experimental and theoretical learning recognised as its final authority the compelling force of *reason*, rather than the coercive powers of church or monarch.

Francis Bacon's works, *The Advancement of Learning* (1605), *Novum Organon* (1620) and *New Atlantis* (1626), announced a bold new attitude to how learning should be conceived and carried out. While showing a deferential attitude to royalty and distinguishing between 'the dignity of Learning' and 'the wisdom of God', Bacon blamed the 'Schoolmen' of scholastic philosophy for retarding the development of scientific learning: 'Their wits being shut up in the cells of a few authors – chiefly Aristotle their dictator – as their persons were shut up in the cells of monasteries and colleges'.[7] The thrust of Bacon's influence, however, was to advance an *attitude towards nature*, and notwithstanding the overt frequency with which he places all learning under the rule and wisdom of God, this attitude towards nature was essentially one of interrogation and domination. The Scriptural warrant quoted by Bacon in this connection was *Proverbs* 20:27: 'The spirit of man is as the lamp of God, wherewith he searcheth the inwardness of all secrets.'[8] Bacon moreover regarded the inductive method he recommended for such searching as a piecemeal progress towards certainty.

The Moravian educator and pastor Comenius (1592-1670) was

deeply influenced not only by Bacon's ideas for the reform of learning in the sciences, but also by his conviction that learning itself should be all-embracing, or universal, as distinct from partial or specialist. Comenius' educational writings, particularly *The Great Didactic*, sought therefore to include in one expansive curriculum what he took to be the entire scope of human studies, and sought also to elucidate a pedagogical method which would make learning a humanising and engaging pursuit for both learner and teacher. More importantly however, Comenius' concentration on the quality of the learner's experience, like that of Erasmus, placed the humanity of learning in a religious context. In a more explicit and detailed way than Erasmus, Comenius viewed educational experience as the pathway for leading the learner towards a wholehearted acknowledgement of the hand of the Divine in all of nature. Viewed critically, this might suggest that Comenius wished to bring the emergent spirit of independent scientific enquiry under the authority of the evangelical, and in a sense this is true. It is more accurate to say however that Comenius viewed religion itself as a freely embraced way of life – inspired by Christian scriptures and governed by a scripture-informed conscience – rather than as being primarily a submission to theological doctrines.[9]

Despite the primacy of religious loyalties in the endorsements of scientific enquiry by influential figures like Bacon and Comenius, the conception of nature as a world that would have to yield up its secrets to the systematic interrogations of human intellect carried with it a different impetus. It accommodated all too uncritically a culture of learning which promoted the attitude of assertive dominance towards nature mentioned above. This culture advanced by building on the tradition of establishing scientific institutes – which had been initiated under church auspices during the Renaissance – but which became a much more independent development in the seventeenth century. These new institutes included the Academia del Cimento in Florence (1657), the Royal Society in England (1660) and the Académie Royale des Sciences in France (1666). These developments advanced learning more than a few steps along a road that was already stretching towards human intellect's independence from the Divine. The traditional idea of learning as a consecrated pursuit had irrevocably passed its noon. As William Boyd concludes in his book, *The History of Western Education*: 'In the new age on which men were entering Bacon took the place of Aristotle as the master of those who sought to know and to teach'. (p.237)

Descartes and the Advent of the Enlightenment

The authority gained by the achievements of empirical science and by the application of strict rational method in the conduct of enquiry also came to have a deep influence on philosophy. For although the masses of ordinary people, and very many in the world of learning, continued to acquiesce in the picture of the universe sanctioned by their upbringing and culture, increasing numbers of thinkers could not do so. Such thinkers were constantly confronted with troubling questions. How, for instance, could the more questioning and discerning among the inhabitants of the post-Reformation world adjudicate between mutually hostile versions of Christianity? Could the doctrines of *either* traditional or reformed religions enjoy any standing as certain knowledge? Couldn't the entire systems of explanation and the entire body of teachings on authoritative truth associated with religion itself be radically placed in doubt? Questions of this kind were being contemplated by the French philosopher René Descartes (1596-1650) at about the time when Galileo was being persecuted by the Inquisition. In 1637 Descartes published a book – *Discourse on Method* – which set out four rules on which the pursuit of certain knowledge might be confidently based. These can be paraphrased as follows:

(1) Never accept anything as true which cannot be clearly shown to be so, beyond all possibility of doubt;

(2) Divide each problem or difficulty into as many simple parts as possible;

(3) Begin with investigation of the most simple and proceed, little by little, to knowledge of the most complex;

(4) Review each step in this procedure, to ensure that all inferences have been correctly made and that none have been omitted.

As an example of this method in action, Descartes reported that he systematically doubted everything that he could possibly doubt, until (by his own reckoning) he had isolated his reflections from all the influences of traditional belief and everyday intercourse and was left with certainty of nothing but his own thinking, i.e. his very activity of doubting. Thus, his first inference from this was to be: 'I think, therefore I am.' Descartes was able to proceed from this first principle to 'think' the existence of other entities, including indeed, God. Some have pointed out that this may not have been possible if he had retained a rigorous insistence on 'I doubt, therefore I am' instead of 'I think, therefore I am'. In any event, his mathematical and argumentative dexterity also enabled him to escape the censure of the Inquisition: he made the Copernican theory respectable by invoking central elements of it in his own, while still accommodating the church's orthodox declaration that the earth does not move. This ambiguity confounded the powers of the Holy Office and was thoroughly conducive to the furtherance of the claims of intellectual independence against those of established authority and tradition in the world of learning.

Descartes' championship of methodical doubt and his application of mathematical principles were enormously influential. Where the revolution in science is associated mainly with the work of Newton, Descartes was the precursor of a revolution in philosophy which was to prove no less momentous. This revolution itself was one of the main features of the European Enlightenment: that unprecedented series of transformations in thought and outlook which took place in the eighteenth century and which opened the way for revolutions of a political kind in America and France. From among the many phases and strands of the Enlightenment, let us now identify a number of themes which were particularly pertinent to education, and to the long eclipsed notion of teaching and learning as an unfinishing search for truth.

* The claims of authority and tradition, in the conduct of learning as elsewhere, can no longer be allowed to go unchallenged but must everywhere be submitted to the judgement seat of autonomous human reason.

* Education must enable learners to have the courage to make full use of their own understanding. Learning must therefore be a means of emancipation rather than an instrument for securing conformity in thought and belief.

* Texts which have previously enjoyed largely unquestioned acceptance, such as Sacred Scriptures, must be seen as historical documents, and therefore the circumstances of their production can become subject to the critical scrutiny of historians.

* Much of what has been invested with authority in European traditions of learning rests on prejudices rather than on rationally established principles. Where authority rests on the prejudices of particular individuals or institutions (e.g. papacy, monarchy) these prejudices can be detected and exposed by critical historical research.

* The use of autonomous reason in a systematic and disciplined manner holds forth not only the prospect of detecting and overcoming prejudice, but also that of major advances in science which will greatly improve the material circumstances and the prospects of happiness of humankind.

* The use of autonomous reason can prove similarly beneficial in examining the social order. Therefore, not only is a scientific history possible; so also is a scientific study of society and politics.

* Artistic activity – such as the composition of poetry – is a creative act which is an expression of the free imagination. Being different from strictly rational activity, the production of such work cannot be said to disclose any truth, but is concerned with arousing and gratifying the aesthetic imagination and emotion of those who seek to experience works of art.

* Rational beings, in virtue of their rationality, have a unique dignity among other beings. Whereas everything in nature conforms blindly to laws, rational beings can *formulate* laws, to which they themselves can then conform or not conform. Humans therefore have a status which is incomparably higher than anything in nature, and this higher status commands moral respect.

* Reason, in its practical use, requires that others be treated as ends, not means. Therefore universal justice is a requirement issuing from the nature of reason itself. This would become more fully appreciated as enlightenment advances. 'Enlightenment is man's emergence from his self-incurred immaturity'.

But the Enlightenment's championship of an unhindered search for truth was different in at least two major respects from that practised and commended by Socrates. Firstly, the informed deference towards long traditions of learning and morality which formed the context for Socrates' critical encounters was bypassed by Enlightenment thinkers, in favour of an adversarial attitude towards tradition. Secondly, in recognising no authority save that of reason, the Enlightenment placed critique above self-critical enquiry, giving it a status which was virtually absolute. Many of the chief themes of the Enlightenment which bear on learning – such as those listed above – found eloquent but ambivalent expression in the educational and political writings of Jean Jacques Rousseau (1712-1788). Unlike the strictly rational standpoint adopted by the prominent authors of the Enlightenment however – such as Hume, Voltaire, Diderot – Rousseau's championship of reason was imbued with romance, and thus with ardent appeals to emotion and sensibility. His accounts of human experience were accordingly more colourful and more dramatic, more erratic, but also more inclusive and more engaging, than were those of his rationalist contemporaries. These features gave Rousseau's radicalism a popular appeal which was as alarming to church authorities as it was captivating to his rapidly growing readership. This alarm broke forth as a vehement storm when Rousseau's famous tract on the freedom of learning - *Émile* - was published in Paris in 1762.

Rousseau's Romantic Revolt

In 1693 John Locke had published a collection of his educational reflections under the title *Some Thoughts Concerning Education*. Three years earlier he had published a systematic treatise *An Essay Concerning Human Understanding*. The famous insistence of this work that humans are born with no 'innate ideas', that the mind is a blank sheet (*tabula rasa*) to be furnished by subsequent experience, provides an insight into Locke's lack of awareness of how different and unique human propensities and predispositions are from earliest childhood onwards. This may also help to explain the disregard for originality and sensibility and the emphasis on utilitarian conformity which are features of his educational writings. Though in no sense a systematic work, *Some Thoughts Concerning Education* contained some key ideas of the Enlightenment: that learning should not be forced on pupils for their own good, that tutors should reason with their pupils rather than command obedience through harsh punishments, that the contents of the curriculum should not be decided on the authority of tradition and custom but should be tailored profitably to the pupil's likely occupation in life (e.g. 'a prince, a nobleman, a normal gentleman's son'). Pursuits of a romantic and imaginative character – such as poetry, music and painting – were discouraged by Locke, in favour of those which habituated the mind and heart to an unfailing and sober industriousness.[10]

Locke's *Thoughts* were translated widely and inspired many similar efforts in the century after his death. Rousseau's *Émile* may have been initially conceived in this vein, but in the course of its construction it became a manifesto of the most challenging kind, and one which pointed in very different directions to Locke's *Thoughts*. The opening words of the *Émile* indicate that this is not just another tract of maxims, but something much more far reaching and indeed subversive: 'God made all things good; man meddles with them and they become evil'. The boldness of Rousseau's rebuke to long-standing puritan influences in church teaching becomes fully explicit in book II of *Émile*:

> Let us lay it down as an incontrovertible rule that the first impulses of nature are always right; there is no original sin in the human heart, the how and why of the entrance of every vice can be traced. The only natural passion is self-love or selfishness

> taken in a wider sense. This selfishness is good in itself and in relation to ourselves; and as the child has no necessary relation to other people he is naturally indifferent to them; his self-love only becomes good or bad by the use made of it and the relations established by its means. (p.56)

The rejection here is emphatic of the Pauline-Augustinian doctrine of the perversity of individual human will. Such a doctrine, which the Reformation had raised to new heights of influence, was a toxic one in Rousseau's view, chiefly because it asserted depravity to be humankind's natural condition. For Rousseau, depravity was to be identified with humankind's estrangement from nature and consequent bondage to the rituals, conventions and tyrannies of 'civilised' society. 'Civilised' society, he claimed, had made education a matter of slavish obedience to an institutional authority which was arrogantly insistent on conformity to its own precepts and also unconscious of its own intransigent prejudices.

The institutional forms of education which Rousseau observed in late eighteenth century France – 'our ridiculous colleges' – were largely responsible, he held, for sustaining such prejudices: for perverting nature's impulses and for blinding youth to the divine origins of these impulses. Not surprisingly then, his sanguine conception of an education in accordance with nature required not just a radical freedom from traditional forms of authority. It also required emancipation from what Rousseau regarded as the abiding hypocrisies which resulted from habitual compliance with such authority, namely the affected manners of society, city and salon. In this much we can see that Rousseau has also broken with Locke's recommendation to tailor learning to the occupational roles offered by social rank, convention and tradition. The break with Locke is even more pronounced in Rousseau's rejection of Locke's advice to 'reason with children'. But this rejection was founded on an insight which showed that Rousseau's understanding of reason in childhood was actually more incisive than that of Locke, or of the later writers of the Enlightenment:

> If children understood reason they would not need education, but by talking to them from their earliest age in a language they do not understand you accustom them to be satisfied with words, to question all that is said to them, to think themselves as wise as their teachers; you train them to be argumentative and rebellious. (p.53)

And to this he adds a little later:

> Childhood has its own ways of seeing, thinking, and feeling; nothing is more foolish than to try to substitute our ways; and I should no more expect judgement in a ten-year-old child than I should expect him to be five feet high. (p.54)

If childhood is 'the sleep of reason', then an authority which seeks to show that its requirements are based even on the most defensible of reasons will miss its mark according to Rousseau. Anything that must be refused to the child must be seen to arise from a refusal which resides in the natural order itself, or in the 'heavy yolk of necessity' which nature places on all humans. Rousseau claimed that to become habituated to this necessity would make the child self-sufficient in due course. It would also make the child's desires more modest than would otherwise be the case, and would prepare the ground for a sense of discernment which was capable of distinguishing valid judgements and inferences from those based on vanity, caprice, or the desire to wield power over others.

Perhaps the most controversial of Rousseau's views on teaching and learning are those which concern questions of faith and religion. These views are put forward in a section of the *Émile* called 'The Creed of the Priest of Savoy' and are related at second hand (by his tutor) to Émile, who is now no longer a child but an adolescent, or youth. Rousseau uses the device of an unfrocked priest's autobiographical tale to undertake a venture which was as dangerous to his own safety as it was disconcerting to the authority of the institutional churches. The Priest's tale is called on to establish the essentials of Rousseau's most seminal critique, which included the following objectives, and much more besides: to castigate what he regarded as the intolerance of the Catholic Church 'which decides everything and permits no doubts'; to highlight the limitations of human intellect – in particular as manifest in acclaimed philosophical and theological wisdom; to decry the church's ritual and ceremony as pomp; to ridicule the doctrine of 'no salvation outside the church'; to affirm the freedom of conscience aided by critical reason; to refute the atheistic materialism of many of his own contemporaries among French men of letters; to proclaim his belief in a personal, divine and all-loving God; to admit his recurring doubts about aspects of revealed religion; to advocate tolerance between different religions; to proclaim simplicity, humility and pastoral concern as the most worthy of religious virtues; and, not least, to call attention continually to the tentative status of the creed itself – its character as a heartfelt but unfinishing quest, as distinct from any body of doctrine established with certainty.

Had Rousseau written from the standpoint of an atheist his work might have provoked less disquiet than it did in ecclesiastical quarters. The faithful could be authoritatively warned against materialist philosophies by church leaders, but the Creed in Rousseau's text took pains to outclass such efforts through its own refutation of materialism and to appeal, by every craft of eloquence, not to the despisers of religion, but to the faithful themselves. His reply moreover to the condemnation of *Émile* by the Archbishop of Paris could scarcely be more dismissive of all that he took the Archbishop's office to stand for: 'My lord, I am a Christian, and a sincere Christian, according to the doctrine of the Scriptures. I am a Christian not as a disciple of the priests, but as a disciple of Jesus Christ.'[11] Here was an idiom which had not only abandoned the cover which Folly had provided for Erasmus's criticisms of the church, but which had also taken up Luther's cry 'I want to be free', not as a short-lived episode, but in a vigorous and sustained way. Most disturbing of all from the point of view of the church's outlook on human learning, Rousseau emphasised conscience not merely as an autonomous inner voice counselled by reason, but also as a voice attuned to the moods of the divine in nature: to *sentiment and romance*. Thus from the orthodox standpoint of the Catholic Church, the Savoyard Priest's advice, 'Seek the truth for yourself, for my own part I offer you only sincerity' (p.259), could only be classed as an invitation to moral turmoil and spiritual anarchy.

Notwithstanding the hostility which greeted its initial publication, or the many inconsistencies in its arguments, or the impracticality of its provisions if taken quite literally, or the volatility of its author's temperament, the ferment of ideas provoked by the *Émile* was to prove immense. Its insights into childhood experience, its declarations on the innate goodness of human nature in childhood, its recasting of the teacher's work in a more sophisticated and subtle role, and its many pedagogical innovations arising from ideas such as these, provided many inspirations for the efforts of nineteenth century educational thinkers, most notably Pestalozzi and Froebel. From these efforts emerged at last a tradition which placed the quality of the pupil's emergent educational experiences at the heart of the teacher's purposeful planning and enactments. But as a tradition it was not until the twentieth century that it came to play a major part in the mainstream of educational practice. In the twentieth century moreover, the various currents of this tradition include the works of authors as different as Montessori and Dewey and a plentiful supply of lesser known figures. Although this tradition can also trace important aspects of its ancestry back beyond Rousseau – to Comenius, Montaigne, Erasmus and even to classical sources such as Quintillian – it is a tradition which still remains controversial in some respects, not least because it has frequently been taken to relegate the importance of the teacher in favour of cultivating unhindered 'expression' among pupils.

These are issues to which we shall return in Chapter Seven. At this stage I am keen to turn to major landmarks in the story of teaching and learning in the era of modernity itself; the era which was inaugurated by the Enlightenment and its revolutionary aftermath and which remains with us in embattled state at the close of the twentieth century.

Notes:

1. See for instance, Johan Huizinga's *Erasmus of Rotterdam – with a selection of the Letters of Erasmus*, translated by F. Hopman and Barbara Flower (London: Phaidon Press, 1952). Huizinga claims that Erasmus, despite his natural piety, 'lacked the mystic insight which is the foundation of every creed'. For reference to further criticism of Erasmus' bypassing of deeper theological issues, see W.H. Woodward's *Desiderius Erasmus – Concerning the Aim and Method of Education* (Cambridge: Cambridge University Press, 1904), pp. 26, 46; and also J. Bronowski & B. Mazlish, *The Western Intellectual Tradition* (Harmondsworth: Pelican, 1963), p.87.

2. See Michael A. Screech's *Erasmus: Ecstacy and the Praise of Folly*, (London: Duckworth, 1980; Harmondsworth: Peregrine, 1988).

3. The text of both essays – 'On the Right Method of Instruction' and 'On the Liberal Education of Children' – is included in Woodward's *Erasmus Concerning the Aims and Method of Education*. See note 1 above.

4. This declaration of Luther's is quoted by Bronowski & Mazlish in their chapter on Erasmus in *The Western Intellectual Tradition*, p.110. See note 1 above.

5. William Boyd quotes from Rabelais' account of life at the Utopian Abbey of Thelma as follows: 'All their life was laid out, not by laws, statutes, or rules, but according to their will and free pleasure. They rose from their beds when it seemed good to them; they drank, ate, worked, and slept, when the desire came upon them. In their rule there was but one clause – Do what you will: because men who are free, well born, well bred, and conversant in honest company, have by nature an instinct and spirit which always prompts them to virtuous actions and withdraws them from vice. And this they style honour.' *The History of Western Education*, p.218. Boyd comments that Rabelais himself didn't fully realise the degree of freedom needed in education to achieve the ideals of life and work described here.

6. Montaigne concludes his essay 'On the Education of Children' as follows: 'To return to my subject, there is nothing like tempting the appetite

and the interest; otherwise we shall produce only book-laden asses. With strokes of the birch we put a pocketful of learning into our pupils' keeping. But if it is to be of any use, it should not merely be kept within. It should be indissolubly wedded to the mind'. Michel de Montaigne, *Essays*, translated with an Introduction by J.M. Cohen (London: Penguin, 1958) p.86.

7. Francis Bacon, *The Advancement of Learning*, (1605) (London: Heron Books, 1866 edition) p.26.

8. ibid. p 5.

9. In a recently published assessment of the life and work of Comenius, Daniel Murphy makes the comparison between Comenius and Bacon as follows: 'Comenius, however, much more emphatically than Bacon, represented all knowledge and wisdom as emanating ultimately from religious faith ... To a far greater degree than Bacon, he insisted that the study of finite reality must be conducted from the ultimate perspective of the infinite, i.e. from the standpoint of the inexplicable, mysterious reality that is knowable only through faith.' Daniel Murphy, *Comenius – A Critical Reassessment of his Life and Work* (Dublin: Irish Academic Press, 1995) p.72.

10. John Locke, *Some Thoughts Concerning Education* (1693) edited by Peter Gay (New York: Teachers College Press, 1971 edition) § 174, § 197, § 203. The mistrust of the human imagination in Locke's educational writings and his subsequent influence on the utilitarian character of educational affairs in Britain and Ireland in the nineteenth century is explored by John Coolahan in an illuminating essay, 'Fact and Imagination in the Battle for the Books' in *Studies in Education*, Vol. 4, No. 2, 1986. (Dublin: School of Education, Trinity College).

11. This extract from Rousseau's reply to the Archbishop's condemnation of the *Émile* is quoted by P.D. Jimack in his Introduction to the Everyman edition of the *Émile*, translated by Barbara Foxley (London: Dent, 1974) pp.xxii-xxiii.

CHAPTER FOUR

Modernity's Combative Progeny

Introduction

To understand the import of modernity for the conduct of education it is necessary to emphasise the distinction between virtues and values. The word 'values' enjoys widespread currency nowadays in debate about moral issues. The word 'virtues', by contrast, has connotations of the past and even a quaintly nostalgic ring. 'Values' are what the modern morally autonomous person freely chooses from a plurality of alternative possibilities for personal identity, ethical commitment and deliberate action. 'Virtues', on the other hand, emphasise a sense of deference towards a particular moral tradition; a tradition which which has *already chosen*, in that it has sanctioned certain commitments and pursuits as worthy and others as discreditable. This distinction between virtues and values underlies the differences between sacred and secular conceptions of learning. These differences occasioned intense acrimony as the long era of Christendom was superseded by new currents of post-Enlightenment outlooks and aspirations. The era of modernity marks the two centuries which separate our own time from the demise of Christendom, and in this chapter we shall attempt to detail some of its more notable educational landmarks and to assess their significance for the concerns of learning in our own day. This chapter thus brings into the present the historical review of the first part of the book.

Cultural Disparity and the Growth of State Influence

The Napoleonic sequel to the French Revolution represented a decisive blow to the authority of religiously sanctioned virtues, but without embracing the ideal of rational moral autonomy championed by the Enlightenment. Indeed the new system of state schools and universities in France signalled that the Bonapartist régime had its own strategic interests in education: that the new priorities were the training of loyal citizens and good soldiers, together with the advancement of technical expertise. Where schooling was concerned then, these interests took precedence over any interests of the church. Not only in France, but also throughout Europe, the nineteenth century increasingly became a an era of rival conceptions of social and political order, in which the rule of established authority and tradition, particularly that of the Christian churches and of royalty, was repeatedly subject to attack. A proliferation of emergent ideologies, including industrial capitalism, utilitarianism, nationalism, democracy, liberalism and communism, sought the loyalties of an increasingly urbanised, an increasingly diverse, and a rapidly growing public.

The critical spirit of modernity was embodied in different ways and in different degrees in these various movements. In other words, contestability and disparateness were already taking root as definitive rather than merely occurrent characteristics of the intellectual and political climate of whole societies and nations. Associated with this was a newly charged political conception of education, which was hardly more hospitable to the claims of sovereignty in learning than were the custodial conceptions of Christendom we have examined in the two previous chapters. This newly political (or politicised) conception of education challenged the traditional authority of the church, but not the proprietorial nature of that authority. It viewed education as a strategic instrument to be fought for, controlled, and pressed into service in advancing the sphere of influence of aspirant ideologies. Control of the machinery of legislation offered the best means of advancing such designs, so a major increase in state involvement in education became a prominent feature of the history of learning in the new era, as did conflicts between the state and other interests, particularly the interests of the churches.

State authorities in more than a few Western states were coming to the view that the illiterate masses of poor were a public liability; that their untutored minds and hearts yielded more easily to public disorder than would be the case if they had a certain minimum of schooling. This concern opened the way for national systems of education, particularly for mass education at primary school level. But precedent was not to point the direction for policy in this development. A national system of education had already been established in Prussia in the eighteenth century during the reigns of Frederick William I and his son Frederick the Great. Johann Bernard Basedow, who was sympathetic to some of the ideals of Rousseau and also an advocate of state control of education, played a prominent part in the Prussian reforms. His Philanthropinum school attracted widespread favourable attention in its early years and his *Elementary Work*, which contained a colourful and expansive curriculum, also excited the interest of a growing body of educational reformers in other European countries.

Immanuel Kant (1724-1804) was deeply moved by Rousseau's *Émile*, and also took an active interest in the work of Basedow. Discarding Rousseau's more extravagant claims and idioms (e.g. 'the noble savage') Kant still shared wholeheartedly Rousseau's conviction that the natural playfulness of children could greatly be turned to profit in improving the quality of their educational experience. In Switzerland, Heinrich Pestalozzi's (1746-1827) imaginative schemes showed that many of the ideas of Rousseau were promising in a practical sense. Although a poor administrator, Pestalozzi's writings and his pedagogical innovations at Burgdof and later at Yverdon showed that the new ideas could best be made fruitful through their modification by disciplined reflections on the teacher's own experience with schoolchildren. The attention Pestalozzi gave to teaching and learning as a field worthy of thoughtful and systematic study was pursued further by Johann F. Herbart, who, as Kant's successor to the chair of philosophy and pedagogy at the University of Königsberg, greatly advanced education itself as a field of higher learning and was influential in the establishment of many colleges for the training of teachers. Friedrich Froebel (1782-1852), who had spent some time with Pestalozzi at Yverdon, made a lifetime's study of childhood experience and developed a deeply spiritual philosophy – inspired by Rousseau, Hegel, Kant and others – which underlay his pedagogy. He sought to advance his ideas in practice through the establishment of Kindergarten schools.

Yet despite the efforts of figures like these to enlighten educational thought and to reform educational practice, the recurrent ascendancy of counter-revolutionary influences in most European countries during the nineteenth century meant that the tradition springing from the inspirations of Rousseau was itself to endure a prelonged infancy and childhood. Far from cultivating any independence of outlook among either teachers or pupils, national schooling stressed very much the requirements of obedience to authority, loyalty to country and conformity to law. In Ireland and Britain its inspirations were not those of Rousseau, but rather those of Locke, Adam Smith, Jeremy Bentham, and the utilitarian thinkers they influenced. A neglect of the dynamics of teaching and learning became a definitive characteristic of the approaches adopted to national education. A system of mass pedagogy devised by Joseph Lancaster (1778-1838) recommended itself for more than one reason. Its industrious but unimaginative drill found favour with the dominant political outlooks in matters educational, and its use of untrained 'monitors', working under the supervision of a master, meant that very large numbers of children could be schooled at a low cost to the state. In making provision for schooling moreover as a rudimentary form of socialisation, the secular authority of the state found successive opportunities for increasing its powers in the field of education, but not without acrimonious tangles with the churches and other interests.

A full account of the educational import of these conflicts in the different countries of the West in which they occurred would be an illuminating and absorbing story, but it is also too detailed a project to undertake here.[1] As the main concern of this investigation is with the claims of sovereignty in learning, I shall confine myself at this point to selecting a few key issues and controversies which illustrate how these claims fared in an era when the prerogatives which had long been enjoyed by the churches were as likely to be attacked as to be acknowledged. We shall look in particular at four developments which were to have influential effects on how education came to be conceived and practiced, not only in this new era, but right up to our own time, which history may yet come to regard as the conclusion of the age of modernity. The four developments are as follows: firstly, John Henry Newman's re-formulation of the place of Christianity in education and his clashes with utilitarianism and liberalism in Britain; secondly, the confluence of nationalism and liberal spirit in German education giving birth to the liberal university; thirdly, the upholding of traditional ideals of authority and coherence against the spirit of the Enlightenment; finally, the recasting of modernity's own ideals of individual autonomy proclaimed by 'postmodernism', but anticipated a century ago by the writings of Friedrich Nietzsche.

Liberal Learning and the Dogmatic Principle – the case of Newman

The controversy which attended the establishment of the University of London in the eighteen thirties provides some revealing insights into how deeply opposed the ancient universities of Oxford and Cambridge were to the novel idea of a scecular education for an English university. The alliance of radicals, utilitarians, and nonconformists which laboured to found the new institution in London – including Thomas Brougham, Zachary Macaulay, James Mill and the Duke of Norfolk – was keen to grant admission to the university to persons of all religious denominations. The intractable difficulties in achieving this aim however made it imperative for the founders to exclude theology of any denomination from the academic programme of the university and to exclude tests of religious belief for any aspiring members of the university. On behalf of Oxford, Sir Charles Wetherell petitioned the Privy Council against the granting of a Royal Charter to the new institution in London. The petition illustrates how seriously one of the central pillars of Christendom – in this case an English variant – had been damaged. The thrust of the petition was that it would be contrary to the laws of England to incorporate any university which did not conform to the doctrines, discipline and worship of the Church of England. It also argued that the title Master of Arts, traditionally conferred by both Oxford and Cambridge, was properly to be seen as the badge of an education conforming to the doctrines of the established church.

These views were shared by John Henry Newman, as is evident from his letter of 14th March 1834 to his friend J.W.Bowden. Referring to the Oxford campaign to prevent London from securing the power to confer degrees, Newman wrote:

> Indeed it does seem a little too bad that the dissenters are to take our titles. Why should they call themselves MA, except to seem like us. Why not call themselves Licentiates etc.? And what is to hinder the bishops being bullied into putting up with a London MA?[2]

Newman at this time was a Fellow of Oriel College, Oxford, for almost twelve years and, as one of the leading members of the Tractarian movement, was a resolute opponent of utilitarian political outlooks, as he was of 'liberalism' in politics and in religion. It is important here to distinguish both of these kinds 'liberalism' from 'liberal knowledge', this latter being a key principle in Newman's own later ideas on university education. Liberalism in politics, which was embraced in the early nineteenth century by the Whig Party, was based on the Benthamite creed of the greatest happiness of the greatest number. The individual was taken as the best judge of his own happiness, so liberalism as a political philosophy aimed to secure the maximum degree of personal liberty and was particularly sympathetic to what Locke had called 'useful' knowledge. Liberalism in religion took the form of a detached tolerance towards the various religions, without necessarily accepting the authority of any of them as a binding force. A coalescence of both kinds of liberalism was discerned by Newman in a widely reported speech by Prime Minister Robert Peel on the occasion of the opening of a new library in Tamworth, Staffordshire, in 1841. This speech called forth from Newman a bold critique of Peel's educational and political philosophy. In a series of seven satirical letters to *The Times*, signed 'Catholicus', Newman accused Peel of relegating the place of religion in education; more specifically, of ousting doctrine and substituting in its place merely the cultivation of intellect and heart. According to Newman's critique, Peel envisaged that this cultivation would be accomplished by establishing physical and moral sciences as the new useful knowledge of higher learning.[3]

Political liberalism had clearly been influential in the efforts to give England a new kind of university in the early eighteen thirties. The founders of London University were not, however, influenced by a spirit of *religious* liberalism. At least this seems to be the case from their own later account of their decision to exclude theology from the university: (they refer to their own efforts in the third person)

> (they) found it impossible to unite the principles of free admission to persons of all religious denominations with any plan of theological instruction, or any form of religious discipline; and they were thus compelled by necessity to leave this great and primary object of education, which they deem far too important for compromise, to the direction and superintendence of the natural guardians of the pupils.[4]

For Newman however, any decision to exclude religion from education was already a compromise, and he therefore saw little effective difference between the views of the London University founders and those of Peel. In his autobiographical work *Apologia pro Vita Sua*, Newman explained that his own religious outlook was shaped from the start by an uncompromising acceptance of a body of revealed religious truths. This wholehearted acceptance of Christian doctrines he described as 'the principle of dogma', and anti-dogmatic standpoints in matters of religion he regarded as being fundamentally mistaken. The mistake in such standpoints, he claimed, was that of 'submitting to human judgement those revealed doctrines which are in their nature beyond and independent of it'.[5] Not surprisingly then, for Newman the words 'dogma' and 'dogmatic' had connotations quite contrary to the mainly pejorative ones which they had for the Enlightenment and which they have in vernacular language today. In the third of his 'Catholicus' letters to *The Times*, Newman reveals how central a place 'the dogmatic principle' occupies in his own educational outlook and also how different that outlook is from that of Liberalism:

> Christianity and nothing short of it, must be made the element and principle of all education. Where it has been laid as the first stone, and acknowledged as the governing spirit, it will take up unto itself, assimilate, and give a character to literature and science. Where Revealed Truth has given the aim and direction to Knowledge, Knowledge of all kinds will minister to Revealed Truth.[6]

The points we have just been considering suggest that Newman's idea of 'liberal education' – which lies at the heart of his Discourses on university education delivered in Dublin in 1852 – signifies something different in key respects from any claims for learning to enjoy any kind of sovereignty, or 'academic freedom'. Yet the arguments of the middle Discourses (Discourses 5, 6, and 7 in *The Idea of a University*) read very much like a defense of the liberty of the university from the claims of the marketplaces of business and politics, and even from the sphere of ecclesiastical influence. This apparent discrepancy calls for exploration, not just with a view to resolving it but also in order to reveal more than a trace of Enlightenment influences in Newman's own arguments. Towards the end of Discourse 5, after arguing that philosophy, or the disciplined 'enlargement of mind', is quite distinct from virtue and faith, Newman concluded that 'Liberal Education, viewed in itself, is simply the cultivation of the intellect, as such, and its object is nothing more or less than intellectual excellence'. The fact that throughout Discourse 5 Newman described this object as 'its own end' lends weight to the impression that he was here arguing a case for the freedom of learning. Further weight is added by his remarks in Discourse 6 on the 'expansion' or 'enlargement of mind', and by his frank answer in Discourse 7 to 'Locke and his disciples', and to utilitarian claims in education:

> I say that a cultivated intellect, because it is a good in itself, brings with it a power and a grace to every work and occupation which it undertakes, and enables us to be more useful, and to a greater number.

In these lines it would appear that Newman was retracting much of his critique of Peel's Tamworth address just over a decade earlier. He now sees cultivated intellect as 'a good in itself'; as something which is itself imbued with ethical qualities – albeit limited, or 'gentlemanly' ones – before the question of religion is even considered.

This apparent liberalism – the 'philosophic habit of mind' which Newman approvingly designates as 'Liberal' in Discourse 5 – shows itself as a keeness for unhindered but self-disciplined intellectual exploration; as a circumspect willingness not to fore-close the investigation of any question by censorship or other decree. Such fore-closure, as we have seen earlier from instances such as the ecclesiastical denunciations of Abelard and Erasmus, the burning of Bruno and the humiliation of Galileo, was an abiding and sometimes a violent characteristic of those custodial conceptions of learning which had their origins in christianised variants of Platonism. Newman's thoughts in *The Idea of a University*, particularly in the middle Discourses, reveal a new tenor of argumentation; one which advocates a marked degree of liberty for the spirit of learning and which in central respects is also in marked contrast to the traditional standpoint of ecclesiastical authorities to learning.

Of course Newman's use of the phrase 'knowledge as its own end' did not signify anything like the radical sense of rational autonomy that the Enlightenment advocated. Nor did it signify the kind of probing questioning of revealed religion and ecclesiastical authority which Rousseau exemplified in the 'Creed of the Priest of Savoy'. Perhaps the best indication of what it did signify occurs at the end of the first section of Discourse 6, where Newman concluded by describing the fruits of the 'philosophic habit of mind' in the following terms: 'It educates the intellect to reason well in all matters, to reach out towards truth, and to grasp it.' This apparently simple formulation, despite its emphasis on 'reasoning well', contains the heart of the discrepancy in Newman's thought which we are attempting to understand. It combines some unmistakably Socratic resonances – in its references to 'reaching out' towards truth, with some equally pronounced Platonist ones – in its assumption that truth is something that can be grasped and possessed by the best efforts of human understanding. This latter assumption makes 'reaching out' merely a preliminary and a subordinate educational activity: something which implies a later stage of consummation and completion, as distinct from the kind of search whose integrity is intimately linked to its own unfinishing character.

Newman's writings have been regularly invoked in defending the claims of academic freedom and the cause of liberal learning. The conviction which such invocation has often carried, the eloquence and practical effectiveness which it has given – and can still give – to attempts to resist the subjection of higher learning to the political and commercial imperatives of the day, must be acknowledged. Newman's significance for the claims of the sovereignty of learning is no less notable than that of earlier Christian figures such as Abelard and Erasmus, each of whom worked in circumstances where the main sources of acrimony lay in attitudes to learning within Christianity itself. The fact that Newman identified the main dangers for learning in his day as residing in conceptions of education which were no longer religious in origin or inspiration makes his embrace of the 'dogmatic principle' more explicit and more urgent than was the case with the educational writers of Christendom. But in Newman's scheme of things, theology was still the queen of sciences and, as such, served an integrating and illuminating function for all of human knowledge. In short, the claims of doctrine remained for him superior to those of research. It was in Germany, or rather Prussia, that this order was soon not only to be reversed but also to be given a nationalist twist.

The Ideal of the Liberal University

Johann Gottlieb Fichte's *Addresses to the German Nation* were delivered in Berlin while the Napoleonic armies were still in possession of the conquered state of Prussia. In these addresses Fichte (1762-1814) focused in a particular way on the possibilities of education as a vehicle for nationalist regeneration and the promotion of a strong, moral and patriotic German solidarity. The strategic-political character of his designs was softened somewhat by his appeal to the Kantian principle of ethical freedom and to the educational principles of Pestalozzi, particularly those which cast the pupil as an active participant in learning rather than a passive and dependent recipient of knowledge and opinions. Fichte sought to incorporate many of the emancipatory insights of Pestalozzi in his own nationalistic designs but neglected to recognise that insofar as Pestalozzi's work had a political character, it was democratic rather than nationalistic. Much criticism has been made of the tendencies towards fanacticsm in Fichte's *Addresses*, but to Prussion authorities humiliated by the French conquest, the bold new call for an educated national solidarity offered the prospect of a cultural regeneration which would lead Prussia out of its darkest hours. Wilhelm Von Humboldt (1767-1835) shared many of Fichte's ideas on liberty, but not the excesses of the latter's nationalism. One of the leading scholars of the nineteenth century, Humboldt was appointed Prussian Minister of Education in 1808 and in his short period of office he quickly set about reorganising the state's educational system. His reforms were inspired by the remarkable confluence of influences which shaped his educational outlook: a keen regard for the literature of classical antiqity combined with a sensitivity to the Romantic vistas opened by writings such as those of Rousseau and Johann Gottfried Herder (1744-1803), a well-versed appreciation of the ideals of the Enlightenment and, not least, a desire to give scientific study, both in the natural sciences and social sciences, a central place in colleges and universities.

The reforms to schooling and teaching which Humboldt set under way included the establishment of *Gymnasium* secondary schools, with a broad curriculum and with the purpose of preparing students for university entrance, the encouragment of Pestalozzi's educational philosophy in primary schools and the establishment of training colleges where professional courses of three years' duration were provided for teachers. Although these moves did much to restrain church influence in education and to admit voices other than ecclesiastical ones into the professional conduct of teaching and learning, Humboldt's most significant achievement as Minister was his action with Fichte and the Protestant theologian Friedrich Schleiermacher (1764-1834) in founding a new kind of university, the University of Berlin, in the years 1807-1810. Whereas Fichte's proposals for the new university emphasised a nationalistic concept of learning, Schleiermacher's emphasised liberal learning. Humboldt's scheme embodied elements of both – more of Schleiermacher's than of Fichte's – but more importantly, it also envisaged the university as a place where research in the various branches of learning was to be given priority and where it could be pursued without interference by the interests of church or state.

Although traces of Fichte's idiom can be discerned in certain phrases of Humboldt's, such as 'the spiritual and moral training of the nation' and 'the intellectual character of the German nation', these seem to be more concessionary remarks than features of Humboldt's own rationale. The kind of freedom which Humboldt sought to secure for higher learning, and the bold new departure which his vision signified, can be more aptly gathered from remarks such as the following:

> The State should not look to the universities for anything that directly concerns its own interests, but should rather cherish a conviction that in fulfilling their real function, they will not only serve its purposes but serve them on an infinitely higher plane.[7]

There are clear parallels between this declaration of Humboldt's in 1809 and Newman's response to 'Locke's disciples', quoted a little earlier. But the freedom from the utilitarian concerns of the state which Newman sought served ultimately to preserve a conception of learning as a consecrated pursuit, under the authority of the church. This latter concern was foreign to Humboldt's philosophy, which viewed knowledge, and in a special way science, not as receiving its imprimatur from ecclesiastical or other authority, but as something 'which has not yet been completely discovered'. Herein lay a definitive break between the viewpoint which saw scientific research as an independent activity and the traditional ecclesiastical conception (shared by Newman) of the sciences as a hierarchy, with theology as the supreme science.

The University of Berlin was to enjoy state funding but also the freedom to manage its own affairs, both in relation to the conduct of academic studies and the administration of its resources. Where Newman's conception was to be the model for many Catholic universities, Humboldt's served as the model for the 'liberal university' of the nineteenth and twentieth centuries, in America, Europe and elsewhere. The concept of academic freedom which the liberal university embodied could not be reconciled with the tests of religious belief which scholars had to undergo before being admitted as members of the traditional university. Hence, in the appointment of its academic staff, the liberal university was to give consideration not to the applicant's beliefs in matters religious and moral, but rather to the applicant's record and promise as a scholar in the field of study in question. Not surprisingly, this led to a much greater diversity of viewpoint than was hitherto present on university campuses, and to greater discord – both in quality and quantity – in the moral climate which attended teaching and learning in places of higher learning. In the twentieth century, the absence of anything like a controlling ecclesiastical voice, and the ubiquity of adversarial standpoints in academic life, have led to recurring questions about the merits of the liberal university. For instance, the capitulation of the German universities to the interests of the Third Reich and the political turmoil on campuses in many parts of the world in the late nineteen sixties and afterwards, are sometimes cited in objection as just two examples of the eventual fruits of the unconstrained liberal spirit in learning, and of the lack of direction and discipline engendered by the Enlightenment's legacy to education.

Objections like these raise problematic issues for any case which might be made for the claims of learning to enjoy sovereignty. Karl Jaspers, for instance, was conscious of the unhappy combination of humiliation and acquiescence which was the experience of the

German universities during the Second World War. But drawing on the strength of his own refusal to yield to Hitler's regime, Jaspers reaffirmed in 1945 the arguments for academic freedom which he had earlier made in 1923 in his book *Die Idee der Universität*. Jaspers' arguments sounded now the same note of boldness amid degradation, of hopefulness amid catastrophy, of independence from any kind of fore-closure of questioning, which distinguished Humboldt's founding ideals in the early nineteenth century. Chapter four of *Die Idee der Universität* grants an unambiguous priority to research among the various activities of the universities. Research, for Jaspers, was conceived as an unconstrained search undertaken by independent minds:

> Since learning and personal initiative go hand in hand, the university aims for the broadest possible development of independence and personal responsibility. Within its sphere, it respects no authority other than truth in its infinite variety, the truth which all are seeking and yet no one can claim to possess in final and complete form. (p.66)

Jaspers' arguments also make clear that research is not an activity which must compete with teaching. Rather he insists that teaching itself – while not neglecting the responsibilities of instruction and explanation – must embody an attitude and atmosphere of research; that is, of a quest jointly undertaken by a teacher whose experience provides a plenitude of questions which are worthy of investigation, and students whose growing engagement with such questions manifests a sincere spirit of enquiry. For the students this would mean a commitment to standards of fluency which, at whatever level of study, makes the asking of genuine questions possible. For the teacher it would mean not only a commitment to keeping abreast of new developments in the field of study in question, but also a willingness to grant whole-hearted recognition and an open-minded presentation to theories, perspectives and arguments different from his or her own.

The moral imperative here, to use a description of Michael Oakeshott's, is that of sustaining a disciplined conversation between different voices, as distinct from jockeying for advantage in a race or an argumentative contest. In his various writings on the liberal spirit in education Oakeshott combines – sometimes in arguments strikingly similar to those of Jaspers – a deeply rooted respect for the authority of tradition in learning with an unqualified endorsement of the freedom of enquiry. In his essay 'The Idea of a University' (1950), from which the distinction just mentioned has been taken, Oakeshott describes conversation as 'the peculiar virtue of a university'; a conversation with no predetermined course, which needs neither chairman or symposiarch, but 'each study appearing as a voice whose tone is neither tyrannous nor plangent, but humble and conversable'. Similarly, in 'The Voice of Poetry in the Conversation of Mankind' (1959) Oakeshott describes this conversation as an event where:

> 'certainties' are shown to be combustible, not by being brought in contact with other 'certainties' or with doubts, but by being kindled by the presence of ideas of another order; ... Thoughts of different species take wing and play round one another, responding to each other's movements and provoking one another to fresh exertions.[8]

The heart of Oakeshott's argument in his various educational writings is that education, properly viewed, is as an 'initiation into the skill and partnership of this conversation'. He adds that such conversation, 'where talk is without a conclusion', is not only the greatest but also the most difficult to sustain of humankind's accomplishments.

Notwithstanding the reaffirmations by Jaspers, Oakeshott and others of the spirit of the liberal learning, the objections raised against this spirit have not been silenced. Indeed as the twentieth century draws near its end there has been a resurgence in attacks on the claims of formal learning to enjoy discretionary scope.[9] By the late nineteen sixties these claims had come to enjoy an expansive degree of liberty in most Western universities, and had also made decisive advances in the curricular and pedagogical policies of very many schools at post-primary and primary levels. Three main sources of the attacks of recent decades can be identified, (though my own selection of these is not an exhaustive survey). Firstly there are objections from those who regret the pluralistic currents of almost two centuries of modernity and who share, in varying degrees, the conviction voiced by Alasdair MacIntyre that the entire 'Enlightenment project' and its legacy of liberal thought was a great mistake. Secondly, there are the criticisms of 'post-modern' thinkers, who are not only hostile to the rationalist tenor of much of modern life, but who also share, in varying degrees, the conviction of writers like Jean François Lyotard that modernity's preoccupations with ideals of freedom and meaning are illusions. Thirdly, there are attacks inspired by a new commercialisation of education. This has been associated with the market ideology which became pervasive in Britain, America and other countries in the eighties, but which has now, in a modified form, influenced the outlooks of most Western governments. It is also increasingly apparent in the publications on education of international agencies such as the Organisation for Economic Co-operation and Development (OECD). We shall briefly review the first two of these in the last two themes of this chapter – the anti-modern and post-modern standpoints – but return to a fuller consideration of all three in Part Two.

The Anti-Modern Critique and its Oversights

In the final chapter of his book, *Whose Justice? Which Rationality* (1988), Alasdair Macintyre laments the demise of the religious influences which controlled the contexts of learning in the long era of Christendom. The demise of the 'preliberal university', he claims, precludes the voices of tradition, other than that of liberalism itself, from being heard. (p.399) He points to the authoritative coherence provided by the religious traditions of the pre-liberal university, not only for the pursuit of enquiry but also for the adjudication of intellectual conflicts among the scholars. He cites as examples of such coherence the regulation of the University of Paris in the thirteenth century and that of the Protestant universities of Scotland and Holland in the seventeenth and eighteenth centuries.

MacIntyre claims that the abolition of tests of religious belief, under the influence of the Enlightenment, did not mean that the universities where such action was undertaken henceforth became 'places of ordered intellectual conflict'. Instead, he insists, the Enlightenment's faith in independent reason promoted the belief that objectivity in learning could be safeguarded by an approach to teaching which proceeded '*as if* there were indeed shared standards of rationality accepted by all teachers and accessible to all students'. (p.399) Such a belief was an illusion according to MacIntyre – since reason-in-use always operates *within* a tradition. But he claims it is an illusion which continues to pervade modern learning in a baleful way. Its effects are less harmful in the sciences he maintains than in the humanities, where the loss of the criteria once provided by the traditional contexts of enquiry (i.e. the religious and ethical orientations of the preliberal universities) has deprived teaching of the appropriate standards of judgement in making appraisals of texts and theories, arguments and viewpoints. MacIntyre's conclusion strikes a stark and downcast note:

> What the student is in consequence generally confronted with, and this has little to do with the particular intentions of his or her particular teachers, is an apparent inconclusiveness in all

> argument outside the natural sciences, an inconclusiveness which seems to abandon him or her to his or her prerational preferences. So the student emerges from a liberal education with a set of skills, a set of preferences, and little else, someone whose education has been as much a process of deprivation as of enrichment. (p.400)

When one reflects on much of the quality of educational experience in modern mass universities, it would be futile to claim that MacIntyre's argument is without substance. MacIntyre himself concedes 'happily' however that not all education in modern cultures is liberal in the sense he described. But to suggest that the unhappy state of affairs he outlines in the quoted passage – insofar as it is a historical fact – is occasioned by the conception of a liberal university, and to imply that things would be much happier if 'liberal modes of debate' could be circumvented or subverted, (p.401) is really to do battle with a contemporary stereotype rather than to tackle with evenhanded criticism a serious tradition of learning. Indeed it is to obscure, albeit unwittingly, what is distinctive in an original vision: the incisiveness and generosity of Humboldt's intellect and the perceptive subtlety of Schleiermacher's insights. The fact that many academics now propagate in their practice an ill-versed or otherwise privative version of the liberal university should no more discredit a defensible ideal than the excesses of progressivism should be blamed on John Dewey, or indeed than the terrors of the Inquisition should be traced to the essentials of Christianity.

MacIntyre's unhappines with forms of enquiry whose outcomes are less than 'conclusive' is evident from the passage quoted above. By contrast, the claims of learning to enjoy an essential measure of liberty are based – from Socrates onwards – on an acknowledgement that the fruits of any merely human form of enquiry must be provisional rather than final. Rather than 'abandoning' students to their 'prerational preferences', however, such absence of finality properly teaches humankind an educated sense of its own ignorance, even in the face of its most dazzling accomplishments; indeed especially in the face of such accomplishments. This is one of the most significant lessons of the Socratic educational practice considered in the first chapter. And it is what makes the Socratic itself distinctive as a conviction worthy of the respect of anyone whose business is education. Of course the eclipse of this conviction and practice which we also considered there, and its supercedence by Platonist and Augustinian influences, meant that this lesson never became a strong feature of Western traditions of learning. In other words the Socratic, in its distinctiveness, failed to become institutionalised as a tradition in Western learning. It is all the more important then to emphasise that wherever this sense of educated ignorance pervades the moral climate where learning is pursued – and this is as true of the sciences and technologies as it is of the humanities, fine arts and religion – it places on each person the responsibility of making defensible personal commitments, of 'reaching up to humanity', as Herder put it. This contrasts in all important respects to an education that encourages commitments to arise from a largely unquestioned acquiescence in one or other outlook which claims for itself the authority of certainty, or final truth.

The emphasis on the personal which is evident here played a central part in Humboldt's elucidation of the ideal of *Bildung* (self-formation, cultivation, education); an ideal which guided his educational thinking and whose distinctiveness he sought to set apart from the more undifferentiated concept of *Kultur* (culture).

> But if in our language we say *Bildung* (rather than *Kultur*), we mean something both higher and more inward, namely the attitude of mind which, from the knowledge and the feeling of the total intellectual and moral endeavour, flows harmoniously into sensibility and character.[10]

Here the connection between education and the unforced appropriation of an inclusive sense of personal identity is made explicit. The kind of educational liberty envisaged by Humboldt signified a shift – or a series of shifts – in the self-understanding of the person, not as something imposed but arising out of a discerning and disciplined encounter with different traditions of learning. Nor was such an encounter an antagonistic standpoint towards religion. As Hans-Georg Gadamer points out in his historical survey of key humanistic concepts in *Truth and Method*, the origins of the word *Bildung* lie in religious mysticism, where 'Bild' (picture, image) signified the likeness of the divine in each person; a likeness which was to be discerned and cultivated through learning. (*T&M* p.12) Hegel, who came to Berlin as professor of philosophy in 1818, insisted that the freedom which was essential to *Bildung* was universal: the right of each and everyone, not the preserve of particular authorities.

Schleiermacher's efforts helped to refine and enrich the spirit of liberal learning which Humboldt had linked to the concept of *Bildung*. Where traditional theology had emphasised correctness of understanding in the study of scriptures, Schleiermacher emphasised the psychological and individual aspects of understanding and traced a close interplay between understanding and interpretation. Because every effort to understand texts, argued Schleiermacher, is so closely attended by individual interpretation, misunderstandings and conflicts arise here more naturally than does correctness of understanding. He therefore defined hermeneutics (the art of interpreting texts) more as one of avoiding misunderstandings than of guaranteeing any final and correct understanding. He also added that what was true of the study of texts was equally true of conversation, and of listening to speech. Where learning was concerned, therefore, the art of avoiding misunderstanding required the learner to attempt to place himself within the mind of the author he was attempting to understand, and to approach the text as the free expression of a creative mind. Later authors have pointed out that such a project could not be carried out with any expectation of completeness and also that the inter-subjective emphasis (reader and author) in Schleiermacher's account does less than justice to the *communal* audience of a text. Yet there is a psychological insight in Schleiermacher's account which sets it apart from the Enlightenment's dogmatic faith in reason and which lies at the heart of any adequate conception of liberal learning: if individuality plays such a central part in understanding, thus rendering it ever likely to some degree of mis-understanding, the same is true of reason itself, for it is through the exercise of reason that understanding – and thus mis-understanding – takes place.

The educational importance of this insight can be gathered from Schleiermacher's own comments on 'meaningful dialogue'. If the possibility of mis-understanding is a universal feature of human experience, then, in contrast to all conceptions of learning as the learner's acquiescence to dogmatically transmitted truths, learning must first be conceived as the effort to bring individuality to an appreciation of its own possibilities and limitations. This enables learning not only to gain a more coherent understanding of its own standing-within-tradition, but also to enter more meaningfully into the to-and-fro of dialogue – with texts which make a claim to truth and with others who do likewise. Schleiermacher's insights thus envisaged not an overthrowing of tradition but rather a redefining of the nature of our relation to tradition. This redefining, when taken together with Humboldt's conception of *Bildung*, provided an instructive, but largely unheeded lesson for the currents of pluralism which were becoming ever more assertive and divisive in the early nineteenth century. It also provided a seminal rationale for liberal learning in pluralist society, a rationale which remains scarcely more heeded, either by liberalism or its critics, in the education of our own day.

Post-Modern Critique of 'Narratives' and Meaning

Where the criticisms of anti-modern thinkers allege that the Enlightenment and its rationalist legacy undermined the coherence of pre-modern cultures, including cultures of learning, 'postmodern' thinkers make the charge that such traditional conceptions of coherence were no more than illusions ('Postmodern' is generally written as one word). They make the additional charge however that the various critical currents of modern thought which owe their origins to the Enlightenment are *also* a pursuit of illusions. Prominent writers associated with postmodernism include Richard Rorty, Jacques Derrida and Michel Foucault.[11] The postmodernist orientation has been given its most concise formulation however by Jean François Lyotard in his book *The Postmodern Condition: A Report on Knowledge*, first published in 1979. But this is not a report in the ordinary understanding of the word. Although Lyotard declares in his Introduction that it was written in response to a request from the President of a government agency for higher education, its idiom is as much a declamatory as an informative one. Intermingled with Lyotard's account of the way things stand with knowledge and its use in the late twentieth century is a polemic against philosophy. Lyotard seeks to dis-illusion any lingering claims that the search for truth can put forth accounts of meaning, rationality, freedom etc. which might be candidates for universal acceptance, i.e. for application to *humankind as such*, even in a provisional sense.

While some of the distinctive projects of modernity, such as those of Hegel, Marx, Freud, shared the pre-modern practice of attempting to establish their findings with the finality of theory, i.e. as the complete picture and objective truth, the more self-critical of writings in both philosophy and science came to adopt a provisional standpoint to the outcomes of enquiry. Despite their radically different attitudes to authority and tradition, however, both pre-modern and modern forms of enquiry shared nevertheless the basic ideal of an understanding that might be universal in its application, i.e. a search for truth about human being *as such*, nature *as such* etc. More specifically, all retained the belief that such a truth might exist (albeit that humans might never get more than an imperfect understanding of it) and was at least worthy of seeking.

It is this latter belief that the standpoint of postmodernism is keen to discard. For instance, Lyotard, although describing himself at one point as a 'philosopher', calls philosophy a 'metadiscourse' which makes appeals to grand narratives, or 'metanarratives'. 'Metanarratives' he sees as accounts on a grand scale of humankind's destiny, or purpose or meaning. Put more simply, a 'metanarrative' is a body of beliefs, writings, and claims which presupposes that human existence as such is purposeful or meaningful. 'Metanarratives' are thus what underlie whole cultures and what justify whole traditions. A religion would be a clear example of what Lyotard means by a 'metanarrative'. So would any political movement or theory which presupposes the liberty, or equality, or solidarity of humankind as a coherent or desirable goal. But so also would economic theories which appeal not to solidarity, but to the individualist tradition of wealth creation, as the best means of advancing the common good. Lyotard defines 'postmodern' as 'incredulity toward metanarratives'. (*The Postmodern Condition*, p.xxiv) On this understanding, religion would be viewed as mythology and the philosophical and political traditions which featured most prominenently in Western civilisation (indeed in most other known civilisations also) would be grouped together as so many human tales of self-deception.

Lyotard claims that the incredulity he describes is a product of scientific progress, and that scientific progress must also presuppose it. That is to say that scientific progress must disbelieve older 'metaphysical' ways of understanding the world and that the advances in knowledge which such setting aside of 'metanarratives' makes possible contributes in turn to consigning 'metanarratives' to obsolescence (p.xxiv). He claims further that the task of providing unity and coherence for knowledge as a whole, traditionally played by philosophy in universities, (and overseen by the Church in the Middle Ages) is now in crisis.

> To the obsolescence of the metanarrative apparatus of legitimation corresponds, most notably, the crisis of metaphysical philosophy and of the university institution which in the past relied on it. The narrative function is losing its functors, its great hero, its great dangers, its great voyages, its great goal. It is being dispersed in clouds of narrative language elements – narrative, but also denotative, prescriptive, descriptive and so on. (xxiv)

The quality of the language here – its formidable terminology and its ambitious embrace – is characteristic of Lyotard's general style in this text and is more that of a manifesto than of a 'report'. It resembles in many ways the kind of grand account which Lyotard himself is keen to descredit. Most critically, however, Lyotard's discernment of trends and patterns turns an unseeing eye to evidence of counter trends. The selective character of his arguments, the summary nature of his judgements, the unrestrained sweep of his conclusions and predictions, these make his analysis questionable on virtually every point at issue. To any standpoint which would seek due weight to be given to the varieties of pluralism which characterise modernity in our own era, it is difficult to avoid the conclusion that in the last analysis Lyotard's account is less a report on knowledge than a tendentious advocacy of *one* outlook; one which is hostile to both traditional and modern conceptions of learning and which seeks to make the most of some notable contemporary developments in order to advance the case for a different conception.

Notwithstanding these criticisms of Lyotard's arguments, his analysis calls attention to a number of important features of how the pursuit of learning has changed in recent decades. The 'dispersion' referred to in the quoted passage identifies one of the consequences of advanced and specialised research: an ever increasing tendency towards disparateness and self-containment among the different branches of knowledge. The argument can of course be made that such advances in research have as much to teach us about the interconnectedness and ultimate unity of scientific knowledge as about the disparateness and 'incommensurability' of knowledge which Lyotard and other postmodernists are keen to emphasise. Consider for instance, the 'order out of chaos' theory of Ilya Prigogine,[12] or the universe-as-an-ecosystem theory of modern biological research. And similar counter-instances can be cited in the case of virtually all of Lyotard's other main claims. Yet, as in the case of the anti-modern criticisms considered in the previous section, insofar as Lyotard's analysis describes tendencies which are historical realities, these realities must be acknowledged and their import for teaching and learning must be considered.

Accordingly, from among the many theses advanced in *The Postmodern Condition*, some are of special relevance to our theme. They are as follows.

(a) the displacement of criteria of justification by criteria of performance, or effectiveness;

(b) the superseding of long-term commitments by temporary contracts;

(c) the divorce of knowledge from the personal qualities nurtured by learning (*Bildung*);

(d) the 'commercialisation', or 'mercantilisation' of knowledge, as a specialist and power-related commodity;

(e) a hostility towards dialogue which seeks consensus and the affirmation, instead, of heterogeneity and contest;

(f) the promotion of aesthetic experience – and in a special way that of avant garde – to a place of prominence over ethical and political considerations;

(g) a disbelief in accounts ('metanarratives') of meaningful ends for humankind as a whole, and the substitution of a conception of human action as an unrelated multiplicity of 'language games' where the participants manoeuvre for power through 'moves' in the game.

The first four of these points identify trends which are undeniably evident nowadays – in greater or lesser degree – in the conduct of public affairs and decision-making, at local, national and international level. The last three identify Lyotard's own orientations, and mark the tendentious element in his report on the contemporary state of knowledge. What is somewhat odd, on a first reading, is the absence of any critique or critical standpoint on Lyotard's part, in relation to developments such as the first four trends listed above. These are developments which are more likely to engender divisiveness in a recurrent way than any enduring sense of co-operation or peaceful co-existence. On more than one occasion Lyotard himself associates them with the exercise of bureaucratic terror (p. xxiv, p.64). But such a critique would presuppose an avowal of something like an essential sense of purpose, or dignity, or ethical coherence, in human existence as such, and this is precisely what the postmodernist orientation of Lyotard (and others such as Richard Rorty) seems to lack. It is precisely what he finds most unworthy of belief in the standpoints of modernity and the premodern era alike.

The coherence in Lyotard's position, if coherence is the proper word to venture in this connection, begins with the disavowal of the possibility of any truth or meaning which might be universally worthy of humankind, or universally applicaple to humankind. Yet Lyotard's report draws on the fact that human undertakings are replete with power struggles. But this seems to be a 'move' to insert the motive of *power* in place of the aspirations towards meaning and truth which he has ousted. But this makes power itself a universal motive, or end, in Lyotard's scheme. Once this is recognised, one can more easily see how the factual components of Lyotard's thesis fit with its advocacy postmodernism *as an ideology*. For if the pursuit and enjoyment of power now provide the *telos* of human action, albeit something unacknowledged as a *telos*, then things are cast in an entirely new light: prowess in performance can quickly put demands for justification in the shade, one's most recent conquests can eclipse considerations of loyalty and long-term commitment, the ethical dimensions of learning tend to appear as a debilitating burden, specialist knowledge receives an unparalleled significance as the most useful weapon in one's arsenal, appeals for dialogue can appear as the refuge of the weak, and the aesthetic enjoyment of novel 'moves in the game' beckons human efforts as the supreme consummation of desire. This last point is more or less admitted by Lyotard himself in his reference to 'the increase in being and the jubilation which result from the invention of new rules of the game, be it pictorial, artistic or any other'. (p.80)

When the educational import of postmodernism is considered, it may seem both to earlier conceptions of education and those of modernity that it represents nothing less than an attempted overthrow of all traditions of learning which have claimed the attentions of generations since classical antiquity. It may also seem that, far from acknowledging any sovereignty of learning, it supplies nothing so much as a recipe for a plunder of the trusting and the innocent. Lyotard's account for instance, is thoroughly disdainful of the project of Humboldt and Schleiermacher in founding the Univesity of Berlin. He dismisses this project as an attempt to give a practical embodiment to yet another 'metanarrative', in this case that of 'the speculative spirit' wedded to 'the intellectual character of the German nation' (pp.32-33). The dismissal strikes of course at pretensions to absolute, or universal knowledge in nineteenth century German philosophy, but it also presumes summarily that the heart of the founders' purposes could be captured in such dubious phrases. Yet it may still be the case that Lyotard has done a salutary service, notwithstanding his own intentions, in identifying the family of motives to which the pursuit of power properly belongs, and in calling attention to how different a preoccupation this is from what educational authorities have characteristically considered themselves to be pursuing. At a time when contests for control of the educational enterprise have witnessed a vigorous resurgence in Western democracies, Lyotard's arguments are not only worthy of our consideration. Equally important, their provenance in the writings of a much earlier critic of modernity, Friedrich Nietzsche, needs to be made explicit, together with an unearthing of more than a few currents of this kind of thinking in contemporary educational reforms.

Notes:

1. The utilitarian-rationalist ancestry of the fear of the imagination which pervaded the outlooks of educational authorities in the late eighteenth and nineteenth century is well illustrated in an essay by John Coolahan, 'Fact and Imagination in the Battle for the Books' in *Studies in Education*, Vol.4, No.2, Autumn, 1986 (Dublin: School of Education, Trinity College) pp.7-21. The Irish national system of education was established before that of many of the Western countries and two studies which examine the church-state clashes and inter-church clashes which constantly attended it are Coolahan's *Irish Education - History and Structure* (Dublin: Institute of Public Administration, 1981), particularly Chapters 1 & 2; also D.H. Akenson's *The Irish Education Experiment - The national system of education in the nineteenth century* (London: Routledge and Kegan Paul, 1970)

2. This extract from Newman's letter is quoted by Fergal McGrath in his book *The Consecration of Learning* (Dublin: Gill & Son, 1962) pp.63-64

3. For an account of the Tamworth controversy and Newman's 'Catholicus' letters, see Ian Ker's *John Henry Newman – A Biography* (Oxford: Clarendon Press, 1988) pp.206-208. See also McGrath's *The Consecration of Learning*, pp.84-91.

4. Quoted by McGrath, *The Consecration of Learning*, p.55

5. John Henry Newman, *Apologia Pro Vita Sua* (1865) See 'Note A', on Liberalism, at the end of Newman's text. The passage I have quoted appears on p.288 of the edition of 1891 (London: Longman's Green & Co.), and on p.193 of the 1973 edition, which has an Introduction by Maisie Ward (London: Sheed and Ward).

6. This passage from Newman's third 'Catholicus' letter, is cited on p.210 of Ian Ker's *John Henry Newman - A Biography*.

7. Quoted by William Boyd, in *The History of Western Education*, p.336

8. Oakeshott's essay 'The Idea of a University' is reprinted in a collection of his essays on education in a book called *The Voice of Liberal Learning - Michael Oakeshott on Education*, editor Timothy Fuller (New Haven: Yale University Press, 1989). The first two short extracts on 'conversation' which I have quoted are taken from this essay (Fuller, p.98). The longer Oakeshott passage I have quoted (indented) and the short ones following it are from 'The Voice of Poetry in the Conversation of Mankind', which appears in Oakeshott's own collection of essays published under the title *Rationalism in Politics and Other Essays* (London: Methuen, 1962), pp.198, 199, 200.

9. Such attacks have been far more common in other Western countries than they have been in Ireland. Yet the new utilitarianism of the eighties and nineties is evident in the economic and cultural life of Ireland scarcely less so than in other Western countries, and it bears on current educational reforms in Ireland in a number of ways. Some of the pertinent issues in this connection have been explored by Kevin Williams in his essay 'Usefulness and Liberal Learning' in *Religion, Education and the Constitution* edited by Dermot A. Lane (Dublin: The Columba Press, 1992) pp.34-59

10. The passage from Humboldt is quoted by Hans-Georg Gadamer in his *Truth and Method* (*Wahrheit und Methode* 1960), translated by Garrett Barden and John Cumming (London: Sheed and Ward, 1975) p.11

11. Some central themes from the works of Rorty and Derrida will be explored in later chapters. Derrida is frequently identified as one of the foremost representatives of 'postmodernism', although this attribution is arguably more inaccurate than accurate, as we shall see in Chapter Nine. Rorty, on the other hand, is happy to describe himself as a 'postmodern bourgeois liberal'. See Rorty's essay, 'Postmodern Bourgeois Liberalism', in Robert Hollinger (ed.), *Hermeneutics and Praxis* (Notre Dame: University of Notre Dame Press, 1985).

12. Ilya Prigogine was awarded the Nobel Prize for Chemistry in 1977. His jointly authored book with Isabelle Stengers *Order out of Chaos - Man's New Dialogue with Nature* (English edition London: Fontana, 1985) presents an account of some surprising reappraisals of key scientific beliefs. The book also envisages inviting prospects for 'reconceptualised' scientific research: prospects which suggest that disequilibrium and entropy can be a source of order, and which also anticipate a new alliance between the sciences and humanities. By contrast, Lyotard's view of science places almost exclusive emphasis on 'parology', and other postmodernist writers place simililar emphasis on the 'incommensurability' of research in the different fields of learning.

PART II

Educational Experience and the Sovereignty of Learning

CHAPTER FIVE

Power, Partiality and the Purposes of Learning

Introduction

Theology in the Middle Ages was the supreme science. As we have seen in Chapter Two, it sought to give to the contents of Christian Scriptures the status of infallible truths, maintaining with Thomas Aquinas that 'it is impossible to use any truth to prove anything that contradicts our faith' and that 'evidence' adduced against the faith must be invalid evidence. (*S.T.*, Ia, q.1, a8) Articles of faith were thus treated as matters of incontestable fact. And this theological account of reality goverened not merely the conduct of the supreme science itself, but also that of all sciences, which had to bring their own findings into conformity with its precepts. Failure to do so was to risk papal censure and the unwelcome attentions of the Inquisition. Of course the findings of scientists like Copernicus and Galileo were not necessarily hostile to the essential teachings of Christianity. They contradicted rather some additional features – like the earth as stationary and the earth as the centre of the universe – which the church built into its picture of the nature of things.

Discoveries such as those of Copernicus and Galileo revealed that the objects which the natural sciences explored were open to radically different interpretations, and also that revolutionary interpretations could now sustain themselves against long established ones. Luther's revolt, unlike the earlier acrimonies and schisms in the church, showed that the same thing was possible in theology itself, and in this it undermined theology's claims to supremacy as a science. The efforts of the leading figures of the Scientific Revolution and the Enlightenment continued to dismantle the picture of objective reality which had come to dominate European learning since the beginning of Christendom, and a plurality of interpretations gradually thronged an arena previously reserved for a single and consecrated world-view. It was still possible however for that single world-view, while acknowledging the achievements of the individual sciences, to assert that, as far as matters religious were concerned, its own explanations and teachings were the objective truth and that conflicting accounts were merely interpretations, mistaken interpretations at that.

In the mid-nineteenth century, philosophers like Ludwig Feuerbach and Karl Marx produced uncompromising atheistic accounts of the world and human society and claimed that these represented the objective truth. Central to their claims was the argument that it was religion and metaphysics that must be regarded as misleading interpretations and that must therefore be rejected. A further decisive advance for the atheistic standpoint occurred with the prolific writings of Friedrich Nietzsche. The bulk of these were published in the 1880s, and although, like the writings of Marx, they had little immediate impact, their longer term influence was no less significant, though considerably less acknowledged than the influence of Marx. The history of Marxist influence in social and educational affairs is well known, including its demise with the decline of totalitarian variants of Marxism in recent years. The influence of outlooks of a Nietzschean character has been somehow more anonymous and has taken a more diffuse route. Yet this influence has become ever more pervasive in the pluralist cultures of Western civilisation in recent years; a point that may still strike many as a mistaken, or even an offensive one. Yet the force of this influence is becoming gradually more apparent with the continuing decline of religion as a feature of culture and with the uncertainties which have befallen Western socialism in the wake of the collapse of the Soviet Union and its satellite states. To bring out this picture more clearly, we need to explore some key Nietzschean themes and discern their effects in present-day cultures; particularly those in which teaching and learning must be attempted.

Nietzsche's Theses on Power

Let us begin by outlining seven of Nietzsche's more notable theses, and then review the measure of their significance for how teaching and learning are currently understood and pursued. The first thesis concerns the radical nature of Nietzsche's attitude to objective truth, or to anything which would claim the status of independent facts. In section 481 of his posthumously published work *The Will to Power* (*WP*) he declares: 'Facts are precisely what there are not, only interpretations.' If this is the case, then an objectively true understanding of the world, of humankind and its prospects, is an impossibility. Essentially the same point is made in his *Beyond Good and Evil* (*BGE*) (sections 5, 8). On this account, each and every science, philosophy, or religion can offer no more than arguments and claims which are provisional at best and which are necessarily partial. Far from any objectivity, these arguments would receive their character, in Nietzsche's view, from the particular backgrounds, values and interests of those advancing them.

This leads us to the second thesis, namely Nietzsche's perspectivism. This holds that every philosophy or viewpoint advanced about the world, and humankind's significance in it, is only one among many possible alternative interpretations. (*On the Genealogy of Morals*, III, 12) Such interpretations, or perspectives, he is keen however to distinguish from relativism, which would hold that nothing can decide what interpretations are better or worse than any others, and which could only be taken as a warrant for anarchy, indifference or arbitrariness. So perspectivism, unlike relativism, has to produce some kind of criteria (i.e. has to '*create values*') for enabling the holders of a particular perspective to distinguish that perspective from inferior ones. For Nietzsche, these criteria would arise from a wholehearted acknowledgement of, and acceptance of, what he regarded as being most 'life-advancing', 'life-preserving' and 'species-preserving'. In this he concludes that from among all the motives and desires which underlie human action, primacy must be given to what he calls the 'will to power'. With this we have come to the third thesis.

In section 13 of *Beyond Good and Evil*, Nietzsche explains the will to power as follows: 'A living thing desires above all to *vent* its strength – life as such is will to power – self preservation is only one of the indirect and most frequent *consequences* of it.' In recurring passages of this book he asserts that falsification, exploitation, envy, and lust for domination pertain inescapably to life as such and not just to so-called primitive societies (*BGE* sections 4, 23, 188, 201, 259). In one such passage he writes:

> Life itself is *essentially* appropriation, injury, overpowering of the strange and weaker, suppression, severity, imposition of one's own forms, incorporation and, at the least and mildest, exploitation. (section 259)

Nietzsche is annoyed however that words such as these, which, he insists, describe a necessary part of life's unfolding and progress, and which often serve to identify the strong and the courageous from the weak and the mediocre, should have about them such a bad odour. Eighteen centuries of morality and religion in Europe are seen as the cause for this state of affairs, so the fourth of Nietzsche's theses to concern us here is his critique of Christianity.

If a will to power is present in humans – and in all living things – as the most primary 'drive', or desire, then, Nietzsche continues, those in whom it is most organised and best deployed will distinguish themselves as leaders, heroes, tyrants, artists, or as otherwise superior kinds of human beings. The rest of humankind – the vast majority – will be the led, the weak and the wretched. Thus things stood, Nietzsche claims, in prehistoric times and in the age of classical antiquity, or in what he approvingly calls 'the pre-moral period of mankind' (*BGE*, 32). The strong were distinguished from the weak by an abyss and a distinct rank order between strong and weak was central to the social order itself. In his book, *On the Genealogy of Morals*, Nietzsche declares passionately that Christianity and its ascetic ideals destroyed this older order: 'One may without exaggeration call it the true calamity in the history of European health'. (*GM* III, 28) To the strong and powerful, according to Nietzsche, Christianity preached that they should be ashamed of their domination of the weak: that their great hopes, their manly conquests, their pride and joy in beauty, should become remorse of conscience, self-destruction, guilt and timidity. (*BGE* 62; *GM* III, 14) To the weak it preached 'thou shalt obey', but also that their shortcomings – e.g. their lack of courage, their herd mentality – should be seen as virtues – e.g. humility, love of one's neighbour. To the sick and wretched it preached that they alone were to blame for their miseries, which were to be seen as a punishment and an atonement for their sinfulness. (*GM* III, 15) The ascetic ideals of Christianity, such as poverty, chastity and humility, drew particular hostility from Nietzsche. Indeed the practice of these virtues would seem to be the very denial of anything like a will to power: a self-denial carried out for purely spiritual motives, an attempt even to bridge the gap between a finite earthly world and an eternal heavenly one. But if, as Nietseche maintained, all such considerations of an eternal world must be ruled out from the start, then the motives of asceticism could only be some kind of conceited perversion of a more basic motivation, namely the will to power. In his own words:

> here rules a *ressentiment* without equal, that of an insatiable instinct and power-will that wants to become master not over something in life but over life itself, over its most profound, powerful and basic conditions. (*GM* III, 11)

The fifth of Nietzsche's theses which I have selected here attacks Christianity not because of its teachings – which as we have just seen he regards as obnoxious – but because of the dogmatic character of these teachings. In other words, in Nietzsche's view, these teachings have been offered not as one interpretation of the world and humankind; nor are those to whom they have been preached been left free to accept or reject them. Rather, Nietzsche insists, they have been proclaimed as the final truth about the whole of reality and such proclamation has furnished itself with powerful means to enforce its own will and to smother any awareness that what it proclaims is just an interpretation. (*GM* III, 14; *BGE* 188) The church as institution thus becomes for him one of the most striking accomplishments, but also one of the most objectionable, of the will to power itself.

The sixth thesis concerns the search for knowledge, including self-knowledge, which Socrates had placed at the centre of philosophy. Nietzsche has a disparaging regard for most European philosophers and an ambivalent attitude towards Socrates. On the one hand, he admires Socrates's uncompromising criticisms of the conventional moralites and the pretensions to wisdom which prevailed in the Greek culture of his own day. On the other hand, he despises Socrates for his humility and 'incapacity' in relation to a more autonomous kind of human conduct and wisdom (*BGE* 191) – a kind which Nietzsche himself identified with what he called 'free spirits' and which would 'overcome' considerations of morality altogether. 'What is needed above all', Nietzsche wrote, 'is an absolute scepticism towards all inherited concepts.' (*WP* 409) Socrates is to be faulted, in Nietzsche's view, because his self-knowledge was not radical enough: it still acquiesced in acknowledging a requirement for a morality which was binding on all and it still retained a deferential attitude to traditional morality, if not to conventional morality. For Nietzsche, then, the self-knowledge of Socrates was still a self-deception. Accordingly, the kernel of this sixth thesis is to be found in the following declaration from *Beyond Good and Evil*:

> I do not believe 'a drive to knowledge' to be the father of philosophy, but that another drive has, here as elsewhere, only employed knowledge (and false knowledge) as a tool … For every drive is tyrannical: and it is as *such* that it tries to philosophise. (*BGE* 6)

So convinced was Nietzsche of the primacy and all-pervasive character of the will to power that the significance of everything living, and in a special way that of all human experience, must be explained by reference to it. So passionate was his insistence on the superiority of the explanations supplied by the will to power, that any philosophical aspiration to a universal meaningfulness, any moral aspiration to solidarity between different classes or kinds of people, any spiritual aspiration to communion with a divinity, were at best self-deceptions and at worst were wilfully fraudulent. With repeated emphasis Nietzsche asserts that 'all meaning is will to power' (*WP* 590)

But if meaningfulness in any primary or universal sense is to be ruled out, if the lot of morality and religion is to be similar, what are the possibilities left for purposful action? for the kind of action which would have a recognisably human character? for educational action? Nietzsche's answer here, which I will present as the seventh and final thesis, emphasises the kind of action that springs from an unflinching, indeed a joyful embrace of a world shorn of the illusions and comforts provided by philosophy, religion and morality. Paraphrasing Nietzsche's arguments, it would in the first place be a courageous acceptance of the horribleness, and the marvellousness, of drives which now thrust themselves forward and back in human experience with an unhindered energy and in all their naked, elemental character. It would, secondly, be a sustained attempt to *create one's own values;* to make one's own prowess confer a meaning on one's actions; indeed to fashion one's own life as a bold and original work of of art. And thirdly, this would mean giving originality of direction and strictness of discipline to those particular drives which, in any particular individual, best enabled him to stand out and embrace distinctiveness and greatness; to become in a word, a superior kind of being, namely an *Übermensch.* (*Thus Spoke Zarathustra*, Prologue 3 ff; II, 12, 13) It is important to note that Nietzsche dismisses females from these higher possibilities.

Moral considerations, insofar as they are present here, are taken over by aesthetic ones and receive their character from them. This is precisely the inversion of values which Nietzsche seeks to promote. He readily acknowledges moreover that the distinctiveness and greatnesss which beckon the human spirit here, might indeed alternate with periodic downfall and torment. He insists, finally, that all 'free spirits' who embrace greatness in this way know and accept that their greatness is inevitably doomed to mortality and extinction. (*Zarathustra*, I, 10, 11)

Let us now recapitulate on the seven theses in summary form. The first asserts that objectively true accounts of the world and humankind are impossible, that all accounts must be interpretations, and that such interpretations are invariably coloured by the background and particular interests of the person giving the account. Following from this, the second thesis maintains that although knowledge is possible only as perspectives, criteria ('values') can be advanced by holders of a particular perspective to distinguish this perspective from inferior ones. The third thesis identifies the 'will to power' as the primary principle of human motivation and argues that a wholehearted acceptance of this would expose what Nietzsche regards as the self-deceptions of religion, philosophy and morality. The fourth thesis is an attack on the moral teachings of Christianity, as being the most influential, the most enduring and the most calamitous of such self-deceptions in eighteen centuries of European history. The fifth thesis challenges the dogmatic character of Christian teaching – namely its insistence that it proclaims the final truth that must be accepted by all. The sixth thesis asserts that the search for truth championed by Socrates is the will to power in another form. Finally, the seventh thesis indicates the kind of action appropriate to those courageous enough to face up to the realities of the will to power. It would be a disciplined fashioning of one's own life as a work of art, an unflinching creation of one's own 'values' in response to one's singular but also transient call to greatness.

Partiality as a Condition of Understanding

It would perhaps be tempting to dismiss Nietzsche's theses as the rantings of a fanatic, or a resentful eccentric. Indeed it would be all too easy to do so. The many contradictions evident in his various arguments and pronouncements, his continual petulance, his neglect of the sobrieties of scholarly writing in favour of aphorism and hyperbole, his failure to match his denunciations of religion, philosophy and morality with a well-worked out and constructive alternative; these may be advanced as reasons for not taking his work too seriously. In addition, his forced retirement from the University of Basel in 1879 due to recurrent illness, his isolation and restless wanderings in the next decade (during which he produced his most important writings), his capitulation to mental illness in 1889 and his failure to recover from this until his death in 1900; all of these may be offered as further grounds for believing that his work bears the marks of instability and volatility, rather than insights of abiding character. Notwithstanding the force of these criticisms, Nietzsche's accusations and claims cannot be finally silenced by such evidence. Indeed it is impossible to deny that many of the features of moral and political life in Western cultures at present have been prefigured in Nietzsche's philosophy, and it is now necessary to make these explicit.

Consider firstly the ill-fortunes of an objective or universalist standpoint, the effects of which are more discernible in moral and political affairs than in the pursuit of knowledge. At an international level, the *United Nations Declaration on Human Rights* is perhaps the nearest thing to a universal moral-political creed that the spirit of modernity could produce. But it is now so widely and blithely overlooked by governments and their agents that its existence has for many almost become an anachronism. In particular, as we shall explore in Chapter Nine, the increasingly fashionable currents of 'postmodernism' in contemporary Western cultures have abandoned anything resembling a universal orientation for moral-political thought. None of this is to say of course that moral considerations of an impartial nature have been altogether jettisoned in the conduct of world affairs; rather that they tend to enjoy scarcely more hospitable treatment under the patronage of many states which avow democracy than they did in an earlier age under emporors, kings, and princes of the church. Turning to political discourse at national level, the kind of utterance which characteristically employed reference to ideals such as 'the common good', or the 'welfare of all the people', has been virtually displaced by a kind of utterance which preoccupies the discourse of public affairs with references to 'the economy', its growth prospects, and its 'performance indicators'. Here, no less than at international level, changing employment and unemployment patterns show that the course of events tends to be influenced more by the interests of powerful corporations and the imperatives of international capitalism than by any efforts at self-determination by communities, regions or national governments.

Turning more particularly now to the issue of perspectivism, it is clear that one of the most notable features of contemporary Western societies is the radical plurality of world-views which has replaced the once dominant world-view of Christianity, including its different denominations. It has been common practice for quite some time to regard different world-views, including religious ones, as *interpretations*, and it is into a world of multiple and often radically conflicting interpretations that today's children are born. So-called 'fundamentalist' societies may be an exception to this, but the modernising and rationalising influences of Western pluralism are ever in attendance on those societies also. The consequences of this multiplicity of interpretations is everywhere in evidence: in politics at all levels; in industrial relations; in statutory, voluntary and executive bodies – such as managements, councils, boards, committees, and public authorities; in relations between colleagues in a workplace; in relations between parents and children; and, in an ever recurring way, in relations between teachers and their pupils. Wherever the decisions of established authorities might previously have hoped for a substantial measure of acceptance, such efforts are now much more likely to meet resistance or contestability: 'I'll do my own thing, you do yours', or 'who are you to say that your way is better than mine?' Or to take another example, the currency of new colloquial phrases such as 'hidden agenda', or 'her words are one thing, where she's coming from is what's important', show that whatever homage is still offered to ideals of objectivity, the attitude of perspectivism and the related concept of sectional interest (declared or undeclared), have become pervasive among the outlooks of the educated publics of the Western world.

The evidence we have so far been considering from patterns and trends of life in contemporary societies seems to provide more in the way of verification than falsification for the third of Nietzsche's theses sketched above: that all purposeful human action proceeds from the will to power. It seems also to suggest, as Nietzsche himself did strongly, that selfishness is one's best ally and strategy in one's affairs in the world. (*Zarathustra*, III, 'Of Three Evil Things') The primacy of self-interest is of course a natural corollary of Nietzsche's thesis on the primacy of the will to power. Although the empirical evidence we have consulted to this point is limited, it would not be a difficult task to add a thousandfold to the uncomplimentary examples we have just considered. Of course it would be a very lengthy task, filling with grim details countless books of historical record.

But do we have to accept that the weight of historical evidence is sufficient to provide verification of Nietzsche's thesis on the will to power, and the other theses associated with it? And must this evidence also force us to the conclusion that his interpretations of Christianity were correct – that religions are really no more than ecclesiastical politics as a form of the will to power? Some of the practitioners of *Realpolitik* (Nietzsche's trem) might simply reply 'yes' at this point, and add merely that the thing must be pursued with some degree of protocol, to give it an air of acceptability or even a certain panache. Nietzsche's many remarks on *style* provide material for just such a standpoint, and seek to give splendid attire to motives which Machiavelli was earlier content to leave in their naked state. Yet is is likely that the majority of people, including many contemporary practitioners of *Realpolitik*, will find something deeply disquieting in Nietzsche's theses and their practical corollaries. I have suggested above that there is enough of verified substance in many of Nietzsche's key arguments to make any question of their dismissal a self-deceiving proposition, despite whatever comforts such a dismissal might give.

I am keen to argue, however, that just where some of Nietzsche's arguments came closest to being most illuminating, they also come closest to obscuring the heart of the matter. I also hope to show that the line of argument I propose to open up here can provide us with an account of the purposes of teaching and learning which is both promising and challenging in a practical sense and which is also a strong candidate for defensibility in a universal sense.

Notwithstanding its plausibility and the support it can muster from historical evidence, Nietzsche's thesis on the primacy of the will to power has a dogmatic, even an obsessive character. In other words, despite his arguments that all knowing is conditioned by the knower's perspectives and interests, Nietzsche's own comments on the will to power are so insistent as to exclude, even to ridicule, alternative interpretations. Recall for instance his characteristic comments on life, on meaning, on the search for truth, and on religion: 'life as such is will to power'; 'all meaning is will to power'; 'every drive is tyrannical: and it is as *such* that it tries to philosophise'; 'I call Christianity the one great curse … the one immortal blemish of humanity'. (*BGE* 6, 13; *WP* 590; *The Antichrist* 22) Nietzsche's writings are replete with remarks such as these, which press themselves on the reader with a passionate intensity. Their insistent and all-inclusive character leave no room for contrary interpretations.

Yet such a contrary interpretation might argue tellingly as follows: that purposeful human action may be occasioned not just by *one* primary source, but by *two*, or possibly *more* primary sources. Against Nietzsche one can put forward a more subtle thesis, however, than the example just cited; a thesis which can be more fully and convincingly supported by the evidence of history and biography than can the thesis on the primacy of the will to power. This more subtle thesis would deny absolute primacy *to any single drive or desire*; it would hold that human beings rarely act from *one* motive, but from a *mixture* of motives, or indeed from a conflict of motives which has only been partially resolved. Such motives could, of course, include power and self-interest, but could also include – to mention but a few – service to others, acknowledgement of one's identity and of one's special contribution to human engagements, a desire for tolerant co-existence, compassion for suffering and bereavement, loyalty to friends or family, solidarity with the exploited and the downtrodden, or indeed love of God and one's neighbour. The central point in the case I am attempting to put forward here is that human experience is characterised by an ever unfolding play of motives rather than by any primary motive which must be accorded a permanently fixed place at the top of a hierarchy.

It would be as dogmatic and one-sided to assert that motives such as these just listed are merely perverse or sublimated forms of a primary will to power as it would be to suggest that the will to power is merely a disappointed or perverse form of any of these latter motivations. It is far from dogmatic however to suggest a shifting hierarchy among motives or to argue that even within a single individual, different motives might struggle with each other for a higher place on the hierarchy, even where the individual in question would seek to keep them in some disciplined and harmonious order. This is just one example of what it means to describe human experience as a *play* of motives. The effort to achieve such a harmonious order would represent, in each case, the individual's best attempt to give a coherent response to the moral or religious interpretations of reality which make a sustained claim on his or her attentions. Of course throughout recorded history, different religious and moral traditions have supplied different hierarchies of virtues, and have done so in both dogmatic and undogmatic manner. Taking Christianity as an example, the two highest virtues it originally preached were love of God and love of one's neighbour. It seems moreover from the four Gospels which give summary accounts of the life and teachings of Jesus Christ, that there was nothing dogmatic in those teachings, although this is still rarely acknowldeged. They were addressed to disciples and multitudes alike, and although they claimed to offer the Way and the Truth, their hearers were placed under no compulsion to accept them.

With the incorporation however of a Pauline-Augustinian theology as the dominant orthodoxy of the Christian church, we have seen that a significant shift occurred in Christianity's hierarchy of virtues. Augustine's unyielding insistence on the essential depravity of human nature established in Christianity a doctrine as onesided and dogmatic as Nietzsche's doctrine of the will to power. Augustine's relentless emphasis on self-denial was a consequence of his belief in the depravity of human nature. His decisive influence on the subsequent history of Christianity gave to asceticism and to authoritarian conceptions of discipline a significance which seems to be quite absent in the teaching activities of Christ himself. Although it was this asceticism and authoritarianism which drew Nietzsche's strongest invective, his own philosophy mirrors Augustinian Christianity nowhere so much as in the dogmatic primacy given to a reversal of Augustine's central theme. In the place of submissive humility and its consequence – ascetic self-denial – Nietzsche asserts the will to power and its consequence – wilful self-interest.

There are some important lessons to be learned from all of this. Perhaps the most important is that the granting of a fixed primacy to a single human characteristic, whether will to power, or depravity or whatever, obscures a proper awareness of the point that human experience is constituted by a *play*, or more precisely an *inter*play of motives – in our engagements with others or with the ideas and thoughts that are addressed to us. And proceeding now to some further lessons to be learned, this conception of human experience as an active interplay has a crucial importance for how we understand the purposes and the practice of education. It provides us firstly with an understanding which is both practical and dynamic, as distinct, for instance, from more theoretical conceptions such as 'man as a rational animal', man as '*homo economicus*', or man as a '*res cogitans*'. Such theoretical conceptions, no less so than Nietzsche's declarations on the will to power, tend to give a fixed priority to one aspect of the interplay, and thus to freeze, or distort it. Secondly, our conception of the purposes of education is further advanced if we understand human experience not just as an interplay of *motives* but also as an interplay of *perspectives, beliefs, aspirations, interests* etc., each of which may have something distinctive to contribute, but also, each of which is in itself partial. Thirdly, we are now in a better position to see that even the most accomplished of human expertise and judgement, the most inspired commitment, policy decision, and so on, still represents only a partial, a provisional and indeed a fallible understanding. Far from promoting any relativism, this awareness provides the enterprise of teaching and learning with a unique and a distinctive orientation; an orientation which views teaching and learning in any field as a disciplined venturing forth of the best efforts of imagination, intellect and sensibility; a venturing forth whose best fruits warrant no vanity or opinionatedness, but serve rather to provide human understanding with a refined modesty, with an educated sense of its own capabilities and limitations.

To conclude these lessons which can be gained from this brief review of Nietzsche's philosophy and its influence, it seems that Nietzsche's dogmatism frequently led him to ignore the real significance of one of his own finest insights, namely the insight that human understanding at its best can never hope to be anything better than interpretation, and that all such understanding is therefore necessarily partial. But we can now recall from the opening chapter of this book that an earlier form of this insight was present in Socrates' reference – during his trial – to the Oracle at Delphi. What was quoted in that chapter now takes on a new significance, in the light of the arguments we have just been considering:

> Real wisdom is the property of God, and this oracle is his way of telling us that human wisdom has little or no value. It seems to me that he is not referring literally to Socrates, but has merely taken my name as an example, as if he would say to us 'The wisest of you is he who has realised, like Socrates, that in respect of wisdom, he is really worthless'. (*Apology*, 23)

If the limitations that Socrates is drawing attention to here are properly understood and acknowledged as the kind of partiality which is inherent and inescapable in human experience, then perhaps human experience can better resist partisan temptations to regard its fruits as a final objectivity or certainty. Perhaps secondly, it can then better articulate a description of human understanding which does justice not only to its limitations, but also to its subtleties and possibilities. Perhaps thirdly, arising from this description, it can provide us with a discerning and durable account of the best purposes of learning and also with a defense of the claims of such purposes to enjoy a judicious measure of sovereignty. Finally, it is important to recall that Socrates would not accept acquittal if it meant that his educational activities were to cease to enjoy the responsible freedom which he had exercised throughout his public life. He produced a defence of the integrity of his life and work which the verdict of history (unlike that of the court) has invariably upheld. That the strength of such a defence could be made on the basis of the kind of considerations we have just encountered here may still seem an exceptional case. There may still be some who feel that the lessons I have drawn from the critique of Nietzsche's theses are similarly exceptional (as distinct from universal) and that they do not provide grounds for granting sovereignty in any significant sense to teaching and learning. To these issues we must now turn in the next section.

The Limitations of Understanding and the Purposes of Learning

What Nietzsche asserted in a sweeping manner – that 'facts are what there are not, only interpretations', and that all knowing is a perspective knowing – provided insights which were to be refined and to become central in the works of some of the most distinguished philosophers of the twentieth century. Karl Popper, Martin Heidegger, Hans-Georg Gadamer and Paul Ricoeur are among those who have argued that human understanding is inescapably interpretative in its nature, who have sought to establish that an understanding which is independent of presuppositions or preconceptions is not possible for humans. Of course there are important and sometimes striking differences between these thinkers, but there is also a crucial distinction to be made between what they share and what sets them apart from Nietzsche's perspectivism. In order to establish this distinction clearly, I want to consider briefly some key insights from each of the four, Popper, Heidegger, Gadamer, and Ricoeur.

Where Nietzsche denied the possibility of objective knowledge, Popper, for instance, takes great pains to testify to its existence and its significance. Popper's arguments however differ from traditional conceptions of objective knowledge in many respects, the most important one being as follows. In his books, *Objective Knowledge – An Evolutionary Approach* (*OKn*), *Conjectures and Refutations (C&R)*, and in many of his other writings, Popper argues that objective knowledge is no longer to be viewed as something which is either complete or irrefutable. It is rather to be understood as the sustainable findings of human conjectures (or theories) about the world. This kind of knowledge then, unlike conceptions of induction from Francis Bacon onwards, is constituted not by theories which have become so verified by evidence as to make them certain facts. Rather it is constituted by theories which have been ventured into the public arena, which remain open to question, and which have so far withstood the best efforts to refute them. In Popper's own words:

> And if we fail to refute the new theory, especially in fields in which its predecessor has been refuted, then we can claim this as one of the objective reasons for *the conjecture that the new theory is a better approximation to truth than the old theory*. (*OKn* p.81)

Objective knowledge, on this account, retains an essentially partial, and an essentially provisional character. It never attains the status of certainty, or absolute knowledge. Popper is not saying here however that this latter kind of knowledge is inconceivable; rather he is suggesting that it is an impossibilility for humans. Popper quotes fragments 18 and 34 from the pre-Socratic philosopher Xenophanes to summarise his arguments that all human knowledge is partial, that it is conjectural and interpretative in character, and that certain knowledge lies beyond the reach of human capability:

> The gods did not reveal, from the beginning,
> All things to us; but in the course of time,
> Through seeking we may learn, and know things better...
>
> But as for Certain truth, no man has known it,
> Nor shall he know it; neither of the gods,
> Nor yet of all the things of which I speak.
> And even if by chance he were to utter
> The final truth, he would himself not know it:
> For all is but a woven web of guesses. (*C&R* 152-3)

Heidegger's arguments on understanding also highlight the point that all human understanding is, inescapably, interpretation. (*Being and Time* §§ 31 & 32) These arguments are particularly incisive and have provided a basis for much further research, not only in philosophy but also in theology and the social sciences. 'In interpretation', Heidegger argues, 'understanding does not become something different. It becomes itself.' He calls attention especially to the point that wherever we understand anything at all, what is understood discloses itself to us *as* something of a particular kind. In other words the *as* is already inbuilt in the act of understaning, even where the understanding is a mis-understanding. And although disciplined study, and criticism of our efforts by others, can take much of the 'mis-' out of mis-understanding, they do so only by bettering our grasp of the *as*; not by getting rid of it but by refining and revising it. But our efforts to understand cannot take all of the 'mis-' out of mis-understanding, because to do so would mean arriving at an understanding from which the limitations of perspective were finally excised, and before which the reality of that which we were seeking to understand disclosed itself in its fulness; in a word, an understanding which was in this respect omniscient.

So on Heidegger's account, we understand, for instance, what is addressed to our attentions *as* agreeable or disagreeable, *as* difficult or easy, *as* biased or evenhanded, *as* funny or sad; we understand what we hear *as* the sound of a car or *as* a car with a faulty silencer, *as* the sound of an angry or a pleading voice, *as* a decent request or *as* an indecent proposal; and so on with the other senses through which our understanding takes place. Something from our earlier experience plays an inescapable part – as an interpretation – in enabling us to understand at all. Even that which we fail to understand still involves an understanding with an inbuilt interpretation: we understand it *as* puzzling or *as* incomprehensible. Our prior orientations, our anticipations, our pre-conceptions necessarily remain active and, far from being ever overcome, or set aside in a so-called presuppositionless understanding, they remain that which makes any kind of understanding possible in the first place.

In each case then, the *as* receives its character in a decisive way from our previous experience: from a totality of involvements which marks that experience as our own rather than someone else's, and which Heidegger simply calls a 'forehaving' (*einer Vorhabe*). Secondly, according to Heidegger, this fore-having is also attended by a 'fore-sight', or inbuilt anticipation (*einer Vorsicht*) which, in the act of understanding, already focuses interest and attention on some features and possibilities rather than others. Thirdly, Heidegger argues, it is attended by a fore-conception (*einem Vorgriff*), namely the pre-conceptions which give to each act of understanding not only the character of an interpretation but also the unavoidable character of a judgement.

Heidegger's observations on the interpretative character of human understanding, and particularly his arguments on the part played by pre-judgements in our efforts to understand, have been richly elaborated and developed by Gadamer and Ricoeur. In a key section of his major work, *Truth and Method*, Gadamer explores in detail the structure of understanding and offers the memorable conclusion that 'the prejudices of the individual, far more than his judgements, constitute the historical reality of his being'. (*TM* 245) In a subsequent essay, he phrases the same conclusion as follows: 'It is not so much our judgements as it is our prejudices that constitute our being. (*Philosophical Hermeneutics* 9) Gadamer acknowledges that this is a provocative formulation, but argues that his intention in putting the matter in this way is to challenge what he calls 'the cold rationalism of the Enlightenment' for believing that it could free humankind from the prejudices of authority and tradition; for holding that 'a methodologically disciplined use of reason can safeguard us from all error'. (*TM* 246) He points out that the Enlightenment drove out of usage a concept of prejudice which could have a positive as well as a negative significance, namely: 'a judgement that is given before all the elements that determine a situation have been finally examined'. On this account, 'prejudice' would mean not merely something arising from overhastiness or from unquestioning attachment to a particular tradition or culture.

More positively, it could also mean a pre-judgement of a provisional character, coloured indeed by one's previous experience and commitments, but also open to other viewpoints and to the evidence which they might have to offer. It is to this enabling sense of prejudice as a pre-judgement which remains self-critically alert and open to dialogue that Gadamer is keen to draw our attention.

But as Gadamer himself points out, all the elements which determine a situation can rarely if ever be *finally* examined. This is so not only in all the main fields of scholarship and research, but even in those 'open and shut' criminal cases where the criminal is judged to be guilty 'beyond the shadow of a doubt', but where the degree of guilt, and the motives underlying the crime, are still open to a multiplicity of perspectives, even to an inexhaustible degree. And here, as in the case of the most rigorous scientific research, interpretations can be *more* or *less* in harmony or in conflict, but none can claim to be the final truth. Commenting on this inexhaustibility and its relation to the limitations of human understanding, Paul Ricoeur remarks: 'It is because absolute knowledge is impossible that the conflict of interpretations is insurmountable and inescapable'. (*Hermeneutics and the Human Sciences* 193) (*HHS*)

Now this conclusion of Ricoeur's may sound initially like a counsel of despair for all educational effort. It seems to suggest that the work of teaching and learning, of research and scholarship is, at the end of the day, condemned to endless acrimonies, where the only victor is the ever recurring spectre of a relativism which rules over all. Doesn't the fact that the world's academies – and individual fields of learning – are replete with such acrimonies bear out these pessimistic conclusions? To venture 'yes' as the answer here would in one sense be correct, but it would also obscure something of greater importance. The crucial point here is that these pessimistic conclusions would hold only for the standpoint which maintained that anything less than certainty would be a *deficiency* where knowledge was concerned. And this of course is the attitude towards knowledge which was paramount during Christendom. The rationalism of the Enlightenment tried to displace the *contents* of this older view, but largely retained the *attitude* that the pursuit of knowledge was a quest for certainty. This current of Enlightenment thought still tends to equate rigour with certainty and is still alive and vigorous in most of the world's centres of learning. By contrast, the entire argument I am advancing here rests on the premise which holds not only that the unattainability of certainty is a basic feature of the human condition, but also that a wholehearted acknowledgement of this is among *the most important of educational virtues*.

To put this in another way, the quest for certainty, and the attempt to establish one's own certainties in a place of prominence over those of one's opponents, represents a standpoint which sees knowledge essentially as power and which gives a Nietzschean ethic of domination and self-interest primacy in the arena of education. It would of course be foolhardy to suggest that such an ethic could be somehow *excluded* from this arena. Only by the most repressive means could schooling be thoroughly insulated from tendencies which are prevalent in society at large. And even then, such measures would be likely to be of only limited success. But what I am suggesting is this. Insofar as the educational enterprise fails to understand its *own essential purposes as lying in the opposite direction* of an ethic of power and self-seeking, it becomes the instrument and accomplice of such an ethic, albeit in an unwitting way. And this is far from making the simplistic recommendation that education should be used to change society's evil ways. It is rather a question of nurturing throughout the various branches of learning the human dispositions which keep alive, and in some sense realise, the possibilities of making significant inroads on those inclinations which all too easily offer accommodation to one or other dogma, and particularly those which enjoy an unquestioned ascendancy. Or to use a maritime metaphor, it is to engage wholeheartedly in the continual play of ebb and flow, but in such a way as to keep tidal waves of partisan origin at bay.

Our explorations to this point have concluded that the unattainability of certainty is an inescapable feature of human experience and that an acknowledgement of this insight is an educational virtue of first importance. Let us now make explicit the practical orientation this two-fold conclusion would have for the purposes of learning. Ricoeur suggests that the failure to make the acknowledgement I have just mentioned gives an unwarranted scope to critical enquiry's faith in its own ability to surmount the limitations of perspective and to provide autonomous critiques and commanding overviews. In this connection he speaks of the 'arrogance of critique', and of the necessity of renouncing such arrogance in favour of an enquiry characterised by more modest aspirations, by more self-criticism and by more joint endeavours. (*HHS* 244-6) In a similar vein Gadamer argues that we realise our best selves when our enquiries proceed from an acknowledgement of the limitations in own perspective, and from an appreciation of the effects of our preconceptions on our outlooks and dispositions. None of this is to disparage the tradition or outlooks which any individual or group might bring to an enquiry. Rather it is to suggest that all perspectives attain a better grasp of their own essentials, a better understanding of contrasting perspectives and a better understanding of the need for their own continual re-education, when the conduct of enquiry becomes a disciplined venturing and listening characterised by dialogue. Such a play of venturing and listening Gadamer grants a special importance. He describes it as 'the dialogue that we are'.[1]

But we become what we 'are' in this sense only when we realise the best in ourselves, and this may be far from an everyday occurence. Insofar as motives of a Nietzschean kind are allowed to enjoy a prominence in our enquiries, and in our intercourse with others, one could indeed speak of 'the *contest* that we are'. So in order to distinguish the motives and practices that describe the 'dialogue that we are' from the motives and practices of contrasting orientations, let us identify the characteristics which might be evident in a practical instance of the 'dialogue that we are'. These can be summarised as follows:

(a) A readiness to listen in a disciplined way to what the other party has to say, including that party's strongest criticisms of one's own standpoint;

(b) a readiness to grant that there may be distinctive insights and points of merit in the perspectives of the other party;

(c) an ability to discern and a willingness to note the most significant points in the other party's perspectives, including any points of agreement with ones' own standpoint, any points of difference, and any areas of new ground;

(d) a capacity to bring one's own standpoint incisively into play and to explore in a self-critical way the merits of the various perspectives which have been offered by the different parties;

(e) a willingness to put the claim to truth in one's own perspective at risk, in the effort to achieve a more inclusive understanding.

From these points we can clearly see that what I have described above as 'the dialogue that we are' has an aspirational character, as distinct from something found in a readymade way in the everyday world. In other words it is a *discipline* to be pursued and practised, in accordance with the requirements just listed. Secondly, we can also see that it differs in crucial respects from what our everyday language calls 'discussion and dialogue', i.e. bargaining and negotiation. The 'dialogue that we are' is rarely attained in such pure form however that it entirely escapes considerations of bargaining and negotiation. Thirdly, it differs even further from what is called political engineering, namely the efforts to contrive and manipulate a social consensus towards a standpoint which has evaded the risks of venturing itself in dialogue; or in other words, a standpoint envisaged and fixed in advance by the social engineers. Fourthly, this rather formal and procedural mode of the 'dialogue that we are' should be distinguished from the more personal, more spiritual, indeed sublime kind of dialogue described by Martin Buber in his book, *Ich und Du*, though the difference is still more one of degree than a difference in nature. Finally, the aspirations embodied in the 'dialogue that we are' have a special significance for the emergence of personal identity in our continual encounters with traditions, customs and the entire range of cultural influences which address human experience as it unfolds. In short, these aspirations have a singular significance for education. But they are frequently distorted, confounded or sidetracked by contradictory practices which have become ingrained in the conduct of education itself. These conflicting orientations have intensified with the pluralistic movements associated with modernity. The following chapter will attempt to unravel some of the main strands in this tangle.

Notes:

1. The short passage where this appears reads as follows: 'We are seeking to approach the mystery of language from the conversation that we ourselves are' *Truth and Method*, p.340. 'Wir suchen von **dem Gespräch** aus, **das wir sind**, dem Dunkel der Sprache nahezukommen' *Wahrheit Und Methode* (Fourth edition,Tübingen: J.C.B. Mohr – Paul Siebeck, 1975) p.360. The German word is Gespräch, which can be translated either as dialogue or conversation. I have put in bold print above the words I quoted from the passage. The passage introduces one of the most significant claims in all of Gadamer's writings. This is the claim that it is through the to-and-fro of conversation – and more especially the kind of dialogue which seeks to understand the other party in the fullness of his or her otherness – that what is most significant about being human is disclosed. The third part of *Truth and Method* explores this claim in detail, and is accordingly titled 'The Ontological Shift of Hermeneutics Guided by Language'. There are strong parallels here with Oakeshott's special emphasis on 'conversation' which we came across earlier. Oakeshott does not make Gadamer's point about the ontological significance of conversation, yet the singular and striking part 'the conversation of mankind' plays in his different writings seems to point implicitly in a direction similar to Gadamer's.

CHAPTER SIX

Personal Identity: Imposition, Creation, or Epiphany?

Introduction

In the first four chapters we reviewed predominant patterns in the history of teaching and learning in Western civilisation. In the fifth chapter we explored the play of motives, perspectives, aspirations and so on, which constitutes human experience itself. These reviews now enable us to confront anew the following question: Are educational institutions in general, and individual teachers in particular, entitled to entertain proprietorial designs on their pupils and students? Or more formally, are they entitled to enjoy proprietary rights over their pupils' sensibilities and loyalties? The question raises for us the kind of issue the critical spirit of the Enlightenment raised against the claims of religious authority and tradition which prevailed during the long era of Christendom. Where the authorities of Christendom would answer this question by insisting that education must seek to stamp on each learner the image of the Divine Creator, the Enlightenment spirit would voice a resounding 'no' to any attempt to impose a sense of identity on the learner. The question could be answered in a different way still by an aesthetically inspired standpoint which holds that one's identity can be chosen, and re-chosen, from an ever-changing range of alternatives. The educational standpoints which spring from the growth of pluralism in the modern era provide yet a further range of possibilities for answering the question.

Indeed the disparaties of outlook which pervade modern western cultures would suggest that education must remain an arena for recurrent battles between competing conceptions of the good life, or progress, or enlightenment. That these battles are now generally carried out in democratic societies does not mean that they are therefore generally governed by democratic norms and procedures. Even if they were, victory could still go to the party with the most political clout rather than to the viewpoint which is most informed and most defensible on educational grounds. But the eventual victor remains conflict itself, and even incoherence, unless the conduct of politics is prepared to grant that education – like other professions – has an integrity which is entitled to an accountable measure of informed discretion, or what I have called in this book, sovereignty.

The following discussion of education and emergent identity is not therefore any politically inspired attempt to champion one approach over another. Rather it will seek to explore three contrasting approaches to the question posed in our opening paragraph, but to do so from an educational perspective; a perspective moreover which attempts to honour the nonpartisan requirements of dialogue considered in the previous pages.

Identity as Imposed

For Christendom, the chief task of education was to shape the identity of a fallen creature to the image and likeness of godliness, while establishing in the learner's understanding both the certainty of God's existence and the certainty of the learner's own unworthiness of God's redeeming grace. In practical terms this meant that the identity of each person was already ordained, in all essentials at least, by the proclamations of religious authority. Accordingly the goal of education was to bring each to an ever more complete acquiescence in this identity and therefore to ever more determined efforts to win eternal salvation. Because of the incontestability which was then generally accorded to theological principles, because of their proclaimed status as objective truth, the rights claimed by educational institutions upon their students' beliefs and loyalties could be viewed as having a formal and an authoritative standing. To claim against such authority a right such as the right of each individual to be different, and the right to assert that difference, would be to make a claim against what was seen as a divinely ordained order and would place the claimant promptly in a position of heresy.

By contrast, one of the chief characteristics of a pluralist age such as our own is its tendency to contest, or even to dismiss, any world-view or doctrine which claims the status of objective truth and which binds its followers to obedience. It is precisely in this tendency that the legacy of the Enlightenment – its temperament and its prejudices – is most influential. And because the Enlightenment temperament sees reason as autonomous and prejudice of any kind as a blemish, it is slow to recognise any prejudices in itself, or in its own appraisals of the world-views of a previous age. Where reason is championed as autonomous, then anything which is regarded as repugnant to this standpoint falls in for particular criticism. Proprietorial rights or designs on the sensibilities of learners would thus be seen here as illegitimate, or more judgementally as indoctrination; as the imposition of an alien identity on the young and the curtailment, explicit or otherwise, of the powers of reason to grow towards autonomy. This explains the forcefulness of the negative answer that the Enlightenment spirit – in our own age no less than in the Enlightenment's heyday – gives to questions like the one about proprietorial designs and rights in the conduct of teaching and learning.

But the dismissive attitude of the Enlightenment spirit towards what it regards as the prejudices of authority and tradition contains in itself some assumptions which should be examined. In particular, it casts discredit on any suggestion that there might yet be some merits in the claims of an authority which sought allegiance above all else, or that there might yet be riches in a tradition which was replete with dogmatic preachings and practices. But just such a suggestion may indeed be a fertile one, and pursuing it here might enable us to consider some illustrations of how legitimate prejudices – i.e. pre-conceptions which remain self-critical and open to new evidence – might be distinguished from illegitimate ones. To provide such illustrations, we can draw on some of the arguments and reviews in the earlier chapters, particularly those relating to Plato and to Aristotle in Chapter One and those relating to Augustine and Pope Gregory VII in Chapter Two.

In the first chapter we saw that the strong convictions of Plato produced a body of thought on moral, religious and philosophical issues whose influence was such that it largely eclipsed the kind of practical commitment which Socrates sought to bear witness to in his life's work. We also saw that Plato's custodial conception of learning was shared in key respects (though by no means all) by Aristotle, and that this kind of conception achieved a place of first importance in the subsequent history of Western education. In the second chapter we saw how Augustinian theology occasioned a similar eclipse – though in this case more a distortion – of the kinds of conviction exemplified in the teaching activities of Jesus Christ. We also saw how, through the work of Gregory VII, an Augustinian-Platonist version of Christianity largely became the official doctrine of the church as an institution. Now in all of these instances the claims of institutional religious authority and tradition are very much to the fore. The institutionalising theme is particularly significant in Plato's work. He is so convinced of the necessity for a body of virtues and practices which is invested with the authority *conferred* by tradition that he invents a 'noble myth' about humankind's ancestry to replace those features of the existing moral tradition which he finds unacceptable. (*Republic* 415a-c) His writings presuppose from the start that it is not merely a question of having designs on the sensibilities of the young (for indeed the differing schools of the sophists had this), but rather a question of having the clear right in law to exercise these designs, once their embodiment of the Good had been established as exemplary. Gregory VII's 'Augustinian' reforms to church structures, procedures and law, showed a similar purpose, but whereas with Plato and Aristotle the purpose was set out in theory only, with Gregory its pursuit became very much a matter of practice, including compulsion.

The strong note of authoritarianism in all of this is undeniable, as is the strategic exercise of censorship. So also is the recasting of selected features of traditions as forceful orthodoxies which now proclaim themselves as the supreme truth. Repugnant as this kind of practice may be to any standpoint which claims autonomy for reason and its exercise, it still does not warrant the dismissal of the tradition in question, or even of an authority which is associated primarily with this tradition. For it may well be the case that such a dismissal precludes us from seeing that there may have been insights of abiding worth and of a defensible character in what has been dismissed; insights which might now be uncovered by a discerning reclamation of what the authoritarian doctrines had themselves taken for granted, or overshadowed, or disfigured. I would like to focus on a few such insights here, to show firstly that our sense of personal identity cannot dispense with tradition and its influence; to show secondly that it misleads itself if, under the banner of rational autonomy, it claims a radical independence of tradition; to show thirdly that such a radical independence cuts itself off from the sources which are most vital to sustain and nourish identity, namely community and 'nativeness'. The insights I wish to explore here have been anticipated in the earlier chapters and are promisingly present in such apparently archaic notions as *telos, polis, ethos*. They are also to be discerned however in a notion which at first sight resembles a proprietorial mentality, namely the notion of *belonging*. But we must now make explicit the interplay of these four characteristics in human experience – *telos, polis, ethos* and *belonging* – and show that it is precisely through an interplay of this kind that personal identity takes shape and becomes intelligible.

Telos, as we saw in the first chapter, can be translated as the 'aim' or 'end' of a particular action, of an entire community or society, or of human life itself. Now many post-Enlightenment critical philosophies are suspicious of the notion of *telos*, particularly of the claim that human life itself has a *telos*. For such philosophies, it is just this claim that opens the way for totalitarian world-views and that denies toleration to human experience to understand itself as autonomous, or as individual; or to understand itself ever-anew as different. Indeed the notion that life as such has an underlying *telos* is the particular target of the critiques of 'metanarratives' by the 'postmodern' standpoints we considered in Chapter Four. But for Socrates, just as for Plato and Aristotle and most of the Western history of learning, something like a *telos* for life as such had to be presupposed, and the very conception of education as a purposeful undertaking would have been incoherent without it. And the same would be true of the related notions *polis*, *ethos* and *belonging*.

The characteristics of a *polis* we also examined in the opening chapter, where it was described as a city-state of small enough size to be a civic community: one sharing a public avowal of certain virtues, a public disdain for certain vices, a public acknowledgement of divinities and their powers and, not least, sovereignty over its own civic, cultural, economic and military affairs. This is not to say that what was acclaimed as virtuous or honourable in the *polis* was always observed by the citizens, or even always unambiguously interpreted. Nevertheless, what were generally acclaimed as virtues or disdained as vices revealed the public's inherited understanding of what was worthy of enduring commitment and what was not; in short, the public's understanding of the *telos* of life as lived in the *polis*. The *polis*, its traditions, its cultural pursuits, its military exploits, provided the citizens with an unforced but a very distinctive sense of their own identity. The ambiguities and differences in interpretation mentioned just here gave rise in time however not only to different schools of thought in places of learning, but also to practices and outlooks which threatened what had sustained that identity in times of crisis. Thus Socrates saw the Athenian *polis* of his later years as being in a state of moral decline and Plato saw it as having reached such depths of decadence that nothing less than a replacement of the prevailing culture – achieved through education as an institutional strategy – could bring before the young again ideals which were worthy of their commitments.

We have seen that Aristotle criticised Plato for seeking the highest human good in a theoretical *idea* (the *idea* of the Good) which lay outside of human practices themselves. The goodness of character which Plato sought to promote through education, should be sought, according to Aristotle in *practice,* or rather in its embodiment in those practices in which the learner had become habituated. Such habitual practices gave rise to a distinctive moral climate, or spirit, and this is what Aristotle called *éthos*. An *éthos* therefore was not something which could be simply decreed – i.e. determined from above – by the legislators. Indeed if it was to become part of the constitution of the *polis,* that constitution could be found in the first place in the spirit which was habitually shown and in the dispositions which were habitually nourished by the citizens. Or as Aristotle himself puts it

> for the maintenance of any constitution, like its first establishment, is due, as a rule, to the presence of the spirit or character (*éthos*) proper to that constitution. The establishment and maintenance of democracy is due to the presence of a democratic spirit (*éthos*), and that of an oligarchy to the presence of an oligarchic spirit. The better the spirit, the better the constitution it gives rise to. (*Politics* VIII, i)

But the insight present in this passage, which views the legislator as the expression of the citizens' will rather than as any kind of despot, is apparently cancelled in another passage a few lines later. This important passage has already been cited in Chapter One, in connection with some initial comments on the fourth notion of interest to us here – namely that of *belonging*. In the light of what has been argued since that chapter, it is worth giving most of this passage a second reading at this point.

> And since the *polis* as a whole has but a single aim (*telos*), it is plain that the education of all must be one and the same, and that the supervision of this education must be public and not private, as it is on the present system, under which everyone looks after his own children privately and gives them any private instruction he thinks proper. Public training is wanted in all things that are of public interest. Besides, it is wrong for any citizen to think that he belongs to himself. All must be considered as belonging to the *polis*: for each man is a part of the *polis*, and the treatment of the part is necessarily determined by the treatment of the whole. (*Politics* VIII, i)

The opening sentence of the passage seems to suggest, like the instance of Christendom cited at the beginning of this chapter, that there is but a single identity for everyone in the *polis* and that this must be imposed on all. This seems to be confirmed by the two final sentences, which apparently make the citizens the property of the *polis* and its rulers. To the critical spirit of Enlightenment the passage must seem significant chiefly as a species of totalitarian spell cast by classical philosophy over the conduct of life and learning in Western civilisations. Yet if this judgement can be suspended for long enough to allow evidence of a more subtle kind to present itself from Aristotle's passage, we may begin to become more clearly aware of the kind of reclamation mentioned just a little earlier. For instance, it must be recalled that, for Aristotle, the 'one aim' for the *polis* as a whole is happiness in its citizens and that this happiness is not something passive. Aristotle describes it, at its best, rather as a conscious *activity of the soul* in accordance with goodness. (*Nicomachean Ethics* I, vii; *Politics* VII, xii) When we recall moreover the rather intimate scale of the *polis* as a city-state, 'belonging to' a *polis* loses most of the anonymous starkness of being owned by the state. Thus, on a more sympathetic, but also a more probing interpretation of Aristotle, 'belonging to the *polis*' could be rephrased as: identifying actively with one's own civic community, with the traditions and customs of one's locality; or alternatively: being identified as a person belonging to a community with a strong sense of its traditions and its collective identity.

But it might still be objected that such identification of self with community is mainly a matter of conformity; that concepts such as *polis, telos, ethos* and *belonging* signify not an emancipation but rather an uncritical acquiescence in the patterns of identity which one's upbringing held forth as acceptable, to the neglect or exclusion of other possibilities for identity and self-understanding. This acquiescence might therefore be regarded as an indoctrination of a more intractable kind, an unquestioned schooling in strongly held 'essentials', with the likely consequence of closing off of any real possibility for choosing an identity or lifestyle which contrasted with the preconceptions of such a schooling. Arguments of this kind are not uncommon nowadays.[1] One of the most notable, which presents a radical case for the freedom to choose, and to re-choose one's identity, has been made by Richard Rorty in his major work *Philosophy and the Mirror of Nature*. Rorty's critique is directed not so much against traditional patterns of schooling and upbringing, but rather against most of the Western traditions of philosophy itself, including those which have provided the foundations of schooling of every kind.

Identity as Chosen

Rorty's philosophy is in many ways strongly reminiscent of Nietzsche's, but where Nietzsche's idiom is largely declamatory and impassioned, Rorty's is generally good-humoured and urbane. For all its urbanity, however, Rorty's philosophy is in some respects even more radical than Nietzsche's. Nietzsche's attack on the notion of objective truth is strongly paralleled by Rorty's attack on 'epistemology' in *Philosophy and the Mirror of Nature.* (*PMN*) Rorty sees 'epistemology', or 'theory of knowledge', as the mistaken attempt to replace the discredited certainties of classical and medieval metaphysics with certainties of a more rational and secure kind. He identifies Locke and Descartes as the founders of epistemology and Kant as one of its early towering figures. As a discipline of thought then, epistemology both *contributed* to the Enlightenment and achieved its rise to prominence *during* the Enlightenment. As 'epistemology', Rorty argues, philosophy sought to provide a systematic account, or 'accurate representations', of the entire of reality. This would be an account grounded on unshakeable foundations; no longer those of theology but those of reason. This spirit of Enlightenment was thus a 'quest for certainty, structure and rigour' in which philosophy, in its new understanding of itself, would be seen as the tribunal of reason. (*PMN* 166)

Like Nietzsche, Rorty is unsympathetic to any suggestion – metaphysical, epistemological or other – that there are objective truths to be known by the human mind. And this includes the suggestion that human beings have anything like 'a common essence'.[2] For Rorty, there are only alternative sets of descriptions, just as for Nietzsche, there were just alternative interpretations, or perspectives. Rorty sees epistemology as a successor discipline to metaphysics; a successor discipline that seeks to discard those certainties of its predecessor that are unscientific, but also to salvage others which it thinks can be grounded for once and for all by reason. Kant's philosophy, for instance, included in this latter category the formal principles of morality, which presented human reason with a 'categorical imperative': 'Act only on that maxim through which you can at the same time will that it should become a universal law.' (*Critique of Practical Reason* 80) But in Rorty's view, all such efforts to salvage or reconstruct some enduring concept or principle which might apply universally to humankind as such, or which might act as a unifying end or *telos*, should be seen as as a pursuit of illusions.

The dominating notion of epistemology is that to be rational, to

> be fully human, to do what we ought, we need to be able to find agreement with other human beings. To construct an epistemology is to find the maximum amount of common ground with others. The assumption that an epistemology can be constructed is the assumption that such common ground exists. (*PNM* 316)

It is just this assumption that Rorty is keen to undermine, so his critique of epistemology carries not only the recommendation to give up the quest for certainty – a recommendation, it should be recalled, which was present in an implicit way in Socrates' famous remark about the 'worthlessness' of human wisdom. Much more radically, Rorty calls for abandoning the search for any truth which might be a candidate for universal acceptance, even if that truth is conceived of in provisional terms. Rorty's dismissal of epistemology then is much more than a dismissal of the claims to certainty which epistemology seeks to establish on behalf of reason. Rather it involves the further step, or more precisely the further leap, of dismissing any claims which would say of humans that they share some essential characteristic worthy of universal respect and dignity. In many parts of *Philosophy and the Mirror of Nature,* Rorty employs a witty irreverance to dispose of the attempts of metaphysics and epistemology to represent human identity, or 'personhood', as something distinctive, or unique. In one such passage where he attempts to minimise the differences between human and non-human entities, he draws on Sartre's distinction between *en soi* and *pour soi,* (viz. *en soi* as being in its totality and *pour soi* as the being of human consciousness and its desires) and argues as follows:

> In a sufficiently long perspective, man may turn out to be less *deinos* than Sophocles thought him and the elementary forces of nature more so than modern physicalists dream. To see this point it helps to bear in mind that there are plenty of occasions on which we do well simply to ignore the *pour-soi* of human beings. We do this in the case of particularly dull and conventional people, for example, whose every act and word are so predictable that we 'objectivise' them without hesitation. (*PMN* 352)

But the question now forces itself on us: what kind of conception of human selfhood, if any, could inform Rorty's argument? Rorty's answer to this is to present a curious argument which separates consciousness, or 'inner life' from reason,[3] and to claim that once this separation is carried out, personhood can be seen for what it is: 'a matter of decision rather than knowledge, an acceptance of another being into fellowship rather than a recognition of a common essence'. (*PMN* 38) This means that one's sense of identity is not something that is disclosed through any fruits of reflection on moral teachings, or on one's relation with a community, or through any knowledge that comes from experience. Rather it is *chosen*, and *re-chosen*, in much the same way that Nietzsche held that one's 'values' must not be appropriated through intercourse with a tradition but must in each case be *created*. Where the 'will to power' (as driving force) supplied Nietzsche's *übermensch* with some kind of criterion for creating his values, Rorty seems to find something similar in what he calls 'conversation', or more precisely, in the effort to 'keep the conversation going rather than to find objective truth'. (*PMN* 372, 377) On this account then, it seems that personhood would be primarily associated with one's ability to participate in the conversation, as would any decision to admit another being into fellowship.

From what has just been said it is hardly surprising that the kind of conversation Rorty has in mind is not just any conversation. In the first place, Rorty avails of Michael Oakeshott's metaphor 'the conversation of mankind' and presses it into service to describe a kind of intercourse which is actively concerned not with the search for 'objective truth', but rather with the 'project of finding new, better, more interesting, more fruitful ways of speaking'. Secondly, it is in this project that Rorty sees the educational, or as he prefers to call it the 'edifying' purpose of philosophy. (*PMN* 359-60) In keeping with his accusation that 'objective truth' wrongly assumes for itself a 'priviliged description' of the way things are, he recommends 'edification' as a conversion from any kind of 'objective truth' loyalties, or *telos* loyalties, to a different kind of outlook. This latter outlook is one which holds that endless sets of alternative descriptions of human selfhood are possible, and that keeping the conversation open means pursuing these possibilities ever anew and preventing the pursuit from 'degenerating' once again into a situation where 'objective knowledge' asserts its supremacy. For such supermacy, in Rorty's view, does violence to the diversity of *different* discourses; it invariably attempts to 'commensurate' what is 'incommensurable', it imposes a hierarchy in the order of being and knowledge, by presuming to adjudicate between the claims of alternative sets of descriptions and by conferring on some more ontological status (viz. a higher place in the hierarchy) than others.

The educational significance of the arts and the sciences lies, for Rorty, not in contributing to any such hierarchies, but in the endless ability of these pursuits to show us new ways to 'remake' ourselves, to 'redescribe' ourselves, to 'become different people' (*PMN* 359) as we give our energies to reading, to writing, to study and to conversation. That such a prospect might invest learning – and the self-understanding which always attends learning – with a supply of inviting aesthetic possibilities seems clear enough. It seems in fact to lift every kind of authoritarian restriction from learning and to grant it instead, not merely the qualified kind of sovereignty I am trying to make a case for in these chapters, but rather an unconditional emancipation. But it is precisely here, where Rorty's appeal might seem most inviting, that his project is most flawed. His championship of 'alternative descriptions' says nothing about how to decide which of these possibilities might be more worth pursuing than others, which might be more defensible than others, whether some might be objectionable, or what kinds of benefits might be expected from following possibilities of one kind rather than another. In relation to validating the fruits of any of these pursuits Rorty argues that patterns of justification are no more than social practices; practices that is, which give us a 'right by current standards to believe', but from which any claim to justification in *universal* terms has been expelled; practices, finally which, like the descriptions they evaluate, have 'possible alternatives'. (*PMN* 385, 389)

The reference here to current standards is therefore a reference not to those which can be the best candidates for universal assent. Rather it refers only to what remains locally after any appeal to the universal has been disregarded. Thus the appeal of the unconditional emancipation mentioned a moment ago – despite Rorty's description of it at one point as 'becoming new beings' (*PMN* 360) – turns out to be something commonplace:

> The sense in which human beings alter themselves by redescribing themselves is no more metaphysically exciting or mysterious than the sense in which they alter themselves by changing their diet, their sexual partners, or their habitation. It is just the same sense: viz. new and more interesting sentences become true of them. (*PMN* 351)

Rorty's distaste for metaphysics is again evident here, but more importantly, there is the further dismissal of any experiences which might disclose insights of a potentially *universal* character. This is a dismissal of anything which might re-orient human understanding towards acknowledging a *telos* for human life as such. It is a dismissal moreover of anything which might even be a candidate for such a *telos*. Finally, it is a dismissal of the *search* for such a *telos*, even where such a search understands its own efforts in a self-critical light and where it grants its findings a provisional rather than a dogmatic status. But this manifold dismissal on Rorty's part obscures just the kinds of lessons through which insights lying beyond the pale of the usual and the novel might be learned and made one's own: lessons, that is, which transcend the 'new and more interesting' and which are quite different from the novelties of 'redescribing ourselves'.

Rorty's conclusions on the choosing and 'remaking' of personal identity place him almost wholeheartedly in a 'postmodernist' position like that of Lyotard, which we considered in Chapter Four. Examining this more closely, Rorty's insistence on the disparateness and 'incommensurability' of different fields or discourses of learning calls to mind Lyotard's deprecation of dialogue, as that which merely seeks consensus by smothering real differences. Rorty's style of writing and argumentation is in itself a dramatic example of Lyotard's affirmation of heterogeneity and contest. Secondly, Rorty's recommending of 'conversation' and 'edification' identify a kind of discourse which turns its back on anything like a joint search for truth and seeks its fulfillment instead in that which is aesthetically new or different. In this it closely resembles Lyotard's promotion of aesthetic experience – and particularly the avant garde – to a place of supremacy over any ethical considerations. Thirdly, Rorty's dismissal not only of metaphysics and epistemology, but also of any 'successor discipline' which might seek a *telos*, or make claims to truth in any universal sense, recalls Lyotard's rejection of all accounts ('metanarratives') of meaningful ends for humankind as such. Finally, where Nietzsche claimed that one's values must be created, the arguments of Rorty and Lyotard make a parallel point that one's identity must be chosen or 'remade' ever anew.

But arbitrariness features just as much in these accounts as it did in the characterisations of imposed identity considered in the first section of the chapter. Where the imposed kind of identity was intended to provide the self with outlooks which retained their unquestioned authority over the course of one's lifetime, identity-as-choice provides us with just the reverse: a conception of selfhood which, despite any appearances of unfettered freedom, remains in thrall to the sweep and sway of the transitory and episodic.

Identity as Epiphany

The preceding explorations bring home to us just how implicated the question of personal identity is with the interplay of educational influences, and just how intractable the justification of such an interplay is in any kind of universal terms. In contemporary democratic societies the traditional conception of identity as something which can be imposed or transmitted finds it difficult to escape the charge of indoctrination. By contrast, conceptions of identity-as-chosen present a picture of individual autonomy which finds it more than difficult to escape the charge of arbitrariness, and which pays scant regard to the necessary features of social life and civic welfare. Educational practices based on the overt imposition of identity have largely broken down in the Western world, with the notable exception of what are called fundamentalist groups. On the other hand, practices influenced by one or other variant of identity-as-chosen have featured quite regularly in Western countries in the present century, but they have invariably given rise to controversies. These controversies have been most acute where upholders of traditional practices alleged that the inculcation of respect and restraint in the young had been abandoned by teachers in favour of permissive ideologies such as 'progressivism', or 'expressionism', or permissive teaching practices such as 'facilitation'.[4]

Recurring controversies between different campaigns and movements have ensured that educational discourse in our own century has been attended as much by acrimony as it has been in any century in the past. Where in previous centuries however the adversaries were clearly evident and generally of long standing – for instance as between ecclesiastical authority and those who were identified as its enemies – this is often far from the case nowadays. The plurality of interest groups which now do battle in public discourse on education have made the struggle for competetive advantage both an immediate and an abiding feature of the discourse itself. The character of the energies called forth by this struggle, the abilities and dispositions cultivated by the struggle itself, means that the metaphysics of power we examined in Chapter Five gains a tacit ascendancy and secures effective loyalties amid the shifting alliances, constellations and lobby groups which throng the arena of discourse. And it is precisely these loyalties which hinder any proper understanding or acknowledgement of that sovereignty of learning which is our main theme here.

Notwithstanding their differences, the common preoccupations of such loyalties *in practice* are largely with the securing of recognised powers in relation to the control of schooling and its declared goals. For the most part, however, this means that the quality of teaching and learning *actually experienced* in schools and colleges – far from being an exercise of sovereignty – becomes secondary and subordinate to such preoccupations. It also means however that the declared aims of schooling may in practice become more ostensible than real: that the sense of personal identity which unfolds through the experienced routines and customs of schooling becomes in key respects yoked and harnessed, rather than emancipated. In this way, emergent identity becomes inured, in an unannounced but habitual way, to the rituals and liturgies prized by what is veritably a culture of power-seeking. This is not to deny the sincerity of any reassuring avowals to the contrary. In fact it is to highlight their innocence of what *ethos* and practice really mean. And it makes only a secondary difference moreover, whether the declared goals of a power-preoccupied educational authority are 'liberal' or 'vocational', or 'spiritual', or 'aesthetic', or whatever. Already at work in such a culture is a 'hidden curriculum' which debilitates the more worthy of convictions and which accomplishes the inversion of 'values' which Nietzsche was keen to make overt, and which he boldly championed in his writings.

This inversion is, in varying degrees, a feature of the educational systems of even the most democratic societies. To the extent that it pervades educational discourse and decision-making in any society moreover, it also becomes an abiding characteristic of educational practice. It remains so, in effect, unless educational practices themselves become self-critical and self-assertive; unless such practices can become, at least in some real and accountable measure, a self-monitoring pursuit, as distinct from a set of practices subordinated in their essential respects to the strategic interests of government, church, commerce, or other powerful group. All of this serves to underline the point that the sovereignty of learning is something which may more than occasionally be in tension with conventional, or otherwise dominant currents of opinion in the society which is called on to grant and uphold that sovereignty.[5] And if it is asked again why the state, or church, or other powerful body should grant such sovereignty to schooling, the answer has to be that this is the best way, perhaps the only way, to make the conduct of teaching and learning hospitable to uncovering each pupil's unique identity and promise – through subtle but accountable practices which embody neither imposition nor arbitrary choice.

If the claim I am making in venturing this answer can be explained and sustained, one of my main purposes in writing this book will have been achieved. But some, who see themselves as anything but 'postmodernists', might still invoke a Richard Rorty type argument at this stage and point out that in very many instances the effort to uncover a unique identity and promise is a waste of time and effort; for example with those who show little or no promise, or who are 'particularly dull and conventional people ... whose every act and word are so predictable that we "objectivise" them without hesitation'. Others might invoke Lyotard and claim that the very notion of a unique identity and promise is a totalitarian one: that it presupposes some kind of missionary 'meta-narrative', or grand presumption, that the life of each individual has a meaning waiting to be discovered, a *telos* waiting to be fulfilled.

In response to these objections, and in support of the argument that everyone has a promise and a sense of selfhood which is worthy of the defensible efforts of educators, I would like to introduce here the notion of *epiphany*, not so much in the biblical sense, but more in the sense given to the word by James Joyce, and expanded recently by Charles Taylor in his recent major study (1989), *Sources of the Self – The Making of the Modern Identity* (*SoS*). Joyce appropriated the word epiphany from religion for his own artistic purposes. In his biography of Joyce, Richard Ellman describes the Joycean connotations of the word as follows:

> The epiphany was the sudden 'revelation of the whatness of a thing,' the moment in which 'the soul of the commonest object ... seems to us radiant.' The artist, he felt, was charged with such revelations, and must look for them not among the gods but among men, in casual, unostentatious, even unpleasant moments. (Ellman, *James Joyce*, p.83)

Taylor recognises a special significance in Joyce's use of the term epiphany, and grants it a wider sense in relation to our experience of works of art. He writes:

> What I want to capture with this term is just this notion of a work of art as the locus of a manifestation which brings us into the presence of something which is otherwise inaccessible, and which is of the highest moral and spiritual significance; a manifestation, moreover, which also defines and completes something, even as it reveals. (*SoS* p.419)

An epiphany in a work of art is therefore something essentially different from art as a mere representation, or copy of something else. It is something essentially more than Plato, for instance, was prepared to allow in his description of art as imitation (*mimesis*). To be brought into the presence of something which is otherwise inaccessible, in the sense described by Joyce and Taylor, is not to escape – nostalgically or otherwise – from the everyday and the ordinary. It is rather to see the everyday and the ordinary from a new perspective; to have one's relation to one or other aspect of the everyday transformed by an unforeseen recognition, and invested with a new, even an invaluable significance. The work of art evokes a mood, un-covers an insight, sets forth a previously familiar world in a way charged with a meaning previously undetected.

One of the most striking examples in writing of what an epiphany means in the experience of works of art is given by Martin Heidegger in his reflections on a painting by Van Gogh of an apparently familiar and unremarkable object – a pair of peasant's boots. The boots are so worn and battered that they are hardly worth a second glance. Their usefulness as equipment shows nothing of the promise or sturdiness of a new pair of boots. They are precisely the kind of object which, from an everyday perspective in modern society, would already be thrown out as rubbish. As Heidegger writes:

> A pair of peasant shoes and nothing more. And yet –
> From the dark opening of the worn insides of the shoes the toilsome tread of the worker stares forth. In the stiffly rugged heaviness of the shoes there is the accumulated tenacity of her slow trudge through the far-spreading and ever uniform furrows of the field swept by a raw wind. On the leather lie the dampness and richness of the soil. Under the soles slides the loneliness of the field-path as evening falls. In the shoes vibrates the silent call of the earth, its quiet gift of the ripening grain and its unexplained self-refusal in the fallow desolation of the wintry field.[6]

Far from being a mere imitation, far from being a projection of 'subjective' or 'aesthetic' insights into the work, the work itself here summons our attentions and invites us to dwell awhile with it. Far from any nostalgia or escapism, the work evokes remembrance and educates identity by re-presenting us with what in our everyday experience has been passed over; that is, by re-presenting the familiar in an unforeseen and newly intelligible way; a way which betters our awareness of that in virtue of which everything familiar is reclaimed in its uniqueness. The work thus embraces us within the stay of the world which it opens up; a world which is in greater or lesser degree already familiar, but is now also newly intelligible *and mysterious*, where the familiar and mysterious are held in a mingling play. So, far from being 'objectivised' in Rorty's sense, and thus rendered scarcely worthy of serious attention, the ordinary and the everyday receive here a special significance. They now suggest themselves as areas where many epiphanies might blush unseen. So also, it is worth adding, does the '*pour soi*' of 'dull and conventional people'.

Epiphanies bring about unexpected and unforced shifts in our understanding of ourselves, of others, and of humankind's common lot. They may identify and call forth abilities and aptitudes of which we were scarcley aware. They may enable us to identify with and share in aspects of a cultural inheritance which previously seemed remote, forbidding or irrelevant. On the other hand, they may bring us face to face with shortcomings and limitations which had remained undiscovered, or else denied, in our experience. Either way, epiphanies are interruptions of the kind of learning which is routine and unreflective in character. They are, in the fullest sense of the phrase, what we mean when we say 'learning from experience', or 'learning through experience'. They call attention, first and foremost, to the *quality of what is actually experienced.* They are, in a special way, the means by which one's ownmost potentials are uncovered and appropriated. In short, they are unforced disclosures and affirmations of identity.

But epiphanies may also remain quite undetected. They call for a reflective refinement of understanding and a subtle attunement of sensibility. Just as Van Gogh's painting may appear to many as nothing more than a dull and uninteresting pair of boots, so also may many pupils and students appear to teachers and educational authorities as no more than dull and uninteresting, or disruptive and hostile. If the epiphanies of the everyday play a crucial part in how learners come to understand or mis-understand the qualities, potentials and limitations which are peculiarly their own, then it is of first importance that the understanding of teachers is attuned to the occurrence of epiphany in the experiences of learning.

A Cultural and Communicative Art

Experiences which become routine, but without the element of critical reflection, are ever likely to produce what we call 'creatures of habit'. In this kind of experience, whether in teaching and learning or in any other walk of life, anything having the quality of an epiphany is likely to remain overlooked. That is not to say that such experience is without merit. In many occupations, the effective performance of important tasks requires a kind of practice where routine supercedes the discovery of new or original insights, where the scope for epiphanies in the performance of the task itself is either small or negligible. Such tasks, which might include assembly line production, simple banking transactions, some forms of transportation, are to a greater or lesser degree being taken over by computerised machines. Few people would be happy to include education, and more particularly teaching and learning, in such a category. There is more than a little irony then in the fact that more than a few pupils find teachers boring and predictable when compared to the interactive information technology which now proliferates in the field of education, opening up worlds which, by contrast, are fascinating, even utterly absorbing.

This example serves to highlight the difference between the familiar picture of teaching as an instructional process, determined and regulated by external forces and, on the other hand, the unfamiliar picture of teaching as a cultural and communicative art, properly so called. A number of points need to be clarified in exploring this distinction. Firstly, the distinction does not imply a mutually exclusive rift between one kind of teaching and the other. For instance, a particular teacher's approach might embody primarily the routines and predictabilities characteristic of a process, but might also embody some genuinely artistic moments and experiences; or indeed *vice versa*. In practice, the difference in any particular teacher's case may frequently be more a fluctuating difference of degree than a clear-cut difference of kind. Secondly, where participation in any process requires a training in the skills appropriate to the process, participation in an art calls for such skills to be creatively joined with the insight, vision and originality appropriate to an art. Thirdly, the distinction receives its real force when we describe teaching not simply as an art, but as a performance art, or more appropriately still, as a special kind of *cultural and communicative art*. Its cultural dimension lies mainly in the teacher's continuing attentions to the voices of the subjects and traditions of learning which are her abiding point of contact with the pupils. More particularly, this cultural dimension lies in the character of the teacher's continuing interpretations of these voices in her own experience – i.e. in her dialogue with her subjects. The communicative dimension reveals itself in the quality of the teacher's presentations and enactments; presentations which seek not only increases in pupils' fluencies and competencies, but which also seek in the everyday experiences of schoolrooms the minor or more significant epiphanies which enable these voices to speak ever anew to the sensibilities and emergent identities of pupils and students.

It may be objected at this point that the kind of art experience being described here is a rare occurrence in everyday life, that it represents even an impossible ideal, and that the history of Western education itself validates the objection. To this it must be replied that if the practice of teaching and learning is to exercise responsibly the kind of discretion to which I have been arguing it is entitled, then it is a practice which must not be confused with the spontaneous occurrences of learning in everyday life. Neither must it be confused with the restrictive routines which have marked most of its own history as a practice. The ideal I am calling attention to here identifies not something impossible but an important shift in how we understand not only the occurrence of teaching and learning but also the nature and conduct of teacher education. It hardly needs emphasing then that one's initial training as a teacher is just a first step, but a crucial one, into the the cultural and communicative art I have been attempting to describe. As an art moreover, teaching itself is something which is refined and deepened through the kind of expericence which becomes the focus for systematic reflection and the uncovering of fresh insights to be shared. In relation to such insights it is worth recalling the failure of the Enlightenment – and of its pluralist aftermath – to recover what many centuries of institutionalised educational practice had consigned to obscurity. It is now time to examine these insights in some detail, with a view firstly to exploring their promise in uncovering teaching as an art, secondly, in illustrating the singular features of this art , and not least, in providing a contemporary example of what the sovereignty of learning might look like in practice.

Notes:

1. See for instance the following articles by Peter Gardner: "Religious Upbringing and the liberal ideal of religious autonomy" in *Journal of Philosophy of Education*, Vol.22, No. 1, 1988, pp.89-105; and 'Personal Autonomy and Religious Upbringing: the "problem"' in *Journal of Philosophy of Education*, Vol. 25, No.1, 1991, pp.69-81. For a contrasting argument, which seeks to reconcile the claims of religious upbringing with liberal traditions of learning, see T.H. McLaughlin's article, 'Peter Gardner on Religious Upbringing and the Liberal Ideal of Religious Autonomy' in *Journal of Philosophy of Education*, Vol. 24, No.1, 1990, pp.107-125.

2. *PMN* p.38; also p. 361. Nietzsche differs from Rorty in one important respect here. Despite his insistence that there are no such things as facts, only interpretations, Nietzsche still seeks to establish his doctrine of the will-to-power as something which applies universally to humans as such. This amounts to a metaphysics of human nature – that humankind has an 'essence', namely to strive for power.

3. *PMN* p.38. For Rorty, 'consciousness' seems to be almost exclusively Cartesian, namely a kind of awareness presided over by reason, but which

employs reason firstly to doubt everything that can be doubted, except the consciousness of one's own existence, and secondly to seek a secure and permanent foundation for all enquiry. But this conception of consciousness is now something of a straw man. Rorty's attempt to deprive 'consciousness' of its status in relation to reason would be confronted with a much more daunting task were he to take as his target a strong contemporary conception of consciousness (for instance Heidegger's). Such a conception doesn't have to prove that there is a world external to the self, but is aware that the self's existence is, inescapabley and from the start, a being-*among-others* which is a continual interplay of the rational and the irrational. Such a conception of consciousness describes much more closely than Descartes' does, what actually occurs in human experience and also calls attention to the fundamental error in Rorty's attempt to divorce consciousness from reason.

4. In the nineteen seventies, for instance, a series of publications in Britain, called the *Black Papers*, launched a sustained attack on 'progressivism'. This series drew contributions from influential figures in literary and academic life. For a critique of 'expressionism' in education, see Roger Scruton's article 'Expressionist Education' in *Oxford Review of Education*, Vol. 13, No. 1, 1987, pp.39-44. For a critique of 'facilitation' see *The Facilitators* edited by Doris Manly et al. (Dublin: Brandsma Books, 1987).

5. For some illuminating comments on this point, see Joseph Dunne's article 'What's the Good of Education?' in *Partnership and the Benefits of Learning – Symposium* edited by Pádraig Hogan (Maynooth: Educational Studies Association of Ireland, 1995) p.61 ff.

6. Martin Heidegger, 'The Origin of the Work of Art' in *Poetry, Language, Thought*, translated and introduced by Albert Hofstadter (New York: Harper and Row, 1975).

CHAPTER SEVEN

The Courtship of Sensibility and the Virtues of Teaching and Learning

Introduction

The ground has now been almost sufficiently prepared to present the case in explicit terms for the sovereignty of learning. This case will not be presented however as an apologia for one or other doctrine, or to canvass support for one or other sectional standpoint. It is concerned rather, with attempting to uncover something which is fruitful in practical terms but which is also a candidate for defensibility in universal terms. Thus it will seek firstly to concentrate on what *unavoidably happens to us in any case*, or what befalls us 'over and above our wanting and doing'[1] in the experience of teaching and learning. From here it will attempt to illustrate what might most *appropriately* happen to us, what might most *beneficially* engage our experience and sense of identity, what might most *promisingly* address our abilities and apitudes, what might most *defensibly* be pursued, when teaching and learning are conducted in a deliberate way.

In approaching these concerns, however, we must first clear away a final obstacle: a prejudice which hinders an adequate understanding of the nature of human understanding itself, particularly the experience of understanding in the contexts of teaching and learning. This is a prejuice which forces a rift between the spirit of the playful and that of work, which holds that education is essentially concerned with the latter and that it can only incidentally, if at all, accommodate the spirit of the playful. In tackling this prejudice, we shall be exploring further the kinds of argument made in Chapter Five, on the inbuilt features of understanding itself, or in other words, the primacy of interpretation and perspective within all understanding. Let us begin then by reviewing the effects of a tradition of educational thought which did *not* have available to it these kinds of arguments – a tradition which attempted boldly, but less than successfully, to get rid of the prejudice against the playful.

Limitations in the 'Child-centred' Tradition

In the historical reviews undertaken in the earlier chapters, detailed attention was deferred in the case of one important Western tradition which made educational practice itself its central concern. The prominent figures in this tradition include Rousseau, Pestalozzi, Froebel, and Montessori. Consideration of this tradition, somewhat misleadingly known as 'child-centred', has been postponed until now, largely because it was not until the twentieth century that it reached its height of influence. The two most significant thinkers of this tradition for the mainstream of educational thought and practice were Rousseau and Dewey. The insights of Montessori and Froebel were mainly taken up and institutionalised in the field of early childhood education. In this way they became more of specialist than of general interest within educational circles. Those of Pestalozzi, focusing on the active use of the senses, found further influence through thinkers such as Fichte and Herbart and also foreshadowed in many ways the work of the Swiss psychologist Jean Piaget. But this latter development, despite its many advances, did less than adequate service to Pestalozzi's own emphasis on teaching. Piaget's main concerns were with the development of understanding in children rather than with the part played by teaching in this development.

Partly for these reasons, the significance of the playful for our understanding of *teaching and learning* remained largely peripheral to the mainstream of educational practice. But there were other reasons as well. Insofar as the claims of the playful *did* enter that mainstream, they were more often than not attended by controversy, giving rise in no small way to the prejudice referred to a moment ago.

The 'child-centred' tradition achieved its most notable effects in the mainstream of modern education through the influential writings of John Dewey. Dewey's abiding concern, like that of Rousseau, was with educational *experience* – the question of what it is that identifies experience which is genuinely educational and distinguishes it from that which is not. Dewey's readings of previous philosophers who shared this concern was perceptive, generous and critical, as one of his more well-known works, *Democracy and Education*, illustrates.[2] Dewey's writings, however, were in the critical tradition of Enlightenment, and in this he differs in important respects from Rousseau. A brief examination of a few of the major points of this difference will help to highlight some key insights of the 'child-centred' tradition and also to illuminate the vexed fortunes of the spirit of the playful in education in the modern period.

Rousseau's passionate appeals on behalf of the playful in the *Émile* – 'Love childhood, indulge its sports, its pleasures, its delightful instincts' – for all their challenges to traditional conceptions of authority, contrast sharply with the dispassionate rationalism of the Enlightenment.[3] Rousseau focused on what was most personal in experience, highlighting in a dramatic and memorable way the crucial importance of *sensibility*, particularly childhood sensibility, in learning. But in doing so, he did at least three other controversial things as well: he disavowed any proprietorial designs on his pupil's loyalties, he disparaged metaphysics, and he invoked the authority of reason rather than that of the church. In relation to the teaching of religion, for instance, he engrosses Émile's attentions in the tale of the unfrocked priest of Savoy through passages like the following:

> My child, do not look to me for learned speeches or profound arguments. I am no great philosopher, nor do I desire to be one. I have however a certain amount of common sense and a constant devotion to truth. I have no wish to argue with you nor even to convince you; it is enough for me to show you, in all simplicity of heart, what I really think. Consult your own heart while I speak; that is all I ask. If I am mistaken, I am honestly mistaken, and therefore my error will not be counted to me as a crime; if you, too, are honestly mistaken, there is no great harm done. If I am right, we are both endowed with reason, we have both the same motive for listening to the voice of reason.[4]

The libertine note in Rousseau's educational writings was, of course, counted to him as the most serious of crimes by the upholders of traditional patterns of authority in education, most notably by the Catholic church. The outrage provoked in some quarters by the publication of the *Émile* was matched by adulation from other quarters, and thus it continued through successive generations to the present time. Indeed the severity, if not quite the tone, of the initial condemnations still finds some echoes in educational writings more than two centuries later.[5] Clearly, Rousseau's celebration of the playful in education has not been fully exonerated from the suspicion of licence.

Dewey of course was aware of the lingering aura of controversy attending Rousseau's writings. Not surprisingly then, in notable contrast to Rousseau, personal appeals and passionate declarations find no place in Dewey's works, where the idiom is invariably urbane and circumspect. Where Rousseau's participation in the Enlightenment was very much an ambivalent one, Dewey's approach was clearly inspired by the scientific Enlightenment's legacy of empiricism, as distinct, that is, from the strict rationalism of the Enlightenment itself. Where Rousseau declaimed loudly against metaphysical philosophy, Dewey quietly eschewed it. Where Rousseau wrote in intoxicating prose of the educational possibilities of the playful, Dewey sought to associate these possibilities with the scientific findings of psychology, and to embrace them in an educational programme which was democratic in intent and optimistic in outlook.[6]

Dewey focused in a new and sustained way on what constitutes quality in educational experience. This quality, he pointed out in his *Experience and Education*, had two aspects: firstly, the immediate aspect of agreeableness or disagreeableness, and secondly, the effects of this on further experience. He thus emphasised the importance for teachers to devise learning experiences in an imaginative way, so that these might live on creatively in the further experiences of learners; so that they might cultivate in the learner the desire to go on learning.[7] In this connection, it is necessary to emphasise, against the claims of Dewey's critics, that his writings offer no warrant for relegating either the importance or authority of the teacher. Indeed no serious study of Dewey's educational writings can escape the conclusion that these works call for, if they do not make fully explicit, a conception of teaching which ranks it among the most demanding, discerning and subtle of learned professions. The opposite conclusion has often been the more accepted one: that Dewey was the main author of an irresponsible 'progressivism' which installed play in the place of work, which swept the schools of America and elsewhere and which did much to undermine the authority of teachers.[8]

Perhaps Dewey should be criticised for not making explicit the radical shift in the conception of teaching which his quite explicit arguments on learning and educational experience imply. Perhaps he should have laid more emphasis on the play of imagination than on play as a physical activity. If these are serious omissions which detracted from the force and proper influence of Dewey's work, which I believe they are, the omissions can be traced not so much to an oversight as to a limitation imposed by Dewey's own philosophical approach. His conception of experience, for all its clarity and promise, is essentially impersonal and is quite incomplete. For instance, it never captures the predicaments which human experience frequently encounters in attempting to come to a just decision, or in deciding on a defensible course of action (say, in dealing with disruptive pupils). It cannot do justice to the shifts of circumstance which attend experience in the contexts of teaching and learning. It takes little account of the kinds of discernment and deliberation which lie beyond the technical and calculative. It cannot accommodate the kind of rationality which is most essential to the playful; which reaches beyond the merely systematic and methodical and which itself involves a disciplined play of the ordered and anticipated on the one hand, and the contingent and unpredictable on the other. In short, Dewey's conception of experience has no room for what Aristotle called *phronesis*.[9] That this is largely due to limitations on philosophical perspective imposed by Dewey's own method can be seen from the following retrospective remark, which he made towards the end of his life:

> For many years I have consistently – and rather persistently – maintained that the key to a philosophical theory of experience must proceed from initially linking it with the processes and functions of life as the latter are disclosed in biological science.[10]

There is a peculiar irony in this comparison of Dewey and Aristotle, in that Aristotle's own philosophical method also sprang from biology. Clearly, however, when Aristotle turned his attention to his *Ethics* and his *Politics*, his methodical outlook embodied a very different principle than that which was later embraced by empiricism – both in the natural and social sciences – in the nineteenth and early twentieth centuries. How sharply Aristotle's approach differed from Dewey's is evident from the following remarks by Aristotle on the science of politics, which appear in the opening book of the *Nicomachean Ethics*:

> Our account of this science will be adequate if it achieves such clarity as the subject matter allows; for the same degree of precision is not to be expected in all discussions, any more than in all the products of handicraft. ... For it is the mark of a trained mind never to expect more precision in the treatment of any subject than the nature of that subject permits. (*Nicomachean Ethics* I, iii, 1094b 11)

In examining politics and ethics as practices then, Aristotle sought to bring within his scope as plentiful a field of enquiry as his grasp of the nature of these subjects would make possible. In examining experience, Dewey's philosophical efforts were, by contrast, circumscribed by what the generally accepted procedures of empirical method would at his time permit. This helps to explains why the experience of *teaching* – which calls for an understanding of what is individual, or essentially personal in experience – does not become a focal point of Dewey's enquiry. It also explains why his remarks on play, valuable though these are in *Democracy and Education* (1916), do not reach the heart of the playful; do not, in fact, reach beyond the insights furnished by what he approvingly describes there as 'modern psychology'.

Despite the considerable influence of the 'child-centred' tradition on practices which are now accepted as uncontroversial or even commonplace in schools, there are still few among teachers who would be comfortable in granting that the nature of their occupation is *primarily* playful. There are few who would readily accept that the professional autonomy and discretion claimed by teachers is intimately bound up with the primacy of the playful – properly understood – in the experience of teaching and learning. It is worth noting moreover that this professional autonomy has been ever vulnerable and has more than occasionally fallen on hard times; that it is something which teachers' representative bodies find it increasingly difficult to protect from governments and other interests at present. In such circumstances the playful tends to be seen as a kind of unfettered impulse which may be indulged from time to time, but which must never be allowed any primacy or control in serious human affairs. It is necessary at this point therefore, to explore the playful at closer range and to make explicit its connection with the sovereignty of learning. In doing so, we shall bear in mind not only the Socratic conception sketched in Chapter One, but we shall also draw on whatever insights Western philosophy has to offer in elucidating the forgotten centrality of the playful in human understanding itself.

Uncovering the Primacy of the Playful

In the third part of Chapter Five, in arguing against the primacy which Nietzsche gave to the will to power, the suggestion was introduced that human action normally proceeds from a *mixture* of motives, among which there might indeed be an order of importance, but among which there might also be conflict for the higher places in this order. Nietzsche had claimed that all human action is driven by a power-seeking motive, to which other motives are necessarily subodinate. Nietzsche asserted this thesis dogmatically and invited no criticism of it. By contrast, the standing of any of the theses I wish to offer here is that of a provisional candidate for universal acceptance; provisional, that is, in the Popperian sense that the thesis itself must fall if it can be refuted by the evidence of what is inescapably common to our human experience. The thesis that human beings normally act from a mixture of motives is itself a provisional candidate of this kind. Our first thesis concerning the primacy of the playful is another. Let us now introduce that thesis directly. Gadamer puts it in the following words: 'The first thing we must make clear to ourselves is that play is so elementary a function of human life that culture is quite inconceivable without this element.'[11] This is an argument with a bold import. It suggests that it is a major mistake for us to regard play merely as an adornment to human culture. It argues that it is nothing other than the presence of the playful itself that makes anything like human culture, and therefore education, possible in the first place. It carries the striking implication that in the absence of this presence, what we have are privative, or impoverished forms of culture.

But these claims seem to overturn what the experience of everyday life teaches us, so it must be asked directly if this thesis on the primacy of the playful can be sustained. Does it not reduce the accomplishments of human culture to the level of the frivolous or the trivial? Can whole inheritances of language, literature, religion, art, music, scientific achievement, as well as the customs and traditions which pervade daily life in any society, be seriously described as the fruits of human play? In venturing a negative answer to the first of these questions, the answer to the second has to be, however surprisingly, *Yes*. But we can sustain these answers themselves only if we overcome the everyday prejudices that play is merely a diversion, or that it is necessarily the opposite to anything serious or earnest.

These everyday prejudices, which misrepresent the nature of play, have their origins in a conception of experience which accords too significant a place to the autonomy of individual consciousness; or to put it in other words, which hold that the subjective self is the autonomous author of its own consciousness. In this conception, consciousness is associated primarily with the self and its concerns. It seeks to oversee and regulate the self's relations with whatever is not self: that is, to maintain, as far as possible, rational and conscious control of the self's relations with others and the world. From this attitude, to become involved in play, or as the popular phrase puts it 'to enter into the spirit of the thing', is to allow oneself to lose this control, and this can only be risked when nothing 'serious' is at stake. Thus, sport and recreational activities become the primary acknowledged domains of play. The more serious affairs of life are seen as spheres where consciousness cannot allow itself to be taken over in this way. So in the popularly acknowledged domains of play (sport and recreation) it is maintained that it is the playing rather than the winning that counts. The players know, after all, that it is *only* a game they are playing. Yet if they do not take the purposes of the game sufficiently seriously, they become spoilsports, rather than genuine participants in the play. On the other hand, if they take the game too seriously, the playfulness of the game may yield to the earnestness of determined combat. Thus the 'spirit of the thing', which took over the consciousness of the players while the play remained sporting, now becomes charged with tension and takes over that consciousness in a more complete, a more personal, and a more intractable way.

These examples suggest that, with proper circumspection, it is possible for consciousness to withstand being taken over by the spirit of the playful, particularly in those domains of life which are not the acknowledged domains of play. Serious engagements – such as industry and commerce, politics, religion, and not least education – might come to mind in this connection. It might be argued, for instance, that these are spheres of activity where consciousness must keep an alert, controlling eye on its own intentions and projects, and must avoid falling prey to the schemes and designs of others.

But the illustrations presented in the last two paragraphs, for all their plausibility, betray an inflated conception of the autonomy of consciousness and an unwarranted primacy for subjectivity in interpersonal affairs. And it is just this mistake that allows the spirit of the playful, in its more combative modes, to urge itself unseen within the conduct of these affairs. But the point we must now face is that *it has invariably urged itself already in any case*, seen or unseen, in one mode or another, wherever human experience finds itself engaged, publicly or privately, with the thoughts and ideas of others, either living or dead.

Our human existence in the world is essentially a conscious *being-amongst-others*, in which self-consciousness also plays a greater or lesser part. It is incorrect, though perhaps philosophically attractive, to think of it as a totality of individually autonomous consciousnesses. To accord primacy to the autonomy of individual consciousness over a consciousness which is already pre-disposed by the history of its interpersonal involvements and cultural experiences from birth onwards, is to deny consciousness its historical character. It is to attempt the impossible, as Descartes did with the best of intentions, by taking consciousness out of its history and regarding it as some kind of purely formal entity. But this, in turn, is to allow consciousness to be delivered over in the most vulnerable way to the prejudices of its own history: to allow it *to be played along* by the unacknowledged influences and the unadmitted effects of that history. (Again Descartes' 'methodical' philosophy serves as a good example.)

Far from being any kind of autonomous capacity therefore, which regulates our affairs with a world 'out there', human consciousness is always and ever *already implicated* in that world, and has in countless ways been influenced by that world, indeed to a much greater degree than consciousness itself can become explictly aware of. Such influences are already at play in the language we learn from our earliest years, as they are already at play in the homes, communities, churches, sporting and cultural pursuits, and not least the schooling, which mark our upbringing. All of these spheres are already characterised by traditions and vocabularies which we join, in greater or lesser degree, as our experience unfolds. All of them already contain practices, attitudes and beliefs, with which we identify, to a greater or lesser degree, as our learning proceeds. They have already furnished us with contexts in which our sense of identity acquires its distinctive features. Even where we do battle with such traditions, even where we wish to overthrow the influence of a particular tradition, we do so very largely by finding ourselves arguing, not from autonomous selfhood, but from the influences already at play in a different tradition; albeit a radical one, or even an avant-garde one.

We are now in a better position to see that Gadamer's remark on the primacy of play in human experience applies not merely to sporting and recreational activities, but to human experience in *all* its modes. Far from presenting us moreover with an upturned account of our experience, it contains an insight which helps to correct the distortions of standpoints which give primacy to subjectivity, or autonomous selfhood. So where play, in the sense of sporting or recreational pursuits is concerned, what we have here is a *derivative* and specialised sense of play. The being who 'enters into the spirit' of the game is not an autonomous conscious subject who is prepared to set aside some of that autonomy for a bit of sport. Rather this is a being who is *already at play* in a more important way in the serious pursuits of everyday life; or more precisely, a being who is *already being played*, and in more ways than he or she can ever be explicitly aware of.

We can also see now that there are strong parallels between these arguments on the primacy of play and those on the fore-structure of understanding in Chapter Five. In fact they are complementary aspects of the same larger argument. These aspects can now be drawn together in the following summary:

(a) Human understanding itself is inescapably interpretative and historical in character. What it accomplishes in any particular instance is not final knowledge but a kind of knowing constrained by perspective.

(b) Such constraints arise from prior influences, or pre-conceptions, which are already at play in the experience of the person in whom the understanding takes place. They now come more actively into play in response to what addresses the human experience in any particular act of understanding.

(c) Without such pre-conceptions and prior influences, the earliest of which may be even be pre-natal, understanding itself would not be possible. There would be nothing like a personal context in which such addresses could make sense and become significant.

(d) The contexts which we bring to any event of understanding include not merely our pre-conceptions in a cognitive sense, but also our pre-dispositions in an emotional sense. That is to say, our sensibilities, and even more delicately, our sense of personal identity.

(e) Much of the interpretative context which we bring with us to any event of understanding will lie beyond our explict awareness, all the more so if we place an unwarranted faith in a method which claims to be neutral, i.e. without bias.

(f) Nevertheless, a potential critical interplay between the accomplishments and claims of cultural traditions on the one hand, and the emergent abilities and sensibilities of learners on the other, remains possible as one of humankind's most distinguishing and promising pursuits.

(g) Although this pursuit may come upon more than a few epiphanies during its course, it retains the character of an unfinished and unfinishing search. For the reasons we have been exploring, it becomes disfigured wherever it is regarded as any kind of completed enquiry with a fixed set of doctrines.

(h) The judicious bringing about of such an interplay, its sustenance and advancement, is a venture which requires co-operative energies, a fluency in one or other of the main fields of cultural tradition (e.g. scientific, religious, technical, artistic, literary), a commitment to generous but critical learning, and not least, a commitment to the requirements of dialogue, in the sense described in Chapter Five.

(i) Such a venture remains in essential respects stillborn, unless it is granted the standing of a distinct and respected office; an office whose sovereignty yet remains accountable to the society in which it is undertaken and whose resources it has been granted in significant measure.

Having presented in outline here the case for the sovereignty of learning, and having attempted to show how this case arises from a proper acknowledgement of the nature of human understanding itself, let us now examine what the practice of teaching and learning might look like when governed by considerations such as these we have just examined. It is important to note then that what will be presented in the next section is *not a theory* of teaching and learning, but an account of teaching and learning as a *practice*, when this takes due account of 'what unavoidably happens to us in any case' and attempts to move on to what might most defensibly and beneficially happen to us as the practice is deliberately pursued.[12]

The Practice of Teaching and Learning – a courtship of sensibility

In the formal language of schooling we are thoroughly familiar with formulations such as 'the transmission of skills and attitudes', 'the passing on of cultural heritage', 'the imparting of knowledge'. Despite the fact that such phrases are very much at home in the vernacular of the teaching profession, they are far from capturing what happens in the actual practice of schooling. When placed under scrutiny they can in fact be seen as half-truths. By beclouding the *more significant* part of the story, however, such formulations can induce a habitual failure of discernment among those who accommodate them uncritically in their educational outlooks. But why are they only half truths? and what do they obscure?

Teaching is *never* a one-way activity of transmission, imparting, or passing on, no matter how purged such activity seeks to be of harbouring proprietorial designs on the loyalties and the emergent sense of personal identity of the young. Teaching, rather, always seeks to bring about learning of some kind, so the understanding of the pupils, in one form or another, remains central to it. Teaching and learning therefore constitute – at a minimum – a *joint* activity: an experience shared, from different cultural standpoints, by teacher and pupils. And, since it is an experience which is in a special way an event of attempted understanding, different perspectives are already actively at play in it. More precisely then, this experience can properly be described as an unfolding *inter*-play between the ever emergent abilities and sensibilities of pupils on the one hand, and, on the other, the voices which addresses these through the presentations and enactments of the teacher. But what is the intent of such presentations? And what does *voice* mean here?

What addresses the pupils through the presentations of the teacher is the voice of one or other tradition of human accomplishment, one or other coherent practice (e.g. mathematics, music, religion, biology, cabinetmaking) which is capable of engaging new practitioners, from the most rudimentary to the most sophisticated levels of participation. In each instance this voice makes *an appeal* of some kind to the pupils' attentions, their efforts, and indeed their commitments. How can such appeals be justified? Is it by calling attention to a test or examination which draws ever nearer from the distance? Such justifications as this may of course have pragmatic effect on sizeable numbers of pupils, but they will have little on others and will be resented by many who may already see themselves among the ranks of the 'also-rans' or even 'non-runners'. None of this is to say that such justifications should be cast aside. To be able to dispense entirely with extrinsic forms of motivation is the happy lot of only a small minority of teachers. But to rely mainly on this kind of justification is to side-step the central *educational* issue and to give pride of place to something other than the authenticity of the voice which seeks to be addressed to the pupils through the work and presence of the teacher.

The authenticity of that voice, and of its appeal, whether it be the voice of history, Irish, science, religion, art, or whatever, might perhaps best be illustrated by describing the activity of teaching and learning not just as an ever-emergent interplay, but as an interplay which is at the same time a special kind of courtship, or wooing. At first sight this may seem bold to the point of audacity, and of course it requires some explanation. So, to begin with, it must be emphasised that *courtship* here is meant as no mere metaphor. It seeks to describe the kind of cultural interplay which the experience of teaching and learning *actually is*, including, as we shall see, those turbulent cases where the teacher's approaches are rebuffed or even ridiculed by the pupils. To describe the experience of teaching and learning as a courtship moreover, is to highlight the pastoral dimensions of teaching and also to make available to us what are, perhaps, the most secure grounds for withstanding the charge of indoctrination.[13]

In the exercise of cultural influence – no less than in the conduct of affairs of the heart – we can identify different kinds of courtship. We can recognise the kind of courtship which declares its intentions with honesty, which recoils from the forcing of a suit, which has the courage to face difficulties as they arise, which prizes both frankness and the dignity of privacy, which seeks to evade the thrall of the habitual, and which draws its special character from the delights and disappointments, the frustrations and surprises of mutual discovery. In short, we recognise something of *a categorical sense of care* here in one person's basic attitude to the other. We are well aware however that there is another, perhaps more common, kind of courtship, where considerations of a more questionable kind are to the fore: where the arts of dissembling and seduction are harboured and nurtured, and where the characteristics of the first kind of courtship are at best secondary to the securing of the prize, or perhaps the imagined prize. And of course a courtship could sometimes alternate between both kinds.

In the kind of cultural courtship which – I am arguing – embodies the heart of education, the authentic voice of the subject (e.g. history) speaks only when the teacher's enactment succeeds in casting that voice in an engaging, yet faithful idiom; an idiom which addresses the sensibilities of the pupils in an inviting and challenging manner. In other words, the idiom is adapted and the manner is enacted to call forth a questioning kind of response from the particular pupils being addressed. It is important to recall what was said above about teaching and learning being an interplay, so some kind of response is going to be forthcoming anyway, even if its true character cannot be discerned on the surface.

Now, if I teach history, or Irish, or science, or religion, or any other subject which has merited a place on the school curriculum, it is entirely proper that I should encourage my pupils to see that I believe that the subject I'm teaching has something rich and enduring to offer. It is entirely proper moreover that I should wish my pupils to share something of my own enthusiasm for the subject: that my occupational commitment as a teacher should express itself – taking the four examples mentioned – in encouraging them individually and collectively to discover something of the historian in themselves, or something of linguistic aptitude and appreciation in themselves, or something of the scientist in themselves, or something of their own religious sensibilities. None of this is to deny that it may take inspired pains, discerning faith and sterling reserves of equity and forebearance on the teacher's part to unearth that 'something'; or to deny that the 'something' may initially look quite puny even when it is unearthed. Such unearthing invariably marks an event of emancipation, or releasement of the pupil, however, from a previously constraining state. It enables the pupil to understand something more of her own particular promise, her own aptitudes and limitations; to take a genuine step in the gradual appropriation of her own identity.

The picture is quite different however, and gives legitimate grounds for disquiet, if, as a history teacher, I seek to inculcate in the pupils a personal allegiance of my own to an officially sanctioned, or otherwise tendentious version of the past; if as a science teacher, I seek to silence any side of the argument on safe sources of energy; if, as a teacher of Irish, I insinuate the view that this language confers the badge of cultural or racial superiority; if, as a teacher of religion, I treat matters of faith as if they were matters of fact; if, in any instance of teaching, my approach presumes some proprietorial claim on the sensibilities of the pupils. Unless the disavowal of such a claim becomes an imperative of professional discipline in teaching, the interplay of influence between teachers and pupils may become rapidly, even irrevocably, disfigured.

The point to emphasise here is that far from being in any way morally neutral, teaching is an activity which invariably reveals the presence of certain virtues and vices in the actual practice of the work itself. We have briefly seen examples of both in the previous paragraphs, but let us now concentrate on making the virtues more explicit.[14] There are virtues of teaching which are *universal*, as distinct from sectional or factional in character: virtues, that is, which are *educational* before they are anything else. Recalling the argument of the last four paragraphs, such virtues can now be seen to include:

(a) a circumspect honesty in declaring one's own intentions as a teacher;

(b) patience and persistence, which are adroit rather than importunate;

(c) the courage, the moral energy, and the perseverance to tackle challenges and obstacles;

(d) frankness, coupled with respect for each pupil's privacy and dignity;

(e) an originality which resists the ruts of habit and returns ever anew to the address of the subjects which are the teacher's abiding point of contact with the pupils;

(f) a judicious faith in pupils, even in unpromising circumstances;

(g) a disavowal of proprietorial designs, coupled with a constructive sense of self-criticism;

(h) a categorical sense of care for pupils as young human beings, recognising the claims of both equity and difference, and with unfailing expectations as a key ingredient.

Again it must be emphasised that these virtues of teaching are human *practices*, rather than merely attitudes. They are still not the same however as the skills of teaching (e.g. classroom management skills) though they can dramatically transform how the skills of teaching are exercised. The virtues of teaching are concerned, first and foremost, with the *releasement* and *enablement* of pupils. This does not mean any kind of releasement or enablement, but rather the *venture of uncovering the tenor and scope of the pupil's ownmost promise*. The specific yet universal character of these virtues of teaching make them worthy candidates for the occupational commitments of teachers *as professionals*. Such virtues are thus to be distinguished from teachers' personal convictions in matters of ethics, politics, religion, etc., although they may well be in harmony with, or draw sustenance from, the latter.

The virtues of teaching just mentioned nurture a commitment to the end-in-view of the kind of courtship we are currently exploring. That end-in-view can now be described as the actual *bringing about* in some sustained measure (not just the facilitation) of a genuine engagement between the emergent potentials of the pupils and the authentic voices of the differing subjects which seek to address these potentials. In the case of all subjects, the attempt to call forth a substantial response from the pupils is, at the same time, an attempt to call forth some accompanying qualities, namely virtues of *learning*. Rather than assert these latter directly, let us consider how they emerge from the practice of teaching and learning itself, when this is conducted as a defensible courtship of sensibility. It should be noted here, in keeping with the reciprocal nature of teaching and learning, that pupils are in some real sense teachers – of each other and of their teachers – and that teachers are in a central sense, learners.

Let us consider the case then where the teacher's efforts on behalf of the subject are spurned by the pupils, or by the majority of them, in any particular class. The teaching of religion might serve us as an illuminating example here. (Christianity is the religion in this context.) The teacher, let us say, has been attempting to follow the prescribed programme, with a group of third year post-primary pupils who are variously indifferent, resistant or hostile. One day things get so bad that he abandons his plan of work and, in exasperation, asks the pupils why they are so determined to undermine his best efforts with ceaseless snide remarks and offensive comments. A few of the more articulate pupils take this opportunity to tell him, equally frankly, that the textbook, his own approach and the whole programme, are offensive *to them*, in presuming that they are Catholics, or Christians, whereas in reality they believe that 'the whole thing is nonsense'. If the teacher has a sufficiently incisive understanding of his own work that he can honestly acknowledge this standpoint, what course of action remains open to him? Can he proceed at all now without forcing a suit on the pupils? Let us examine these questions directly, as they are the kind which really put to the test, the kind of understanding we are attempting to elucidate.

Suppose the teacher draws now on his own fluency in religious studies and points out that in every generation some people have been unable to accept the beliefs of Christianity (or other religions for that matter); that many have, in each generation, taken just the view that 'the whole thing is nonsense'. Suppose the teacher now goes on to state the following points very clearly and frankly.

* The voice which is the genuine voice of Christianity promises to fulfil the deepest yearnings of the human heart, however outrageous that promise might sound.

* This voice claims moreover to be a Divine voice, not a human one, and the teacher is clearly prepared to acknowledge this – as a teacher of religion. The same claim is true of all major religions.

* This voice is one of invitation, not compulsion – despite any appearances or claims to the contrary. And this will be quite clear in the religion class from now on.

* The invitation is to explore, to consider, to learn the actual details of what the voice says; to weigh up, and indeed to share in the beliefs and teachings explored. But also, this is an invitation which respects the individual's entitlement to decline it, or to reserve his/her position.

* An authenticated request from parents to the school to have their children absented from the religion class will immediately be honoured. (In the Republic of Ireland this is a Constitutional obligation.)

* Those who want to reserve judgement, or who wish to decline the invitation, are still welcome to stay, provided they do not disrupt the class. They are also welcome to contribute to the class, including questions and criticisms.

* The class will be handled differently from now on, with the textbook playing a less important part (subsidiary); but everyone in the class, including the teacher, must observe rules of conduct which will make it possible to carry on a coherent programme of work on the basis of the points just made.

The educational requirements just spelt out might be described as the rules of honourable courtship, as these apply in the teaching of religion. They embody the discipline of dialogue, as described in

Chapter Five. They constitute the practice of the virtues of teaching *in a particular case*. But of course they may also need to be worked out in the case of other classes studying other subjects. And in every case, they must be worked out in relation to *the particular circumstances* in which that teaching takes place. In all practical instances where such rules are worked out and applied, a distinctive *ethos* arises quite naturally, not as something imposed from on high. In this *ethos*, the growing commitment of pupils and teacher to such rules not only helps to build a sense of solidarity and belonging. It also helps the teacher by challenging her to present her subject (or subjects) in a manner best adapted to her pupils. She is called on moreover to provide a robust defence of her subjects, and to have her own understanding of them challenged to further efforts by the pupils' questions and comments. This is the fruitful interplay of a cultural courtship in action.

Teaching and learning have been described here not as different experiences, but as an experience shared, from different perspectives, by teachers and pupils. Accordingly, the virtues of teaching, outlined first in paragraph 9 above, can now more clearly be seen to be paralleled by *virtues of learning*, which the kind of *ethos* just described seeks to sustain among the pupils. Chief among such virtues of learning, which can now be listed, are the following:

(a) a commitment to effort in the pursuit of fluency;

(b) tolerance and co-operation among pupils, in relation to each other's attempts;

(c) method and growing discernment in their efforts to understand;

(d) acknowledgement of the claims of balance in the exercise of critical judgement;

(e) acknowledgement of the claims of equity in all aspects of teaching and learning;

(f) receptive openness by pupils to what is decently addressed to them;

(g) readiness to ask questions or raise critical queries;

(h) willingness to take responsibility for their own learning.

It might be tempting to object here that the virtues of teaching and learning are nothing less than a shortlist of the requirements of sainthood. This would be a glib objection, however, showing little appreciation of what we have argued concerning the predisposed structure of understanding, and the modest aim of making inroads; as distinct, that is from changing the world. When taken together moreover, the virtues of teaching and learning carry the interplay of understanding which occurs in education *beyond* the fact of what inescapably happens to us and *towards* the disclosure of defensible criteria; criteria which enable teachers to make more discerning appraisals of their own occupational commitments and their own professional practice. One of the major benefits of engaging in this kind of work is that it nurtures professional solidarity and reassurance. These are essential in dealing not only with pupils and colleagues, but also with the expectations of parents, society and indeed marketplace. This kind of work, it must be recalled, is nothing theoretical, but rather a Socratic kind of conviction in parctice. Bearing this in mind, it is important to emphasise that the criteria identified by the virtues of teaching and learning seek to be universal in character, and therefore seek to serve as the basis for a universally defensible ethic for teachers. Accordingly, in the groundwork undertaken so far, an attempt has been made to found these criteria not on the doctrines of one or other religious denomination, or on one or other sectional standpoint, but rather on a philosophical exploration which seeks to articulate the basis for a *universally defensible* educational practice in an increasingly pluralist democracy.

There are however, more serious objections to the practices outlined in this chapter than the glib one quoted briefly above. The first of these concerns the possibility that the traditions which come to presence in the experience of teaching and learning, together with the existing institutions which accommodate and preserve them, may already have undetected distortions lodged deeply in the play of influences which is already at work in them. In this case the efforts of teaching and learning to emancipate each pupil's sense of identity, in harmony with the cultivation of that pupil's ownmost potentials, might unwittingly be also a form of imprisonment (e.g. the tradition which holds that certain subject are 'girls only', or 'boys only' subjects, including the institutional arrangements which preserve this state of affairs; or the belief that ability-grouping is the best means of matching the contributions of teachers to the potentials of pupil, including the institutional arrangements which sustain this as a practice). A second kind of objection would allege that any attempt to tie the play of influences in human experience to a programme which, in any subject, has already chosen certain voices and texts as canons, is in fact a more subtle variant of that medieval metaphysics which constrained learning to acquiesce in established conceptions of truth. Both objections represent significant cultural currents in contemporary society and must be answered before the arguments we have been making for the sovereignty of learning can be sustained. Chapter Eight takes up the first objection and Chapter Nine takes up the second.

Notes:

1. This is a phrase used by Gadamer in the Foreword to the second edition of *Truth and Method.*

2. John Dewey, *Democracy and Education* (New York: Macmillan, 1916,1944).

3. Jean Jacques Rousseau, *Émile,* tr. Barbara Foxley (London: Dent, Everyman's Library, 1974) p.43.

4. ibid., p.228.

5. See, for instance, R.T. Allen's critical study *The Education of Autonomous Man* (Aldershot: Avebury, 1992).

6. See in particular Chapter Fifteen of *Democracy and Education.*

7. John Dewey, *Experience and Education* (New York: Collier Macmillan, 1938) pp.27-28, 48.

8. Robert R. Rusk points out that Dewey's educational philosophy was condemned by President Dwight Eisenhower in 1959. For his own part, Rusk makes the misleading claim that Dewey 'more than anyone displaced the teacher from the centre of his classroom'. See Rusk's *Doctrines of the Great Educators* (fifth edn, Ed. J. Scotland; London: Macmillan 1979) p.231.

9. See the section on Aristotle in Chapter One above. For a particularly illuminating exploration of Aristole's *Phronesis* and its application in both modern life and modern philosophical literature, see Joseph Dunne's *Back to the Rough Ground – 'Phronesis' and 'Techne' in Modern Philosophy and in Aristotle* (Notre Dame: University of Notre Dame Press, 1993).

10. John Dewey, 'Experience, knowledge and value – a rejoinder', in *The Philosophy of Dewey,* P.A. Schilpp (ed.) (New York, Tudor Publishing Company, 1951), p.530.

11. Hans-Georg Gadamer, 'The Relevance of the Beautiful' in *The Relevance of the Beautiful and Other Essays,* tr. Nicholas Walker; ed. & intro. Robert Bernasconi (Cambridge: Cambridge University Press, 1986) p.23.

12. The account in the section which follows is drawn mainly from notes I made on my own experiences during two different periods I spent in recent years teaching in a large post-primary school in Dublin. The account is also influenced by some of my seminar sessions with university students, but because its inspiration is mainly the post-primary school, where my classes were mostly in the age range 12 to 15, I have decided to use the term 'pupils' rather than 'students' in describing the learners. Some details have been changed from my notes. For instance, although I have taken the teaching of religion here as my main practical illustration, I never taught religion and am not formally qualified to do so. I chose it because it is a subject which is more than usually vulnerable to the charge of indoctrination and also because it is one that meets with a more than usual degree of resistance and apathy from pupils at present, at least in the post-primary schools of the Republic of Ireland.

13. The notion of teaching and learning as a courtship of sensibility struck me some years ago, arising mainly from my refelctions on my own teaching and my work with student teachers. It could fairly be described as one of the epiphanies of the everyday that I described in the previous chapter. What I have experienced and read since then makes me stronger in the view that this description is much more fruitful than most of the textbook descriptions by which teachers are encouraged to think about their work. I am happy to acknowledge however that the seeds of this notion are already present in Montaigne's essay 'On the Education of Children', mentioned in Chapter Three above. In our own day it also finds echoes, though in a somewhat different vocabulary to mine, in a recently published collection of 'conversations' on teaching by Margret Buchman and Robert E. Floden, entitled *Detachment and Concern – Conversations in the Philosophy of Teaching and Teacher Education* (New York: Teachers' College Press, Columbia University, 1993). I should add, for the sake of clarity, that the 'courtship of sensibility' must not be confused with any kind of erotic engagement.

14. The concentration here on the virtues which reside in educational encounters with the voices of tradition has some parallels with an argument presented by Kevin Williams in a recent essay, where he writes as follows: 'Initiation into the traditions or metaphorical languages of human understanding involves the acquisition not only of understanding, but also of the qualities associated with the possession of intellectual skills or "connoisseurship" and of the intellectual virtues.' Kevin Williams, 'Usefulness and Liberal Learning', in *Religion, Education and the Constitution*, edited by Dermot A. Lane (Dublin: Columba Press, 1992), p.48. Williams' argument explores a rich vein opened up by Michael Oakeshott's writings on education, which in turn has some striking resemblances to the work of Hans-Georg Gadamer on tradition and human experience.

PART III

The Integrity of Education amid the Currents of Public Discourse

CHAPTER EIGHT

The Claims of Radical Critique

Introduction

Let us begin Part Three by revising briefly some of the main themes of the last few chapters. Human understanding, even at its best, is inescapably partial in character. It is also inescapably interpretative in character. It is invariably influenced by the pre-suppositions which have become significant in our experience hitherto and which remain at play in our efforts to understand anything new. Human understanding cannot therefore escape the bounds of perspective and interpretation into some absolute, pre-suppositionless, or pure kind of knowing. It can however make advances in any field, by attempting to become aware, as far as possible, of its own pre-conceptions and by inviting constructive criticisms of its most considered opinions and its best theories to date. In each case this requires a readiness to engage with traditions of learning, to become fluent in those which call forth one's ownmost potentials, to resist allowing our learning to become too narrowly focused, or dominated by one perspective, to listen to and learn from the perspectives of others. A disposition towards dialogue is more hospitable towards this kind of pursuit than is any assertiveness associated with scholarly prowess. Where the practice of teaching and learning is concerned, however, even more crucial is a *discipline* of dialogue, the main features of which were sketched towards the end of Chapter Five.

In Part Two as a whole, we have explored the main implications of these insights, elaborating along the way arguments on the disclosure of identity, on the distortion of this through traditional practices of imposition, or more recent ones of 'remaking ourselves'. We have focused on the unforced engagement of identity through the epiphanies of teaching and learning. We have also attempted to restore the primacy of the playful in educational experience, not as anything self-indulgent or lacking in seriousness, but as the very spirit which makes cultural engagements and pursuits possible in the first place. We have finally brought all of this to bear on the practice of teaching and learning, by considering this practice as an honourable courtship of sensibility and by identifying a list of defensible virtues which are central to the practice itself.

The arguments pursued in these chapters have sought to make explicit 'what unavoidably happens to us in any case' in the experience of teaching and learning. From here they proceeded to a consideration of what might most defensibly happen to us as we engage with tradition in its various modes. This way of arguing attempts to retain a self-critical focus and to offer arguments which seek to be universal – though also provisional – in character. Yet it falls foul of two influential clusters of contemporary thought – on the one hand, some of those which are Marxist in origin and on the other, the deeper claims of postmodernism. In this chapter I propose to deal with the first cluster and in the next chapter to deal with the second. Neo-Marxist currents have been particularly strong in modern sociology of education, if less so in educational practice itself. They have, however, drawn the ire of Conversative politicians in more than a few Western countries in recent decades and have thereby helped to provoke educational 'reforms' which tend to make their own theories into self-fulfilling prophecies. For instance, one of the main arguments in the neo-Marxist standpoint runs as follows: the most significant thing educational systems do is reproduce the kinds of social relations which maintain the inequities of capitalism, and which capitalist societies need in order to perpetuate themselves. There have been many variants of this theme in recent decades, but most of them would share the criticism that the emphasis on dialogue and courtship in the arguments I have advanced is a form of 'consensualism'. Consensualism, in neo-Marxist theory is a kind of engineered acquiescence, a 'false consciousness' which covers over and even denies the existence of deeper conflicts between different interests in society. In this connection the most important conflicts are generally attributed to the differing interests of dominant classes on the one hand (upper class and 'bourgeois'), and disempowered interests on the other ('working class').

The neo-Marxist theory of schooling has been articulated in a particularly striking form by French sociologists Pierre Bourdieu and Jean Claude Passeron in their book *Reproduction in Education, Society and Culture.*[1] Differing variants of this theory have been published in America by authors such as S. Bowles and H. Gintis, Michael Apple, Jean Anyon; in Britain by Michael Young, Madan Sarup; in Australia by M. R. Matthews, and in Ireland by Kathleen

Lynch. It is not possible to review all of this literature in this chapter, but as Bourdieu's and Passeron's study has been one of the strongest articulations of neo-Marxism in educational discourse in recent decades, we shall begin by examining some of the main theses of *Reproduction in Education, Society and Culture*.

A Taste of Total Critique

In this book, Bourdieu and Passeron (B&P) employ a range of specifically chosen concepts – such as 'pedagogic action', 'pedagogic authority', 'pedagogic work', 'school authority', 'educational authority' and 'the work of schooling'. They give each of the above an abbreviation (e.g. PA, PAu, etc) and proceed to discern in each of them connotations which are chiefly invidious. For instance, in one of their opening propositions they announce: 'All pedagogic action (PA) is, objectively, symbolic violence insofar as it is the imposition of a cultural arbitrary by an arbitrary power.' (B&P 5) 'Symbolic violence' is explained as the 'power to impose meanings' and in such a way that the action seems legitimate, because it conceals 'the power relations which are the basis of its force'. (B&P 4) The phrase 'a cultural arbitrary', in which the word 'arbitrary' is used as a noun rather than as an adjective, suggests an arbitrary selection of meanings from cultural traditions, for imposition on learners through 'pedagogic action'. The selection is claimed to be arbitrary because Bourdieu and Passeron hold that it represents the meanings and interests of 'dominant groups' in society.

The term 'insofar as' is employed frequently by Bourdieu and Passeron in advancing their earlier propositions, and invites the impression that the authors are taking care through its use not to be sweeping in their judgements. This initial impression is also prompted by their suggestion that the work of schools is not totally determined by external forces, but is relatively autonomous. For instance, in their proposition on 'pedagogic authority' they claim that:

> pedagogic action 'insofar as it is a power of symbolic violence' and 'insofar as it is the imposition of a cultural arbitrary ... necessarily implies, as a social condition of its exercise, pedagogic authority (PAu) and the relative autonomy of the agency commissioned to exercise it'. (B&P 11-12)

This initial impression that 'insofar as' might signify '*only* insofar as', begins to weaken however as one reads further. The proposition which introduces the concept of 'pedagogic work' argues that 'insofar as it is the arbitrary imposition of a cultural arbitrary presupposing pedagogic authority (PAu) ... pedagogic action (PA) entails *pedagogic work*'. Pedagogic work is then described as:

> a process of inculcation which must last long enough to produce a durable training, i.e. a *habitus*, the product of internalisation of the principles of a cultural arbitrary capable of perpetuating itself after PA has ceased and thereby of perpetuating in practices the principles of the internalised arbitrary. (B&P 31)

The absence of any 'insofar' to qualify these latter clauses makes 'pedagogic work' itself nothing less than indoctrination, or more precisely, a form of indoctrination which is more covert than overt, and all the more lasting in its influences on that account. Qualifying terms are now dispensed with, allowing the judgements to become all-embracing in character. That this is how Bourdieu and Passeron view the work of educational systems as such, is clear from remarks they make in their fourth major proposition, asserting that the 'essential function' of every institutionalised educational system is the 'inculcation' and 'reproduction' of a 'cultural arbitrary'. (B&P 54) Towards the end of the book, this is stated even more bluntly, and no attempt is made to distinguish better educational systems from worse ones: 'Thus the most hidden and most specific function of the educational system consists in hiding its objective function, that is, masking the objective truth of its relationship to the system of class relations.' (B&P 208)

Two further concepts introduced in the book are those of 'cultural capital' and 'linguistic capital'. The authors suggest that these are more appropriate descriptions of pupils' capacity to derive advantages from education than are considerations of the learner's personal abilities and aptitudes. These latter considerations are dismissed as 'the ideology of natural "gifts" and innate "tastes"'. (B&P 208) Cultural capital is defined at one point as 'the cultural goods transmitted by the different family (PAs) pedagogic actions'. (B&P 30) The term 'capital' is borrowed from the treminology of economics and business and it refers to an individual's accumulated cultural benefits, which place him or her in an advantageous position for acquiring further cultural benefits from the educational system. For instance, compare a child who has read a goodly portion of books from the well-stocked shelves of a household where reading is encouraged with a child whose home contains few if any books and where visits to the library are rarely or ever considered. The former child stands to gain substantially more benefits from schooling than the latter. To put it in Bourdieu's and Passeron's terms, the former child is well furnished with 'cultural capital', while the latter is deficient in it. 'Linguistic capital' refers to parallel accomplishments in the field of language: the range of one's vocabulary, the polish of one's accent, one's command of idiom, the confidence to voice a question in a classroom or lecture theatre, and so on.

Bourdieu and Passeron assert that the selections from culture which feature in the work of schools incorporate a content and a manner of communication which are systematically biased against those whose cultural and linguistic capital are not those of the 'dominant classes'. They make the further point that schooling promotes a 'misrecognition of the symbolic violence' it exerts, by promoting the 'ideology of natural gifts and tastes' and by 'monopolizing the legitimate use of symbolic violence'. (B&P 67) On this account, failure at school is not something attributable to shortcomings in students themselves but is rather a systematic 'elimination from the educational system' of certain categories of students. Failure is the lot of those – particularly 'working class' students— whose own cultural and lingustic capital is not recognised by the official school culture, and who are therefore at a double disadvantage. In order to succeed, not only would they have to accommodate themselves to a culture which is alien to their own backgrounds; they would first have to become at home in an alien vocabulary and idiom through which such a culture is communicated.

The analysis presented in Book I of *Reproduction in Education, Society and Culture* provides a theoretical framework from which the most severe critiques of educational systems can be carried out. Despite its many insights, however, it is not an analysis of *practice*, or a faithful account of practice. Many of the insights the authors present are of an absolute character, carrying the suggestion that an educational system does *nothing but* accomplish the operations of reproducing cultural hierarchies and perpetuating social inequities. In other words, the features of educational practice which do not correspond to their critique, or which would call into question aspects of that critique, are ignored to a surprising degree.[2] This gives to their critique a one-sided character, a lack of self-criticism towards their own pre-conceptions which may be as serious as any inattention to built-in bias in the standpoints they are criticising. This becomes clearer if we examine more closely now a number of prominent features of the analysis presented by Bourdieu and Passeron. I have chosen the following six, because they are the ones that express most strongly a conception of education which is at odds with the case for the sovereignty of learning which I have been arguing.

Firstly, the only relations which are credited by Bourdieu and Passeron as being important in education are power relations; more specifically, the power relations between 'dominant' and 'dominated' social classes. Relations arising primarily from care, concern, solidarity, or indeed professional duty, go unrecorded. Yet, action arising from motives like these features prominently in the everyday work of teachers, and not least in the case of those pupils who are at a disadvantage in the circumstances of schooling. Similarly ignored is the evidence of the often-voiced demands of teachers, and indeed of many managerial bodies in education, for the provision of extra resources from the public purse for such pupils. These omissions are all the more serious when we recall that one of the main purposes of Part II of the book is to present 'empirical' evidence. Evidence which would disconfirm, or seriously qualify the propositions of Part I is omitted.[3]

Secondly, and related to this first point, is an old assumption of orthodox Marxism which underlies the entire book. This assumption takes it for granted that conflict between different social classes is the basic mode of human relation. With this goes the suggestion that other modes of relation, such as dialogue in the sense described earlier, or even negotiated agreements, are forms of consensualism: in other words forms of ideology which mask the hidden influence of violence in communications between 'dominant' interests and any other interests which might threaten this dominance. This assumption of the primacy of conflict is just as dogmatic however as Nietzsche's insistence on the primacy of the will to power, which we examined in Chapter Five. It does away with a distinction which is a crucial one in any practical educational context: the distinction between authority and power. It suggests, just as much as Nietzsche's theses do, that conflicts of power are primary to everything else in human relations. The claim that conflicts of power define humans' relations with one another should not be confused however with the more sustainable thesis (considered in Chapter Five) that a conflict of *interpretations* is an inescapable feature of human life itself. That thesis suggested that the conflict could, in certain circumstances, become productive. It could do so by putting the claim to truth in one's own perspective to the critical test of dialogue and by being prepared to accept and incorporate criticism from other perspectives; in other words, by recognising the *authority* of those perspectives which can best withstand refutation in the arena of critical questioning. Such recognition, we have argued, is properly seen as provisional rather than absolute, though not the less committed for that. By contrast, in claiming that authority itself is nothing other than the 'legitimated' power of 'dominant' interests, and by seeing 'legitimation' as part of the masking function of ideology, the primacy-of-power-conflict thesis seeks to remove the grounds for defensible argument from the person who wishes to claim a legitimate authority to teach, or to secure the co-operation of pupils and parents, for the pupils' own benefit.

Thirdly, the benefits of learning seem to be conceived by Bourdieu and Passeron in extrinsic rather than in intrinsic terms. In other words, education is important primarily because of the *social* and *economic* purposes it serves in reproducing the 'dominant' classes, because of the opportunities it gives to its certificated recipients to be part of such classes and its systematic denial of such opportunities to the children of 'dominated' classes. I do not wish to deny in any way the social inequities which are all too apparent in even the most 'developed' countries, or to minimise the part played by schooling in perpetuating these inequities. Analyses inspired by neo-Marxist traditions have done much (as we shall consider in the next section) to highlight the often hidden and often intractable nature of these inequities. To claim however that the reproduction of unequal social relations is 'the most specific function' of an educational system is to regard that system's intrinsic *educational* purposes either as secondary, or as a masquerade. As distinct from the 'relative autonomy' which Bourdieu and Passeron claim to discern in schooling systems, this claim amounts to denying sovereignty *of any educational kind* to teaching and learning.

Fourthly, the concept of cultural capital, whatever utility it may have in analyses of the economic and social effects of education, is a hindrance to a proper understanding of the intrinsic purposes of education. This is so because the pre-conceptions it carries with it misrepresent the nature of cultural tradition itself. Accordingly, it disfigures those encounters with cultural tradition through which the benefits of education emerge. Capital of any kind is a *commodity*, and a quantifiable one at that. Culture, by contrast, is a manifold of *accomplishments* and *pursuits*, which it is impossible validly to quantify and which, to a greater or lesser degree, already inhabits our beliefs and attitudes, our experience and practice. Cultural activity can indeed produce commodities: works of art, scientific theories contained in books, musical compositions, and so on. These become cultural *goods* however (i.e their commodity aspects become secondary) only when they are *understood* and *appreciated* in human experience; only when they engage human experience in their own peculiar ambience. But the concept of 'capital' is inappropriate in another way also. A circumspect deployment of capital in business ventures provides the means for securing the best return on investment. This activity is governed by considerations such as confidentiality, competitiveness, knowledge of the market, and the overriding awareness that one person's gain (of market share, of dividend) is likely to be another's loss. By contrast, when cultural traditions are genuinely engaged through teaching and learning, an enlargement and enrichment of human experience takes place, and through a *sharing* and *questioning* made possible through increases in the relevant fluency, rather than through strategic manoeuvres made possible by a manipulative 'inside' knowledge. Participation in cultural activity, in short, identifies a way of being human in which *all* can benefit. The experience of teaching and learning is properly conceived not as something which concentrates benefits in few hands, but as that which, through co-operative effort and sustained commitment, *enables and widens* such participation by ever greater numbers in any society.

Fifthly, the twin concepts of cultural capital and linguistic capital are identified by Bourdieu and Passeron as attributes associated with different social *classes* rather than with different individuals. These concepts are then used to discredit ones such as individual 'talents', or 'giftedness', which are in turn regarded as the means whereby an ideology of meritocracy legitimates its discriminatory practices. The criticisms of the notions of talents and giftedness are not, however, without foundation. Although they do not identify the psychological term 'IQ', or even 'intelligence', as a target of their criticisms, it is clear enough that Bourdieu and Passeron are attacking a commonly accepted viewpoint in educational circles that intelligence is a quality with which one is endowed, amply or otherwise, from birth. This viewpoint not only neglects the importance of the cultural factors in human experience which may continually challenge one's abilities to further efforts and achievements, or, on the other hand, which may habituate such abilities to indolence of one kind or another. It also neglects the plural nature of human abilities and aptitudes. That is to say, it fails to take proper account of the way one's experiences influence one's potentials, and it relegates some potentials to the margins, or leaves them out of the account altogether. Sometimes these might be a person's most promising, or most singular potentials.[4] But with these last remarks, we have identified one of the most serious shortcomings in the account of 'pedagogic action' contained in Bourdieu's and

Passeron's preoccupations with distinctions based on social class, namely the neglect of personal attributes, contrasting sensibilities and individual differences. Yet such differences, and the difficulties in dealing with them in classroom circumstances, are among the most urgent of practical matters with which teachers have to deal.

Finally, Bourdieu's and Passeron's arguments are a form of theory which gives pride of place to analysis and criticism, and which highlights the influence of social forces and interests that are embodied in institutionalised structures. But it is a form of theory which ignores the need for constructive suggestion, and also the importance of human agency, in any social undertaking. The fact that their theory is a sociological one does not provide sufficient reason for this one-sidedness. Their frequent references to what is 'objectively' the case seek to establish a scientific status for their propositions, and indeed provide some penetrating insights into inequities (overlooked or concealed) which are perpetuated through schooling. But the linking of this 'objectivity' almost exclusively to the concept of *class* interests and social forces views human society in mechanistic terms and obscures interests of other kinds which are ceaselessly at play in any case in the circumstances of teaching and learning (e.g. interests and preoccupations arising from subjects of study, from personal friendships, from extra-curricular activities, from family and kinship relations, and so on). Their theory of 'reproduction' offers as a scientific account of education a theory which focuses primarily on extrinsic rather than intrinsic dimensions of the enterprise, a theory which offers only one family of perspectives (neo-Marxist) on that dimension and finally, a theory which is less than critical of its own underlying assumptions.

Some more recent contributions to educational thought from the neo-Marxist tradition have been critical of analyses like that of Bourdieu and Passeron, faulting them for their absence of a transforming vision, their neglect of human agency, and their doctrinnaire mis-understanding of the subtleties of pedagogical action. This suggests that, unlike the total critque of Bourdieu and Passeron, constructive accounts of communicative practice itself might play a central part in neo-Marxist conceptions of education. And this emphasis becomes increasingly evident in the more recent writings in the Marxist tradition which deal with education, or with the play of influence and interests more generally in human relations. It is appropriate then to consider how our account of educational practice and the sovereignty of learning stands in the light of some of these more recent writings.

Human Agency and the Hidden Curriculum

In his book *Education and Power* (1982 *E&P*), Michael Apple emphasises the necessity for neo-Marxist critiques to press beyond the analysis of structural deformities in educational systems and to concern themselves more with practical possibilities of change. Towards the close of the book he argues as follows:

> Criticism of the way our system works is not enough, however. It needs to be accompanied by specific proposals for an alternative social model (which we may call socialist if we like). These proposals should not be borrowed whole from other countries, but need to be both adapted to the current conditions of, in my case, the American people and contrary to the interests of capital. Without this, again, little in the way of serious and progressive structural change can be expected. (*E&P* 173)

Apple calls into question moreover any analysis which suggests that schools more or less automatically reproduce the unequal relations of capitalist society. He does not reject the concept of 'cultural capital' but argues that it is one of two forms of culture. The first of these, he suggests, is culture as lived: the experience of culture embodied in the day to day lives of people. The second form however is the transformation of culture into a commodity by certain groups in society, to accumulate it and employ it as a form of capital. (*E&P* 19) The most highly prized form of cultural capital produced by educational institutions, according to Apple, is technical and administrative expertise. By this he means the kind of knowledge which is perceived as indispensible not only for controlling mechanical and electronic systems, but which is has largely come to control the conduct of management and politics as well. This kind of cultural capital might thus be described as technocratic. Although Apple does not pursue the connection, this is none other than the knowledge-as-power conception which we considered in the early part of Chapter Five. We can now clearly see that this conception gains its peculiar application in these contexts where interests of power and control have gained the upper hand among the play of motives which attend human experience. In other words it is a view of knowledge which, whatever sway it may hold in those arenas of life where a market outlook is accommodated, works against the more defensible interests of education. To the extent that this view becomes institutionalised in the practices and attitudes of schooling, the integrity which belongs to teaching and learning has already been compromised.

In turning to consider culture-as-lived, particularly within the context of schooling, we might thus expect Apple to elucidate more emancipatory forms of cultural experience; forms which might approximate or shed some critical light on the characterisation of teaching and learning put forward in Chapter Seven. This however he does not do, and it remains unclear how he would regard such an attempt. His main concern in exploring culture-as-lived is in detailing different forms of resistance to the official curricula that schools offer, including the hidden curricula which carry discriminatory assumptions and practices. He draws in particular on Paul Willis' study of a group of disaffected pupils in a British comprehensive school, Robert Everhart's study of minimally compliant pupils in junior high school, and Angela McRobbie's research on a group of working class girls, both in America.[5] He also draws on a study by Mike Brake on youth sub-cultures, including non-white youth cultures.[6] In different ways, these studies show how pupils' attempts (largely successful ones at that) to resist the official cultures and routines of schooling actually contribute to what different orders of capitalist society require. Thus reproduction is served obliquely rather than directly.

In the case of Willis' 'lads', the counter culture they build and inhabit rejects mental work as effeminate, prizes 'having a laff' and other orchestrated forms of disruptive behaviour, and progressively orients their sense of identity to that of factory shop floor. In the case of Everhart's 'kids', their compliance with the requirements of schooling is sufficient to obtain successful grades, but the main features of their lived culture in school are its diversions. These include attempts to place their own stamp on the pattern of daily routine, a consuming interest in sport, in discussing their own leisure activities, and things non-academic. Everhart's comment on the chief kind of reproduction which takes place here is quoted as follows by Apple: 'Students are reproducing forms that will damn them to expressions of reaction, but will not foster critical opposition.' Thus, he claims, they are participating in shaping patterns of dull conformity coupled with ineffective reaction 'that make it likely they will suffer the same fate elsewhere, especially in the workplace'. (*E&P* 106-7) In the case of McRobbie's 'working class girls', they 'knew' instinctively – like Willis' 'lads' – that they were not destined for those occupational opportunities highly regarded by the school cultures. Their opposition to school culture expressed itself in a preoccupation with their own femininity, talk of boys and romance, seeing themselves as very different from the 'snob' girls who 'sucked up' to the teachers. In her remarks on the significance of the girls' peer culture, McRobbie remarks: 'Marriage, family life, fashion and beauty all contribute massively to this feminine anti-school culture and, in doing so, nicely illustrate the contradictions inherent in so-called oppositional activities.'[7] As Apple points out, the relative sense of autonomy provided by the counter cultures in each case is a temporary one, and serves in the longer run to confirm distinctions based on social class and aggravated by distinctions based on colour and ethnic origin.

There are many incisive insights supplied by Apple's critiques, and these are all the more convincing because they reveal a knowledge of the day to day realities of schooling which is largely absent from more abstract critical studies, such as that of Bourdieu and Passeron. Yet some of the same criticisms which were pertinent to *Reproduction in Education, Culture and Society* apply also to Apple's *Education and Power*. Two of these merit particular attention. The first concerns the primacy given to the relations of schooling to the wider society, or more precisely, the neglect of the core purposes of education that results from this. The second concerns the nature of Apple's understanding of the experience of teaching and learning. In relation to the first criticism, perhaps any approach which is Marxist in an orthodox sense must subscribe to the doctrine of class struggle as the most basic characteristic of human intercourse. The perspectives issuing from such a doctrine would almost inevitably collide with any perspective seeking a sovereignty on *educational* grounds for teaching and learning. This is so because the benefits intrinsic to education have a personal-cum-interpersonal character which is overshadowed by the class struggle doctrine in a Marxist analysis. It is important to recall that, far from any individualism, *personal* here signifies the Socratic educational characteristics outlined in Chapter One and the virtues of teaching and learning described in Chapter Seven. It still seems likely however that doctrines of an orthodox Marxist cast would regard as an ideology of concealment any account which gave a prominent place to the dynamics of a *personal* encounter with cultural tradition. The influence of social prejudices is of course always and everywhere already at work, in pronounced or milder ways, in 'what befalls us in any case' in these encounters. But the argument advanced for the sovereignty of learning has sought to keep an *alert and critical eye* on the pre-judgements (and not merely social class ones) which feature in all human understanding. Accordingly, the account of teaching and learning which accompanied this argument placed special emphasis on a self-critical discipline, the to-and-fro play of which endeavous ever anew to unearth such pre-judgements, to give a generous ear and a critical eye to what is addressed to us through educational encounters. It thus seeks to be a form of cultural intercourse which is a candidate for defensibility in a universal sense.

In relation to the second criticism – Apple's neglect of any constructive account of teaching and learning – it should be noted that he calls at one point for 'the building of a clear pedagogical and curricular model' along socialist lines, and towards the end of the book sketches some suggestions for a 'political pedagogy'. But he does not give details of any such pedagogical model and the tentative proposals he sketches for a political pedagogy are mainly concerned with forms of adult learning for groups such as 'the membership of unions, feminist collectives, "rank and file" educational groups and so on'. (*E&P* 128, 174-5) Curiously, the 'relative autonomy' which he claims schools enjoy in the reproduction of unequal economic and social relations, doesn't seem to feature in his thinking where the constructive and educational purposes of schooling are concerned.

These omissions in Apple's work are addressed by some further studies in the Marxist tradition of educational thought. Two of these call for our attentions here because they pass beyond critique and concern themselves in a major way with constructive proposals. These two works are *Education Under Siege*, by Stanley Aronowitz and Henry Giroux (1985; *EUS*), and *Becoming Critical* by Wilfred Carr and Stephen Kemmis (1986). Aronowitz and Giroux are concerned to develop a critical pedagogy, and in this effort they are clearly inspired by the pioneering work carried on by Paulo Freire with illiterate and downtrodden adult communities in Brazil and Chile.[8] Freire constructed a curriculum of ingenious literacy exercises as a means towards giving his learners a critical and emancipatory perspective on the hidden curriculum of their daily lives. This hidden curriculum had for long pervaded their outlooks with the acquiescent belief that they were inferior beings and that their poverty was part of the natural order of things. It had thus imprisoned them in a fatalistic view of their own identity and their own future. Freire's overt themes (such as slum-dwelling, poverty amid wealth, 'the culture of silence' etc.) through which his adult students became literate, therefore served as an emancipation and nourished a critically alert communal solidarity with significant implications for political action.

Inspired by Freire's work, Aronowitz and Giroux articulate what they call a radical pedagogy, with a view to cultivating a social and political movement both within and outside of American schools (USA). The purpose of such a movement would be to free schooling from domination by ideological interests and, in their own words, 'to restore education to an honourable and autonomous place in our culture'. (*EUS* 20) In place of the 'de-skilling' of teachers by educational reforms which make them little more than 'proletarian' workers, Aronowitz and Giroux envisage them as 'transformative intellectuals' who can collectively organise in order to analyse and to change 'the role that educators play at all levels of schooling in producing and legitimising existing social relations'. (*EUS* 41) Pursuing the theme of teacher as transformative intellectual further, the authors envisage a kind of literacy which would not merely be a functional literacy, but a critical literacy achieved through the quality of teachers' engagements with their pupils:

> Critical literacy would make clear the connection between knowledge and power. It would present knowledge as a social construction linked to norms and values and it would demonstrate modes of critique that illuminate how, in some cases, knowledge serves very specific economic, political and social interests. (*EUS* 132)

Aronowitz and Giroux not only provide a more informative and more circumspect analysis than do Bourdieu and Passeron of how schooling becomes implicated in furthering social inequities, they also write earnestly of strategies that might help to counter this state of affairs and stress the necessity for constructive action. But the constructive side of their argument does not give the same emphasis to the actual work of teaching and learning as it does to initiatives such as alliances between teachers and activist parents and community groups. In this they differ from Freire, whose account of the teaching and learning activities his work actually involved is one of the more striking features of his writings. Of course the cultural circumstances were very different for Freire. In addition, the learners in his literacy schemes were themselves adults, parents and potential community activists. Where the actual practices of teaching and learning are concerned, however, it remains the case that the Aronowitz and Giroux make only brief suggestions relating to students' projects on political, social and cultural issues, and to 'autobiographical essays that focus on conflicts between peer interaction and interaction with authorities such as parents and teachers'. (*EUS* 54) Apart from brief indications such as these, the authors say little on how the conduct of teaching and learning might be pursued as an emancipatory and practical discipline between teachers and pupils. Systematic attention to such a discipline might also bring to light, and help to guard against, any tendency for radical pedagogy to pass over into a form of courtship which becomes too zealous; which neglects to ensure that more than one side of an issue gets heard, explored and submitted to appraisal. Recall for instance the comments on tendentiousness made in the 'courtship' section of the previous chapter.

The faith placed by Aronowitz and Giroux in teachers as 'transfromative intellectuals' is questioned by Kathleen Lynch in her book, *The Hidden Curriculum – Reproduction in education, an appraisal* (1989; *HC*). While admitting that at a personal level she adheres strongly to the ideals put forward by Giroux, she claims that as a sociologist she has serious reservations about them. (*HC* 16) This is because the 'sociopolitical status of teachers' curtails any wide-scale likelihood of transformative work taking place in schools. This seems to suggest that the majority of teachers are less than radical in their political outlooks. Sensing something of 'Hegelian idealism' in theories like those of Aronowitz and Giroux, Lynch claims that such theories present solutions at the level of the ideal and pass too lightly over the material circumstances of teachers. She argues moreover that the 'human agency' in teachers' work might frequently be of a conservative rather than a radical character, that it may reinforce the status quo rather than advance the notion of 'education as social transformation' canvassed by Aronowitz and Giroux. (*HC* 16)

This may or may not be the case, but sociological observations on teachers' political attitudes places the focus of attention elsewhere than on the more important question of teachers' *educational* outlooks: their commitment to the *intrinsic benefits* of education, particularly in the case of 'resistant' pupils who are predisposed to distrust and disrupt the efforts of teachers. The constructive proposals of Aronowitz and Giroux can be criticised in this respect also. Their preoccupation with the quality of the *socialising* tendencies of schooling, important though such work is in identifying inequities, neglects another kind of work, namely *educational* work: the kind of emancipation which is the outcome of successfully accomplished encounters with cultural traditions. As we saw in the previous chapter, such encounters can take place in all fields of study, from the most practical to the most abstract, and can range from the most rudimentary to the most advanced. The reservations of the sociologist are reservations about something other than the essential business of schooling; a business which requires not so much 'transformative intellectuals' as the insightful and professional commitment of teachers to defensible *educational* purposes, notwithstanding the teachers' own political persuasions.

The Precedence of Practice

The possibilities for emancipation through educational action are a key concern in the critique undertaken by Wilfred Carr and Stephen Kemmis in *Becoming Critical* (*BC*). They emphasise however that in order for these possibilities to be properly identified and availed of, the practical contexts of schooling, rather than theories of academic origin, must be the source of critical insights. While remaining within a tradition of enquiry which could still be described as Marxist, the standpoint taken by Carr and Kemmis is dramatically different from that taken by Bourdieu and Passeron, as the following passage shows:

> The gaps between theory and practice which everyone deplores are actually endemic to the view that educational theory can be produced from within theoretical and practical contexts different from the theoretical and practical context within which it is supposed to apply. (*BC* 115)

On this view, the practical activities undertaken daily in schools must themselves provide insights for critical reflection among teachers. But Carr and Kemmis claim, like most of the authors we have just been considering, that such activities might often embody ideological mis-perceptions. They therefore advocate critical reflection by teachers on their own practices and describe the approach they recommend as a form of 'action research' which is at the same time a 'critical social science'. Leaving aside for a moment its theoretical character as a 'science', this approach contains a conception of practice which is guided by a critical discipline showing some parallels with the discipline of educational dialogue we considered in the previous chapter. Carr and Kemmis point out that teachers 'are already committed to some elaborate, if not explicit set of beliefs about what they are doing'. (BC *110*) One of the chief purposes of 'action research' would thus be to provide a strategy for teachers to make such beliefs more explicit, to subject them to critical review, to identify contradictions and inconsistencies in their own practices, to loosen as far as possible the grip of institutional constraints and uncritically received attitudes on their professional work. The critical educational science being recommended would therefore require a continuing deliberative discourse among teachers about 'the nature of educational values' and that of their own occupational commitments.

There is a significant shift of emphasis here from traditional Marxist themes to more recognisably Socratic ones. To present such a discipline as a *theory* however, or indeed as a science, is to act against the most promising and most practical possibilities of emancipation in teaching and learning. It may even occasion a disregard of such possibilities by the great majority of teachers. It is to confirm 'action research', however unwittingly, as the property of theoreticians, even if this includes those minorities among teachers who are prepared to get involved in theorising about teaching and to read theoretical material on teaching. It is to remove the discipline precisely from the context where it belongs, namely that of the professional practice of *all* who are teachers. It is worth recalling here that one of the major benefits of Socratic educational practice is its non-theoretical character. This practice includes from the start a self-critical reflection on experience (for instance, on decisions taken, mistakes made, breakthroughs achieved, predicaments handled, opportunities missed or grasped, and so on). Far from recasting practice as a theory, reflections here remain practical through and through. Theory, on the other hand, seeks not only to explain but also to control practice. This may be acceptable enough if the theory is an engineering one, where the practice of building a structure or monitoring an electronic process must follow the blueprint and specifications to the most precise detail. In like manner, much of medical diagnosis and treatment is methodically controlled by theory. The nature of teaching and learning is such, however, that sovereignty is effectively replaced by technocratic control if theory is given a similar status here.

It is also worth recalling that one of the chief effects of the Platonist eclipse described in Chapter One was a flight from practical reflection to the construction of a metaphysics which claimed that theory could supply superior insights to those arising from the to-and-fro play of practice itself. One of the leading exponents of the action research approach to education, John Elliott, has suggested that Carr and Kemmis have done something of this kind by taking the inspiration for their critical social science and 'theory generation' from an 'external source', most notably the critical theory of Jürgen Habermas.[9] This gives a normative orientation of a critical-democratic kind to the theory put forward in *Becoming Critical*. Yet this general orientation shows a certain reticence on the part of Kemmis and Carr to identify the specific character of commitments and virtues which are *educational*, before being anything else. In other words, by allowing 'the nature of educational values' to be essentially a matter of debate, Carr and Kemmis seem to identify no 'values' that are *inherently* educational. Thus, unlike the attempt to specify some defensible criteria for appraisals of educational practice (e.g. the substantive candidates offered earlier on as virtues of teaching and learning) they offer teachers no guidelines for distinguishing those educational activities which might 'change people in certain desirable ways' from those activities which might change people in less desirable ways.

To tackle substantive issues in education however is not only to acknowledge certain procedures of discourse, whether of a critical-democratic or other origin. It is indeed to employ such procedures perceptively in encounters with traditions of learning; traditions which seek to engage our sensibilities and which seek to influence in one way or another our outlooks, our commitments and our choice of worthwhile pursuits. It is to give due recognition to the fact that in all learning we are not only acquiring concepts, skills, and fluencies. We are also being canvassed, or as I put it earlier, courted. This is why it is so apt to speak of the different subjects of learning as so many *voices* of tradition. And it is probably impossible to make fully transparent to our critical attentions the prejudices, the perspectives conditioned by unstated interests, which remain active whenever any of these voices seeks a hearing through the experience of teaching and learning. Not surprisingly then, standpoints of Marxist ancestry remain systematically suspicious of any deferential or generous engagement with these voices. Accordingly, in any constructive proposals for educational action emerging from such standpoints, a critique of ideology is likely to feature as a methodological imperative.

In different ways, such critique informs but also *constrains* the approaches we have been considering in this section of the chapter. The constraint remains present as a hindrance, moreover, unless the primacy given to social class interests yields the place of first importance to an inclusive consideration of *educational* purposes. This is not to lose sight of critique, or of the inequities it seeks to identify. It is rather to ask the question: Critique for the sake of what? and to answer it in a way which grants to educational purposes an integrity which is based on a particular kind of rationality. This rationality, as we saw in the previous chapter, gives a special importance to certain virtues, commitments and practices. It seeks to defend these in universal terms and it is on this basis that it lays claim to a measure of accountable sovereignty. The integrity and sovereignty of learning seek acknowledgement moreover not only from governments and other major interests in society. They seek it no less from radical social criticism.

These remarks now bring us directly to the arguments of a thinker who is perhaps the most constructive, and clearly one of the most incisive, in the entire tradition of radical social criticism. The thinker in question is Jürgen Habermas, whose writings are an enterprise of remarkable proportions in the effort to answer the question 'Critique in the name of what?' Habermas has developed a 'theory of communicative action' and an accompanying 'discourse ethics' which attempt to allow a critique of ideology its full scope, which seek secondly to restore worthiness to consensus, and which seek also to combine these features in a philosophical account of emancipatory human action. As distinct from action which is oriented towards the seeking of power or the manipulation of others, Habermas sees communicative action as 'action oriented towards understanding'. He attempts to distinguish the rationality which characterises such action from the rationality of technical control. More boldly, he views this 'communicative' rationality as being very much in the tradition of Enlightenment and modernity, and accordingly he seeks to defend it in universal terms. The autonomy sought by Habermas for the domain of communicative action is paralleled in some key respects (though by no means all as we shall see) by the case I have been advancing for the sovereignty of learning. Many of the attacks which have been directed against Habermas' work by postmodernist critics might find similar targets, perhaps even more obvious ones, in my own case. In the following chapter then I will briefly join a few strands of Habermas' work to the case I have been making for the sovereignty of learning and then appraise the fortunes of this case in a debate with the more prevalent manifestations of 'postmodernism'. Following this, I will then consider how the case I have been arguing differs from what Habermas' reflections have yielded.

Notes:

1. Pierre Bourdieu and Jean Claude Passeron, *Reproduction in Education, Society and Culture*, translated by Richard Nice, with Foreword by Tom Bottomore (London: Sage, 1977).

2. In Part Two of their book, Bourdieu and Passeron present empirical evidence to support the propositions they advance in Part One. The empirical examples chosen however are ones which confirm these propositions, or which are interpreted in such a way as to confirm the propositions. As we

have seen from the remarks of Karl Popper, a truly scientific approach would have Bourdieu and Passeron actively seeking evidence to *refute* their propositions, thus subjecting them to the more rigorous test. In this connection, there is ample evidence to show that schools do a great variety of things that are different from reproducing social inequities.

3. In his Foreword to the book, Tom Bottimore writes: 'Hence, this kind of research may lead, as in the studies contained in the second part of the book, to a confirmation (or in some cases a questioning) of a theory of class relations initially taken for granted'. (p.vii) Little evidence is offered, however, which would seriously call into question the assumptions of the first part of the book.

4. These comments on the plurality of human potentials call to mind Howard Gardner's theory of multiple intelligences, namely: logical-mathematical, linguistic, bodily-kinesthetic, spatial, musical, inter-personal and intra-personal. See his book *Frames of Mind – The Theory of Multiple Intelligences* (London: Paladin, 1983). I haven't employed Gardner's categorisation in my own arguments. Gardner's insights provide many welcome perspectives on educational practice in my view, but I prefer to remain with the term 'potentials', because it is a better reminder to us that the different 'intelligences' could be co-present in a single individual, and indeed that they could even pull in contrary directions as the person's educational experiences unfold. Other reasons for not using Gardner's scheme is that human 'intelligences' could exceed the seven he identifies (e.g. the intelligence associated with historical-archeological insights) and also, that among the different potentials that a person may have, there may be some which call forth better than others a sense of identity which best enables that person to flourish as a human being. This is a philosophical point, or more precisely, an *ontological* one, which Gardner regards as lying outside the psychological character of his own enquiries. (Howard Gardner at a seminar in University College Dublin in January 1995).

5. Paul Willis, *Learning to Labour – How working class kids get working class jobs* (Aldershot: Gower Publishing Company, 1977, 1980). Robert Everhart *The In-Between Years: Student Life in a Junior High School* (Santa Barbara: Graduate School of Education, University of California, 1979). Angela McRobbie 'Working Class Girls and the Culture of Femininity' in *Women Take Issue*, Women's Studies group (Ed.), (London: Hutchinson, 1978) pp.96-108

6. Mike Brake, *The Sociology of Youth Culture and Youth Subcultures* (London: Routledge and Kegan Paul, 1980)

7. From an extended passage quoted by Apple, *Ibid.*, p.111

8. See Paulo Freire's *Cultural Action for Freedom* (Harmondsworth: Penguin, 1972), and his *Pedagogy of the Oppressed*, translated by Myra Bergman Ramos (Harmondsworth: Penguin, 1972).

9. John Elliott, *Action Research for Educational Change* (Milton Keynes: Open University Press, 1991), p.116. Elliott's work, like that of Carr and Kemmis, produces many incisive insights. The practical promise of these insights is somewhat curtailed however unless the insights themselves are clearly identified with practice rather than with theory. Elliott goes farther in this direction in my view than Carr and Kemmis do.

CHAPTER NINE

Postmodern Playfulness and the Dialogue that We Aren't

Introduction

We have seen that the critique of education carried out by Bourdieu and Passeron contained little in the way of constructive alternatives to what they viewed as the arbitrary embodiments of culture which their critique sought to lay bare. But a critique carried out from a Marxist standpoint is presumably undertaken in the name of some kind of social solidarity. *Reproduction in Education, Society and Culture* remains silent however on the question of solidarity. Indeed its adversarial idiom throughout invites the suggestion that continual class conflicts are both the reality *and the goal* of human action. By contrast, Habermas' later philosophy lies at the opposite pole of critical social theory. It is a sustained exploration of a kind of solidarity which involves, but also moves beyond, critique. In his earlier work, most notably *Knowledge and Human Interests,* Habermas already emphasised that his own critique was guided by an interest in the emancipation of human thought and action from domination by ideology (both political and scientific). The notion of a critical social science envisaged by Habermas in that book mingled a Kantian conception of reason (i.e. the autonomy of rational self-reflection) with a political concept of rationality (i.e. critical self-reflection as the source of enlightened emancipation from ideologically induced dependencies).[1] In his middle and later writings Habermas subjected this notion of a critical social science to criticism and debate and reformulated it firstly as a universal pragmatics of speech and later as a large-scale theory of communicative action.

In this present chapter I hope to show that these influential developments in the work of Habermas and other philosophers of the social sciences have been guided by an insight which we encountered in the opening pages of the first chapter. This is the Socratic insight that the most defensible forms of human action, and human learning, are those which view *and pursue* such action and learning as an unfinishing dialogue. And to say this is to suggest that despite the suspicious attitude which critical social theory characteristically adopts to tradition, and despite his own disclaimers, Habermas has brought the tradition of critical theory itself significantly beyond the threshold of suspicion; that his work has in some key respects made of this tradition a virtual embodiment of Gadamer's claim that what it means to be human is best disclosed in dialogue. In Chapter Five we saw that Gadamer expressed this claim boldly in the words 'the dialogue that we are'. But these suggestions can perhaps best be illustrated by exploring, in the first section of this chapter, one of the most dominant and fashionable currents of contemporary thought which assert a contrary conclusion: the 'deconstruction' enterprise associated mainly with Jacques Derrida. Following a critical review of this current in the second section of the chapter, we can then in the final section review our theme in the light of Habermas' arguments on communicative action and attempt a more conclusive appraisal of learning's claims to sovereignty.

The Play of Différance *and Deference*

The standpoint of suspicion adopted by critical theory towards tradition becomes with Derrida nothing less than a suspicion of speech itself as a form of human action. In this, Derrida sees himself as discovering fresh and unforeseen turns on a radical path of thinking which had been opened up by Heidegger. Heidegger had criticised the entire tradition of Western metaphysics for domesticating the relation between human being on the one hand, and on the other, the unfathomableness of that in virtue of which anything could be at all, namely Being. In Heidegger's critical view, metaphysics was a quest not for a truth which sought to do justice to the mysterious nature of this relation. Rather it was a quest for doctrines of comfort and reassurance which sought to render familiar the strangeness of Being; to render the different similar, to deny *the play of presence and absence* which characterised the relation between human being on the one hand, and, on the other, that which was incomparably beyond human being's best efforts to fathom with concepts. Heidegger saw his own later work as a series of efforts to undo an oppressive domestication which many centuries of metaphysics had established. But his purpose in this was to uncover a more original thinking which enabled the truth of being to be *un*concealed. The very term 'unconcealment' moreover (*Aletheia* [Greek] *Unverborgenheit* [German]), which Heidegger settled on as the most appropriate to describe truth, does not signify any permanantly achieved state of enlightenment. Rather it signifies an event of illumination within a larger, enveloping mystery. In his various woodland images Heidegger compares it to a clearing in a forest which enables shafts of light to shine through but which is reclaimed again by the forest's enveloping darkness.[2]

Derrida gives the undoing of metaphysics a radical twist. Where Heidegger's poetic language attempts to reclaim an understanding of the original interplay of presence and absence which metaphysics had obscured, Derrida seeks to undo, or to 'deconstruct' this interplay itself. Despite Heidegger's attempts to overcome metaphysics, Derrida claims to detect in Heidegger's intimations of 'presence' too much of that comforting sense of 'at-homeness' which Western metaphysics employed to keep at bay anxieties about the possible groundlessness of Being. For Derrida then, the very suggestion of any original belonging-together of human being and Being has to be declined. In his essay, 'The Ends of Man', for instance, Derrida distances himself from what he views in Heidegger's discourse as:

> the dominance of an entire metaphorics of proximity, of simple and immediate presence, a metaphorics associating the proximity of Being with the values of neighbouring, shelter, house, service, guard, voice and listening. (*Margins of Philosophy*, p.130)

Derrida is keen to undermine any 'homely' suggestion of humankind reposing in the bosom of Being. He is also keen to set 'trembling' any quest for an original meaning which might furnish humankind with a sense of origins, foundation, ground, or what he calls *arche*. In particular, Derrida attacks what he calls the 'logocentric' character of Western philosophy for making canonical this concern with origin, foundation, or *arche*. Although Derrida's terminology takes more than a little pleasure in ambiguity, by 'logocentric' he seems to mean the assumption – contained in the Greek word *logos* – that *there is truth and meaning to be disclosed* through philosophical discourse. According to Derrida, not only has this assumption been embraced by the main traditions of Western philosophy, it has also pervaded the more significant traditions of Western learning and civilisation. For Derrida however, such dis-closure is already a *closure* of questions which should remain radically open. It is a hunt for definitive accounts and meanings which has the consequence of establishing invidious hierarchies and canons, thus marginalising whatever remains 'other' or different; whatever the hunt has failed to bring within its assured grasp. Thus the Western tradition must be 'deconstructed' to release the play of alternative possibilities, to keep open the play of differing perspectives which the search for 'truth' seeks to restrict and institutionalise in 'logocentric' traditions of learning.

Derrida believes that 'logocentric' assumptions inhabit the spoken word in a more intractable way than they do the written word. Accordingly, in his book *Of Grammatology*, he suggests that the overcoming of metaphysics, which (he claims) Heidegger failed to accomplish through the poetic turn taken by his later philisophy, might be more successfully undertaken by a 'deconstructive' reading of texts and canons. For Derrida, such an enterprise takes the following form.

> [I]t inaugurates the destruction, not the demolition but the deconstruction, of all significations that have their source in that of the logos. Particularly the signification of truth. All the metaphysical determinations of truth, and even the one beyond metaphysical ontotheology that Heidegger reminds us of, are more or less immediately inseparable from the instance of the logos. (*Of Grammatology*, p.10)

Central to this enterprise is what Derrida calls the play of *'différance'*. In a 1968 address carrying the title *Différance*, Derrida announced that this coinage of his described neither a concept nor a word, but rather a two-fold *strategic theme.* Firstly, *différance* (in the sense of deferring) seeks to counter philosophy's preoccupation with definitive meanings by putting off until later, by deferring indefinitely, any definitive disclosures of meaning or 'presence' in the relation between human beings and Being. Secondly, *différance* (in the sense of difference) seeks to keep in play an unsecured plurality of possibilities, even an endless undecidability, with a view to resisting all attempts at an authoritative pinning down, all efforts to give certain meanings the status of a canon, or of 'truth'. (*Margins of Philosophy* p.7ff).

The startling radicalness of Derrida's 'theme', and its iconoclastic import for any conception of education as an enlightening encounter with cultural traditions, comes home to us when we realise that the path he takes is a continuation of Heidegger's only for the first few steps. It then breaks decisively with Heidegger and strikes out in a direction which recalls Nietzsche's declamations more than anything else. Let us examine the contrast more closely. Heidegger's critique of metaphysics is marked not by *différance*, but by a sense of deference and reverence towards what he claims the tradition of metaphysics has eclipsed: 'the undisclosed abundance of the unfamilliar and extraordinary'. (*Poetry, Language, Thought* p.76) Heidegger's is an attempt to bring something of this abundance within the stay of humankind's dwelling on earth, to recover a more original relation between beings and Being than what the conceptual complexities of metaphysics had installed through the routines of scholarship and institutionalised tradition. It is just this deference towards eclipsed origins that Derrida's *différance* wants to break apart. His 'theme' is one 'which is no longer turned towards the origin'; his 'strategy' is one which, in his own words,

> affirms play and tries to pass beyond man and humanism, the name of man being the name of that being who, throughout the history of metaphysics or of ontotheology – in other words through his entire history – has dreamed of full presence, the reassuring foundation, the origin and the end of play. (*Writing and Difference* p.292)

The 'postmodern' features we noted in the writings of Lyotard (in Chapter Four) and Rorty (in Chapter Six) are again called to mind here. In the first place, Lyotard's incredulity towards any enquiry which 'seeks the truth' in a universal sense ('metanarratives'), and Rorty's polemic against what he calls 'the universal human aspiration towards objective truth' (*PMN* 376), are paralleled by Derrida's dismissal of 'logos', truth and the search for meaning. Secondly, and with each of the three, in the conduct of enquiry aesthetic considerations enjoy the prominence traditionally enjoyed by considerations of truth-seeking. Thirdly, this elevation of the aesthetic gives play a central importance in 'postmodern' sensibility. For Lyotard, human action – including all forms of enquiry – is recast as a play of competitive 'language games', where what counts as noteworthy is the performance of new moves, or 'the increase of being and the jubilation which result frrom the invention of new rules of the game'. (*PMC* 80) 'Performativity' replaces justification as the chief criterion of credit. For Rorty, enquiry (particularly philosophy) becomes the conversational pursuit of 'becoming new beings' through finding more interesting ways of 'redescribing ourselves'. Such redescribing is not placed under the auspices of any 'search for truth', or the disclosure of any enduring sense of identity, but under 'the relativity of descriptive vocabularies to periods, traditions and historical accidents'. (*PMN* 358-362)

At first sight Derrida seems to go even farther than other postmodernists in his wholehearted embrace of the aesthetic. Taking his effective inspiration more from Nietzsche than Heidegger, Derrida champions a kind of play which seems to betoken a carefree demolition of anything revered by tradition. He criticises what he sees as philosophy's saddened nostalgia for 'the lost or impossible presence of the absent origin' and in an idiom which betrays more than a little intoxication, he celebrates instead

> the Nietzschean *affirmation*: that is, the joyous affirmation of the play of the world and of the innocence of becoming, the affirmation of a world of signs without fault, without truth, and without origin which is offered to an active interpretation. (*Writing and Difference* 292)

Declarations like these have the effect, whether intended or not, of placing Derrida's variant of postmodernism at a more extreme remove from tradition than those of Lyotard and Rorty. Derrida's apparent disavowal of any and every candidate for 'truth', even such truth-substitute candidates as Lyotard's pragmatic 'performativity', or Rorty's liberal-aesthetic 'edifying philosophy', invites criticisms that his is a philosophical anarchy on an unprecedented scale, an unrelenting abandonment of human learning to the destructive dance of chaos.

The practical consequences of this have been considerable, and are directly pertinent to any claims to sovereignty on the part of learning. 'Deconstruction' has become a very widespread if controversial fashion, in fact a thriving cultural (or anti-cultural) industry, in the West's academies. In America and France especially, but also in other countries, 'deconstruction' has been a leading issue in academic acrimonies of the last two decades. While Derrida would probably be happy to be regarded as the *enfant terrible* of the academic world – in the sense of a latter-day Socrates – he seems clearly unhappy that he has become the *bête noire* of university authorities in a number of countries. The accusations abound that 'deconstruction' has spawned an unbridled abuse of academic freedom, a rampant indulgence of the most anarchistic of intellectual energies. For his own part, Derrida has refuted the label of 'nihilism' which has been frequently ascribed to his work and has castigated the 'great professors' and 'representatives of prestigious institutions' who, he claims, have forgotten the principles of academic freedom and have rushed to 'heap insults' on texts of his 'that they obviously have never opened'. In a 1984 address titled 'The Principle of Reason: The University in the Eyes of its Pupils', Derrida responded to professorial denunciations in the above terms and claimed that his own entire strategy was an upholding of the principle of reason against irrationalisms both of a traditional and 'postmodern' kind.[3] In this moreover, he sought to distinguish and rescue 'deconstruction' from the irresponsible fashion he acknowledged it had become in the field of literary criticism, particularly in America.

This latter standpoint would seem to mark a decisive development from the unhindered play of undecidability in Derrida's early work towards a more circumspect and *decision-taking* kind of play in his more recent writings. In the next section we shall review some of the chief features of this development, tracing their contrasts with self-professed postmodernist standpoints. In this review we shall seek to uncover some convincing reasons why education in the current day should, more than ever, be accorded a sovereign, responsible and critical office.

The Playful – Scandalous or Sacred?

George Steiner is one of the more notable of literary figures who have subjected 'deconstruction' to criticism. The provocative title and subtitle of his 1989 book, *Real Presences – Is there anything in what we say?*, carry the suggestion that too many have already answered the question in a negative manner. Accordingly, it soon becomes clear that the internationally fashionable practice of 'deconstruction' becomes a chief target of Steiner's arguments. Derrida is credited by Steiner with an incisiveness that cuts through the aesthetic-philosophical preoccupations of much modern literary theory; preoccupations which Steiner claims becloud, or otherwise fail to detect, the aspirations towards *meaning-fulness*, towards resonances of the divine, which he himself discerns in the human word. (*RP* 119-120) Steiner then proceeds however to charge that the radicalness of Derrida's 'deconstruction' strikes at the very heart of these aspirations:

> The issue is, quite simply, that of the meaning of meaning as it is re-insured by the postulate of the existence of God. 'In the beginning was the Word'. There was no such beginning says deconstruction; only the play of sounds amid the mutations of time. (120)

Continuing in this vein, Steiner describes 'deconstruction' as a 'counter-theology of absence' (*RP* 122), a subversive current which replaces traditional theological accounts with a conception of humankind as a gaming species disporting itself in a sea of nihilism: '*homo ludens*'. (*RP* 124) In this kind of cultural landscape, Steiner maintains, the scope for new interpretations becomes infinite. And he adds that this enlargement of scope removes significance, in any definitive sense, from any and all interpretations. Undecidability reigns supreme where every reading of a text is an *un*reading of other readings, where any sense of indebtedness or deference to a tradition is replaced by an imperative which states that all definitive meanings must be deferred so as to prevent the 'arrest of play' and to allow space for futher possible interpretations. Although this sounds quite bizarre from both conservative and radical standpoints on education, Steiner's critique suggests that it still 'does not entail the abandonment of our reading and study of forms'. If meaning is indeterminate for 'deconstructionists', he declares wryly, it is still 'investigable'. The educational purposes of literary enquiry are therefore not abandoned, but are now cast in a different light. 'The good reader or critic or explicator will aim to make the text *more* difficult to read.'

> He will elicit the strategies which the author has employed, consciously or unconsciously; he will make visible the cunning, the ruses, the displacements between signs and emptiness inherent in the author's game and in the language with which, alone, the game can be played. What all parties must remember is this: the games of meaning cannot be won. No prize of transcendence, no surety, awaits even the most skilful, inspired player. He in fact will be the one in whom the displacements, the deferrals and self-subversions will be the sharpest. (*RP* 126-127)

On this account, the kind of activity sanctioned by 'deconstruction' would be a negation of the very core of the Socratic conception of learning which the foregoing chapters have attempted to elucidate. It would be a dismissal of the claim that, through the discipline of dialogue, our enquiries and researches can disclose to us something decisive, if not definitive, of the truthful, the universal, the enduring; can even bring intimations of that which is beyond our ability to fathom. For 'deconstruction', the insights offered by the suggestion 'the dialogue that we are' – insights which Gadamer develops as a practical philosophical theme from the writings of Heidegger and the poet Hölderlin – get turned on their head. The educational quest characterised by dialogue gets recast as an endless working out of the suggestion that *we aren't anything* other than a play of possibilities, some aesthetically appealing, others less so, but possibilities bereft of any definitive sense of meaning and presided over by the very absence of such meaning.

These are the conclusions to which Steiner's critique of 'deconstruction' points. But is Steiner's account correct? Does 'deconstruction' enthrone the absence of meaning to such an extent that all educational effort becomes a play of 'possibilities', 'performances', 'unreadings' and 'redescriptions', no longer governed by responsibility or reason? There are appraisals of 'deconstruction' which offer contrasting conclusions to those of Steiner, and we shall consider one of the more probing of these shortly, but first, it is worth considering the verdict of Habermas, whose championship of a universal rationality has drawn the fire of postmodernists and whose own work has been one of the most staunch defences of the Enlightenment legacy against postmodernist standpoints. Pressing to its conclusion the infinite scope for novel interpretations which 'deconstruction' opens up, Habermas' judgement is as succinct as it is forceful. Writing on Derrida in his book, *The Philosophical Discourse of Modernity*, Habermas declares: 'The labour of deconstruction lets the refuse heap of interpretations, which it wants to clear away in order to get at the buried foundations, mount even higher.' (*PDM* 183)

But isn't this effort to uncover foundations just the effort that 'deconstruction' wants to expose as an illusion? Isn't the point of the whole 'deconstuction' enterprise one of showing that there are *no* foundations? Habermas gives a kind of 'yes and no' answer to this question, as do some other prominent philosophers who have addressed the challenges posed by postmodernism – like John Caputo, Thomas McCarthy and Richard J. Bernstein. Unlike Steiner, Habermas discerns in Derrida's arguments an avowal of an authority as old as Western tradition itself. In a bold and perceptive appraisal he suggests that the undecidability and the deferral of definitive meaning championed by Derrida's 'deconstructive' thinking have a *religious* ancestry. Like the thinking of the later Heidegger, this 'deconstructive' thinking, according to Habermas, lands at an empty, formula-like avowal of some indeterminate authority. It is, however, not the authority of a Being that has been distorted by beings, but the authority of a no longer holy scripture, of a scripture that is in exile, wandering about, estranged from its own meaning, a scripture that testamentarily documents the absence of the holy. (*PDM* 181)

Pursuing this 'testament' note in Derrida further, Habermas maintains that Derrida's inspirations, 'all denials notwithstanding', owe much to the tradition of Jewish mysticism; a tradition which has been in the margins, if not altogether excluded, by the mainstream of Western civilisation. This tradition, Habermas points out, attests the inexhaustibility of the Torah (the will of God revealed to the chosen people) and the inability of human effort to comprehend God's revelation to Moses on Mount Sinai. Habermas cites a commentary by Gershom Scholem which describes this as 'a mystical revelation, pregnant with infinite meaning, but *without specific meaning*'. (*PDM* 183) The *specific* meaning, and the authority attaching to it, became inseparable from Moses' translation of this revelation into human language. On this view, the authoritative teachings of a religious tradition would be human interpretations of something which in itself trancended everything human. Tracing Derrida's familiarity with the Jewish tradition, Habermas concludes that Derrida's work, far from being any 'New Paganism', 'renews the mystical concept of tradition as an ever *delayed* event of revelation'. (*PDM* 183-84)

In his book, *Radical Hermeneutics*, John Caputo shows himself to be considerably more hospitable to Derrida's 'deconstruction' than are Habermas, McCarthy, or Bernstein. In Caputo's appraisal of 'deconstruction' the case is forcefully argued that 'the whole thing is a work of emancipation, a strategy or praxis of liberation'. More specifically, Caputo explains that 'Deconstruction is an exercise in disruption which displaces whatever tends to settle in place.' (*RH* 193) The complacency and the sense of comfort and security provided by established routines of enquiry are justified targets of Derrida's attacks, according to Caputo, who also goes on to probe the issue of the 'undecidability' of meaning in a more direct way than Derrida himself does. In response to the question 'What is all this undecidability doing?', Caputo claims that it 'keeps our questions astir', that it 'keeps us faithful to the flux', that it 'closes off escape routes' traditionally provided by metaphysics. Caputo presses this line of argument home by pointing to the reversal of traditional hierarchies of knowledge achieved by 'deconstruction'. For instance, where Plato's metaphysics criticised mere opinion (*doxa*), proclaimed the Good as the highest object of knowledge, and enthroned it in a relam of changeless truth, Caputo joins with Derrida in celebrating the overthrow of this order. 'Undecidability consigns us to the *doxa*, wandering two-headed in a maze of differential interweavings, with no footing, on constantly shifting, slipping grounds. It keeps us off balance, in the *ébranler*; the trembling.' (*RH* 188)

Arguments like these abound in Caputo's text, which contains detailed explorations of Derrida's major themes. When taken with Caputo's obvious relish for the Nietzschean elements in Derrida's thought (*RH* 145, 155ff) these kinds of argument prompt the conclusion that not only is Derrida's a philosophical irrationalism or anarchy, but that Caputo shares in this anarchy. Many might be perplexed then to discover that Caputo's most significant answer to the question 'what is all this undecidability doing?' presents a claim with a radically *religious* character. Drawing on the negative theology of the fourteenth century German mystic Meister Eckhart, Caputo argues that 'the soul's relationship to God should be "without why"', that the calculating 'machinery of metaphysics' and 'the mean desires of egoism' should be put away. 'That means', says Caputo, 'that the soul should not act on the basis of demonstrated or even revealed truths *about* God, or for the sake of what it wants to gain *from* God, for these are both "why"s ... and as such treat God as some exterior principle'. So on Caputo's account, the radical absence accomplished by 'deconstruction' makes way for an even more radical presence; one which seems to set aside both truth, as traditionally understood, and the *search* for truth, in favour of a quietist mystical experience, a *letting be* (*Gelassenheit*) in its otherness of that which is other. 'Living without why, with *Gelassenheit*, means seeking nothing exterior or outside – or, better, not seeking at all – but simply letting God's love well up in us and flow through us as an inner principle of life'. (*RH* 265) Here the irreverent play of *différance* yields overwhelmingly to a reverence beyond deference.

Clearly, Caputo goes much farther than Habermas does in tracing religious motifs in 'deconstruction'.[4] Viewed from the different standpoints of either Derrida or Habermas, he also brings it in a direction which has some possibilities that are more than a little problematic. For instance mysticism – as a singular kind of communication with an Other who is absent yet powerfully present – might draw human experience not towards a letting-be of human others, but into certainties of a more captive and ominous kind than metaphysics does. It can become a decisive form of closure which is hostile to the discipline of dialogue in learning. Recall for example the intense acrimony between Bernard of Clairvaux and Peter Abelard considered in Chapter Two. Recall also the mystic Luther's impatience with Erasmus and the sidelining of the interpersonal requirements of Christianity in his vehement denunciation of the peasants.

And there are further appraisals of Derrida's 'deconstruction' which help, like those of Habermas and Caputo, to discern in it something more than the ruinous tendencies identified by critiques such as Steiner's. Two of the more prominent of these appraisals – Thomas McCarthy's and Richard J. Bernstein's – dwell on the political and ethical significance of Derrida's enterprise. McCarthy's essay, 'The Politics of the Ineffable – Derrida's Deconstructionism' (in his *Ideals and Illusions* 1993), gives Derrida's project both a sympathetic and a critical reading. On the sympathetic side, McCarthy sketches Derrida's account of Western 'logocentric' culture, (viz. a culture which confidently makes the metaphysical assumption that there is ultimate meaning to be discovered and then parcelled as learnable truth) and credits him with underlining some of the chief faults of Western rationalism. In particular, McCarthy notes Derrida's emphasis on the 'Western' assumption that experience and reality would properly disclose themselves to a reason which imposed a hierarchical ordering on what it explored, which classified in such a way that marginalised or excluded whatever it identified as not being central, which 'homogonised or colonised in the name of the universal'. (*I&I* 197) McCarthy concludes as follows from this, and also introduces here his own criticism of Derrida's arguments:

> As the bad conscience of an imperialistic logocentrism, deconstruction speaks on behalf of what doesn't fit into our schemes and patiently advocates letting the other be in its otherness. There is undoubtedly something to this reading, but even so, deconstruction can hardly give voice to the excluded other. The wholesale character of its critique of logocentrism deprives it of any language in which to do so. (*I&I* 107-8)

McCarthy emphasises moreover that the tolerance of differences which would seem to be one of the chief political implications of 'deconstruction' 'requires that we inculcate universal principles of tolerance and respect and stabilise institutions that secure rights and impose limits.' (*I&I* 113) Such a political implication presupposes of course that the language in which these principles are voiced and enshrined is a meaningful, a decisive, and a binding language. It is precisely here that McCarthy finds Derrida's philosophy silenced, or to use his own word, 'ineffible'. To engage in constructive argument at all, Derrida would have to rely on presuppositions which he couldn't rationally ground. So whatever promise the ineffible may have for mystical experience, McCarthy claims that it is singularly unpromising for any arena of moral-political action.

Richard J. Bernstein includes two essays on Derrida in his book, *The New Constellation – The Ethical-Political Horizons of Modernity/Postmodernity* (1991). In the first of these essays, 'The Ethical-Political Horizon of Derrida', Bernstein traces a passionate political and ethical note in Derrida's writing but argues that the context needed to see this coherently is that of the 'outsider', that is, the viewpoint of the one who has been excluded and exiled by the mainstream of Western civilisation, and we might also add,

Western education. In this connection Bernstein, like Habermas, calls attention to Derrida's Jewish background. Unlike Habermas, however, who focuses on scriptural motifs of Judaism in Derrida's work, Bernstein focuses on the historical memory of the Jew as the outcast who is condemned to wander homeless.[5] 'Some of Derrida's most moving and passionate prose' writes Bernstein, 'shines forth in his perceptive descriptions of the dynamics of exclusion and his *apologia* for what is exiled'. (*NC* 180) Concentrating on the 'positions' evident in Derrida's later writings rather than on the wholehearted embrace of undecidability evident in his writings of the nineteen sixties and early seventies, Bernstein highlights Derrida's keen awareness that snares and traps await us in taking a position, and points out that Derrida has sought to avoid these while still 'taking a position'. But Bernstein concludes that this valiant effort on Derrida's part remains impotent when it comes to *warranting* the position taken; that the very taking of a position now 'hangs over an abyss'. Bernstein comments:

> Derrida knows all too well ... how a self-deceptive violent dogmatism awaits those for whom *archai* [foundational certainties] do not tremble. But even if we learn this lesson over and over again, we are still left with the unanswered question: *how can we 'warrant' (in any sense of the term) the ethical-political 'positions' we do take*? This is *the* question that Derrida never satisfactorily answers. What is worse, despite the overwhelming evidence of his own moral passion and his willingness and courage in 'taking positions', he seems to call into question the very possibility of 'warranting' ethical-political positions. (*NC* 191)

In his second essay, which is a comparative review of the later work of Habermas and Derrida – 'An Allegory of Modernity/Postmodernity' – Bernstein defends Derrida 's work against charges of relativism and irrationalism and holds that, far from any indifference or nihilism, 'undecidability' for Derrida is what keeps a space open for the kind of decision which lies beyond what Derrida himself calls 'the calculable programme that would destroy all responsibility'. For Derrida, metaphysics would be an example of such a programme, where everthing worthy of question was already decided, or closed. Bernstein cites with appoval Derrida's conclusion that 'there can be no moral or political responsibility without this trial and this passage by way of the undecidable'. (*NC* 222) This 'trial and passage', if it is to be anything other than an abstract notion, must identify some *practices* whereby moral and political responsibility are realised. But this is what Derrida persistently fails (or rather declines) to do and he is faulted for it by Bernstein and McCarthy.

At its most 'responsible' then, 'deconstruction' is not a romp of intellect towards chaos. Rather it is itself a critique of ideology, if by 'ideology' we understand a *universal* tendency of established tradition and institutionalised reason to exclude, to dominate, or to domesticate, the otherness of what is other, whether that be 'otherness' as race, as gender, as culture, as religion, or whatever. In its embrace of the playful moreover, 'deconstruction' (particularly as evidenced by Derrida's later work) does not invoke a carefree, a-moral frolicking for which nothing is sacred. Rather it sets in play an upsetting of the ordinary which calls attention to, or even testifies to, that whereby the sacred may properly come into its own. But beyond such calling attention to, and pointing out the possible exclusions and violence involved in practices which have acquired the stamp of established authority and tradition, 'deconstruction' has little by way of *con*structive suggestion to offer. Its 'ineffibleness' in this regard may on the one hand be seen as a kind of moral-political impotence, or alternatively as clearing the way for that before which all speech that is merely human falls silent. The first of these alternatives confronts educational effort with an impasse. The second may help to break that impasse in the most unexpected ways.

Derrida himself can shed some light on this ambiguity. Notwithstanding the fact that he has been regarded as an advocate *par excellence* of a postmodernist outlook, the radical sense of openness which he persistently defends is itself a kind of unending search. In a 1981 interview with Richard Kearney (*Dialogues with Contemporary Continental Thinkers*), Derrida acknowledged that his stance was critical towards criteria of absoluteness provided by philosophical notions like *telos* (aim, meaningful end), or theological-prophetic ones like *eschaton* (the announcement of the coming reign of God). 'But that does not mean', he declared, 'that I dismiss all forms of Messianic or prophetic eschatology.' He added moreover: 'I think that all genuine questioning is summoned by a certain kind of eschatology.' (*Dialogues* 119) These and further similar remarks, together with the later Derrida's sustained attention to the 'principle of reason' in the Enlightenment legacy, place his work at a distinct remove from self-professed postmodernists like Lyotard and Rorty, and still give the deferential an abiding place within the play of *différance*. What is distinctive in postmodernist standpoints, by contrast, is that for these the notion of an unending search has become *passé*, just as much as have the concerns traditionally marked by 'metaphysics', 'epistemology' and 'truth'. If Derrida's reluctance to embrace any criterion of universality makes his acknowledgement of the principle of reason 'hover over an abyss', postmodernist standpoints have already abandoned any appeal of reason to the universal, in favour of what is most acceptable locally (Rorty), or what is currently seen to win acclaim for itself because of its effectiveness in performance (Lyotard).

Communicative Reason and Discourse Ethics

In the light of this it is not surprising that such a stalwart defender of the Enlightenment legacy as Habermas should view postmodernism not merely as a bankrupt ethical and political philosophy, but as a conformist mentality which declines the challenge of 'connecting our convictions with a transcending validity claim which goes beyond merely local contexts'. Habermas insists on the importance of a distinction that Rorty wants to abandon – that 'between valid and socially acceptable views, between good arguments and those which are merely acceptable for a certain audience at a certain time'. (*Habermas and Modernity* 193-4) Mindful of postmodernist objections – under Nietzsche's inspiration – that practices of dialogue are a self-deceptive form of consensualism which conceal the play of power and domination in human relations, Habermas' later philosophy has put forward a conception of *communicative* reason (as distinct from instrumental, or technicist reason), the goal of which is to elucidate the logic of action which is oriented towards reaching undistorted mutual understanding.

In the opening essay in his book, *Communication and the Evolution of Society*, Habermas identifies four features of a 'universal pragmatics' of speech; in other words, presupposed requirements which must be present in any serious attempt to communicate without distortion. These four requirements are:

(a) *comprehensibility* (that the articulations of each are understandable in the language being used);

(b) *truth* (that what is articulated corresponds to what is the case, according to the best available criteria of evidence);

(c) *truthfulness* (that each participant remains sincere in making and responding to contributions);

(d) *rightness* (that the contribution of each is in accord with the norms of moral rightness held by each). (*CES* 3)

The point here is not that these four features will guarantee the reaching of agreement, but rather that any serious effort to seek a mutual understanding must proceed from requirements such as these. That is to say, they are necessarily embodied, consciously or otherwise, in any genuine attempt to reach such an understanding. By making these features explicit and then exploring them in detail, Habermas marks the transition from a philosophy which stops short at critique to one which includes not only a constructive practical dimension, but which also incorporates some substantive virtues in the form of procedural requirements.

In Habermas' two-volume book, *The Theory of Communicative Action*, this detailed exploration is followed through into what is probably modern philosophy's most comprehensive analysis of human communication. Here he takes considerable pains to clarify a crucial distinction. This is a distinction between validity claims which respect the four requirements just mentioned, and on the other hand, those claims embodied in less transparent kinds of communication.These latter would include any acts of communication which were less than attentive to the merits of the claims they put forward, or which sought to inflate or otherwise conceal the real nature of these merits. Validity claims *announce* themselves as articulations which *must be overtly redeemed* in any situation of communicative action and this distinguishes them from any articulations or pronouncements which seek to make themselves effective through manipulation, coercion or violence, whether overt or covert.[6]

Habermas has added a further dimension to his theory of communicative action with the 'discourse ethics' he introduces as a response to Alasdair MacIntyre's claim 'that the Enlightenment's project of establishing a secular morality free of metaphysical and religious assumptions had failed.'[7] The extended essay under the title 'Discourse Ethics' and those that accompany it in *Moral Consciousness and Communicative Action* (1983 German text, 1990 English) comprise a concentrated effort by Habermas to defend the principle of universality in moral-political argument. He does this by relating the principle of universality to *practices* of argumentation and justification. In this vein he proposes: 'As long as moral philosophy concerns itself with clarifying the everyday intuitions into which we are socialised, it must be able to adopt, at least virtually, the attitude of someone who participates in the communicative practice of everyday life'. (*MCCA* 48) The principle of 'discourse ethics' Habermas then states as follows: 'Only those norms can claim to be valid that meet (or could meet) with the approval of all affected in their capacity as participants in a practical discourse'.

(*MCCA* 66) This principle is complementary to, but also distinct from, the principle of universalisation, which Habermas sets as the criterion that every valid norm must fulfill:

> All affected (by the norm) can accept the consequences and the side effects its *general* observance can be anticipated to have for the satisfaction of *everyone's* interests (and these consequences are preferred to those of known alternative possibilities for regulation). (*MCCA* 65)

Of course Habermas acknowledges that the requirements of communicative action and 'discourse ethics' are an ideal, and that they may be more often honoured in their breach than in their observance. Nevertheless they represent for him the most promising possibilities provided by the Enlightenment legacy for responding to the challenges posed by the radical pluralism which now constitutes most of the cultures of Western civilisation. Habermas rightly points out that these are challenges which the different variants of postmodernism either decline or evade. Equally important, the significance of his arguments for the conduct of learning can be seen in the fact that they draw attention to a form of action which embodies a continual commitment to open-ended enquiry and which cultivates an abiding disposition towards critical dialogue.

But as regards practice, there now comes a hesitant note in Habermas' later philosophy. The hesitancy is all the more strange when we consider that the entire Marxist tradition in philosophy has been that of a philosophy with practical intent, a philosophy with a commitment to bringing about change in society and its institutions. In the closing section of his essay, 'Morality and Ethical Life',[8] Habermas draws the attention of his readers to the limitations of the discourse ethics which he has championed. One of the questions he raises here is 'whether it is reasonable to hope that the insights of a universalist morality are susceptible to translation into practice'.[9] Acknowledging that what he has to say on this question may come as a disappointment, he sees it as incumbent on moral enquiry to explain and ground the moral point of view in some universalist ethic. And, despite his earlier acknowledgement that moral philosophy must concern itself with 'clarifying the everyday intuitions into which we are socialised', he sees this explaining and grounding as an essentially *theoretical* task.

But it must be argued against Habermas here that it is inescapably the case that the insights of a universalist morality arise in the first instance from practice itself, or from the experienced worlds ('lifeworlds') of those who hold these insights. In this connection, there is a keen insight in MacIntyre's arguments on the secularisation of morality by the Enlightenment; arguments which Habemas views as hostile to his own work. Consider, for instance, MacIntyre's claim that judgements issuing from the ostensibly autonomous sphere of morality – and he has Kant in mind in particular – are in fact 'linguistic survivals from the practices of classical theism which have lost the context provided by these practices'. (*After Virtue* 60) That is to say, vestiges of the practices of classical theism live on in a secularised form in the dispositions *and* the arguments of the modern Kantian moralist. Or, more precisely, the morality proposed by the Kantian moralist wants to preserve and refine some essentials of the substantive orientation of the traditional theistic morality, but to replace its particularist character and its teleological programme with a universal formula. This kind of insight seems in fact to underlie, consciously or not, Habermas' acknowledgement of the moral significance of 'the everyday intuitions into which we are socialised'. It seems to be more consciously present in his arguments on 'lifeworld' knowledge, or 'pre-reflexive', 'background' knowledge in *The Theory of Communicative Action*. There he describes 'lifeworld knowledge' as having the three following remarkable features:

> It is an *implicit* knowledge that cannot be represented in a finite number of propositions; it is a *holistically structured* knowledge, the basic elements of which intrinsically define one another; and it is a knowledge that *does not stand at our disposition*, inasmuch as we cannot make it conscious and place it in doubt as we please. (*TCA* I, 336)

What this amounts to is that the distinction between concrete ethical life on the one hand – which is invariably pervaded by the quality of our upbringing and everyday experience – and, on the other hand, the claims of rational critique and moral theory, is a distinction which distorts our understanding of human understanding itself. So to argue, as Habermas does in the following passage, seems to me to be to take a wrong turn:

> What moral *theory* can and should be trusted to do, is to clarify the universal core of our moral intuitions and thereby to refute value scepticism. What it cannot do is make any kind of substantive contribution. (*MCCA* 211)

This passage, with its heavy emphasis on a circumscribed domain of rationality for theory, seems to overlook the fact that the moral intuitions theory needs for its clarification activities, are themselves virtues (and indeed vices) which enter human character by way of tradition; virtues and vices moreover, which – as Gadamer has shown – invariably make human sensibility and outlook *pre*-disposed in one way or another. Only by an oversight of this kind can there arise the task which Habermas envisages for moral theory – that of an autonomous court of purely procedural enlightenment, for which the 'intuitions of everyday life' are available for inspection in an unbiased rational manner. There is a rationalist turn here which tends to obscure the inescapable part played by tradition in all human experience. It is also a turn which seems to push Habermas' philosophy, against the thrust of much of his work, into a kind of scientism which he himself criticised from his *Knowledge and Human Interests* onwards.[10] By contrast, I would maintain that insofar as there *can* be such a court of reason, it is necessarily a court of *rationality in action,* of 'impure' rather than pure reason. So its procedures themselves always owe something to the background perspectives and orientations of its participants and its autonomy in this sense is never more than partial. Its inspirations and judgements therefore remain in some inescapable sense indebted to, or encumbered by, substantive pre-judgements of a moral-practical character. Such pre-judgements can overcome much of their sectional or blinkered character however, and can thus seek to be *candidates in practice* for universal worthiness – as I attempted to show in making explicit the *virtues* of teaching and learning in Chapter Seven.[11]

Let us now draw together some conclusions from the present chapter with a few observations on our general theme. This chapter has sought to show that the effort to articulate virtues of teaching and learning, and to identify them as candidates for a practical action which is defensible on universal grounds, is a practical effort, worthy of the sustained attentions of teachers and learners. It does not represent any kind of latter day programme for sainthood any more than it represents any kind of return to a Platonist metaphysics. We have considered here the kind of criticisms brought by postmodernist standpoints against the kind of educational practice whose claims to sovereignty rest not only on the promise of the discipline of dialogue in enquiry, but also on the *universal defensibility* of that discipline. During the course of this review a distinction was made between the strictly posmodernist standpoint of thinkers like Lyotard and Rorty on the one hand, and on the other, the more ambiguous cultural movement inspired by the work of Derrida and widely pursued as the controversial practice of 'deconstruction'. While postmodernist approaches abandon any concern with learning as a search for truth, and happily embrace both the creed of 'performativity' and an appetite for what is aesthetically novel, this combination has not drawn anything like the fire which 'deconstruction' has. This is so despite Derrida's efforts to distance the earnestness of his enterprise from his more fashion-conscious followers in a few continents. This is so secondly, despite the fact that most of the major educational administrations in the Western world have followed the postmodernist example in relegating the search for truth in favour of goals such as performance and effectiveness ('performance indicators' *become* the primary educational goals). Thirdly, and even more ironically, this is so despite the fact that it is degenerate variants of 'deconstruction', particularly the mercurial fashions of postmodernist scholarship, that have brought the seminal spirit of the playful into disrepute in the eyes of educational authorities.

What results from this is the danger of a double eclipse. Firstly, the more promising possibilities of the Enlightenment heritage, particularly the conception of learning as a critical dialogue which seeks to uncover personal identity in the context of an active solidarity (Gadamer, Habermas, Ricoeur, Popper and others) tends to suffer the same fate as the Socratic conception of learning did at the hands of Platonism. Secondly, those metaphysical conceptions of learning which Platonism itself helped to make central to Western traditions of education fall victim to a similar fate. Hand in hand with this double eclipse the darker side of the Enlightenment legacy – its tendency towards total rationalisation – commends itself anew in the affairs of life more generally. It renders more pervasive and more plausible a technicist mentality which increasingly furnishes thought and sensibility with an acceptable picture of life itself as a sphere of self-seeking and manipulative relations. And where both a commitment to dialogue and a belief in metaphysics have been discarded, motives associated with power now achieve a widespread acceptability and a new importance in the play of cultural influences. Insofar as the double eclipse described here becomes a cultural and political reality, modernity's championship of reason in human affairs is undermined. Thus in a technological version of the Nietzscheanism we first examined in Chapter Five, life itself becomes conceived for all practical purposes as a social market, where the more powerful performances – of self, of product, of economy – are what command the highest acclaim, and the highest price.

In the international educational reforms of the last two decades variants of this mentality have made considerable strides and have exerted a forceful influence on the conduct of public education in more than a few Western countries. We can discern here a new custodianship of learning, which is different in inspiration from, but scarcely less ambitious than, that ancient and medieval custodianship we examined in Part One of this book. Notwithstanding the continuing concern of Western countries with reforms to education, these new ambitions are far from being fully realised. Indeed in some countries some of the excesses associated with the zeal for competitive individualism have given policy-makers pause for thought.[12] Bearing these developments in mind, the final chapter will address the priorities of educational policy and will attempt to show in outline the promise and authority these priorities receive when they take their primary character from the kinds of argument we have been advancing up to this point.

Notes:

1. Richard J. Bernstein suggests that Habermas failed to distinguish adequately between these two conceptions of rational reflection in *Knowledge and Human Interests* – between the conditions of possibility for pure (theoretical) reason on the one hand and the normatively laden employment of practical reason on the other. See Bernstein's Introduction to *Habermas and Modernity*, R.J. Bernstein (ed.) (Cambridge: Polity Press, in association with Basil Blackwell, Oxford) p. 10. In fact what is called for here is the abandonment of the Kantian concept of 'pure' reason and an acknowledgement of the point that all human reason is already coloured by outlooks, customs, traditions, ideologies, etc. which may be less or more explicit. Habermas seems to acknowledge this in his later work, although he retains (rightfully in my view) the Kantian idea that the conditions for the employment of reason can claim universality among humankind.

2. Heidegger uses a variety of poetic metaphors in his prose to describe truth as an event of illumination (*Lichtung*). In the same vein he has also written some striking short philosophical poems. Some of these convey more memorably than do prose metaphors, the experience of the 'thinking of being' which his later philosophy attempts to elucidate. The following opening lines from one of these poems are a good example:

> When through a rent in the rain-clouded
> sky a ray of sun suddenly glides
> over the gloom of the meadows . . . .
> We never come to thoughts. They come
> to us.

See 'The Thinker as Poet', 'The Origin of the Work of Art' and the other essays in the collection of Heidegger's later writings published as *Poetry,*

Language, Thought translated and introduced by Albert Hofstadter (New York: Harper and Row, 1971).

3. For Derrida's refutation of the label 'nihilism' see his 1981 interview with Richard Kearney in *Dialogues with Contemporary Continental Thinkers* (Manchester University Press, 1984) p.124. For his response to professorial denunciations see the text of his address, 'The Principle of Reason: The University in the Eyes of its Pupils', published in *Diacritics*, Vol.XIX, 1984, pp.3-20.

4. It is quite unclear, however, how this kind of religious mysticisism can be reconciled with Caputo's embrace of Nietzsche's philosophy, whose central tenet – 'the will to power'– vehemently repudiates a religion which preaches anything like 'letting God's love well up in us'. It is also unclear how either Caputo's mysticism, or any kind of philosophy with strong Nietzschean roots, can be reconciled with Caputo's 'ethics of dissemination' which 'is directed at constellations of power, centres of control and manipulation, which systematically dominate, regulate, exclude'. (*RH* 260).

5. Both Habermas and Bernstein call attention to studies by Susan Handelman which support the argument that Derrida's writings are influenced by the cultural memory of Jew as outsider. Habermas refers to a paper 'Jacques Derrida and the Heretic Hermeneutic' in M. Krapnik (ed.) *Displacement, Derrida and After* (Bloomington: 1983). Bernstein refers to Handleman's book *The Slayers of Moses* (Albany: The State University of NewYork Press, 1982).

6. See Habermas' *The Theory of Communicative Action*, Volume One, trans. Thomas McCarthy (Boston: Beacon Press, 1984), in particular Chapter III. See also his essay, 'What is Universal Pragmatics' in *Communication and the Evolution of Society*, translated by Thomas McCarthy, (Boston: Beacon Press, 1979).

7. See Habermas' essay, 'Discourse Ethics: Notes on a Program of Philosophical Justification' in his *Moral Consciousness and Communicative Action*, translated by Christian Lenhardt and Shierry Weber Nicholson (Cambridge: Polity Press, in association with Basil Blackwell, Oxford, 1990).

8. 'Morality and Ethical Life: Does Hegel's Critique of Kant apply to Discourse Ethics?', in *Moral Consciousness and Communicative Action*, pp.195-215.

9. ibid., p.210.

10. Joseph Dunne pursues this kind of criticism of Habermas in a sympathetic yet incisive way in his book, *Back to the Rough Ground – 'Phronesis' and 'Techne' in Modern Philosophy and in Aristotle* (Notre Dame & London: University of Notre Dame Press, 1993) pp.216-226. See also Habermas' *Knowledge and Human Interests* translated by Jeremy J. Shapiro (London: Heinemann 1972), particularly Chapter 11. The original German text was published in 1968.

11. An argument along somewhat parallel lines, including its implications for students of non-Western ethnic background in Western schools, is advanced by Nigel Blake in an article entitled 'Modernity and Cultural Pluralism' in *Journal of Philosophy of Education* Vol.26, No.1, 1992, pp39-50.

Defending the universal character of the kind of discourse which Habermas develops from the modernising tendencies of the Enlightenment heritage, Blake argues that this is not just different from traditional forms of discourse. He concludes that 'it could be acknowledged by any member of any culture as a positive human achievement'. p.46.

12. For instance, in the Republic of Ireland, a Government Green Paper on education, *Education for a Changing World* (issued in 1992), betrayed more than a little admiration for the attitude of competitive individualism. In the national debate which followed the Paper's publication it was pointed out by respondents of widely different standpoints that the Paper's uncritical commendations of individualism and 'enterprise culture' were unacceptable, and were incompatibible with the Paper's declared commitment to disadvantaged groups. Very many of the formal responses to the Green Paper showed a keen awareness of the many unhappy consequences of education reforms in England and Wales and elsewhere since the late nineteen eighties. The Goverment's White Paper, *Charting our Education Future* (issued in 1995), includes an explicit rationale for policy which the Green Paper lacked and which is quite different in tenor from the Green Paper's championship of competitive individualism.

CHAPTER TEN

Educational Policy and the Quality of Learning

Introduction

The waves of reform to schooling undertaken in many Western countries within the last two decades have been prompted primarily by a concern for quality. In the early nineteen eighties a Conservative government in Britain indicated its dissatisfaction with what it took to be the consequences of the socialist educational policies of the sixties and seventies. In particular it criticised what it perceived as a widespread decline in standards and it associated this with the drive towards equality of educational opportunity of the comprehensive school movement, but also with what it understood as a socialist and progressive creed embraced by newly qualified teachers. Not surprisingly then, one of that government's early publications on education was a report issued in 1983 called *Teaching Quality*, and this identified teacher education as a priority area for reform. More significantly, however, as educational reform became a central issue in Britain during the eighties it also became clear that control of the reforms would not be left in the hands of educational institutions themselves, but would increasingly be assumed by the government.[1]

In 1983 a number of reports sounding a note of alarm on the quality of schooling appeared in the United States, the most notable of which was *A Nation at Risk – The imperative for educational reform*. A similar theme was evident here. Schools and colleges could not be left to reform themselves. If reforms were to be effective, strong legislative measures would have to be imposed and compliance with these would have to be enforced. The state therefore would have to intervene directly in matters which were previously left to the professional discretion of teachers and school authorities.[2]

In 1989 the OECD reviewed educational reforms in a number of countries and published its findings in a book called *Schools and Quality – an International Report*. This contained little that was critical of the interventionist policies of governments but it also attempted to regain a sphere of influence for teachers and school managements. In outlining the reasons for concern about quality, moreover, it gave particular importance to 'economic imperatives' and social context, but little or none to cultural traditions. By 1991, an OECD Report on educational policy in Ireland was able to speak, without any evident sense of criticism, of the international swing 'towards instrumental and utilitarian values', and indeed to identify this trend with preparing young people for 'effective social participation'.[3]

The first section of this chapter will examine some consequences of this continuing trend of policy, particularly those flowing from a conception of quality influenced more by market considerations than by educational ones. The second section will then explore the claims of the economic in a way which seeks to place these in harmony with the more defensible concerns of learning. Arising from this, the third section will examine how a revised conception of liberal education might inform decisions relating to balance in the curriculum, and promote in schools the kind of practice explored in this book. The final section will then review briefly how the question of balance becomes again lopsided if a technological mentality achieves primacy in place of the metaphysical-custodial attitudes which were once dominant in Western traditions of learning. The Epilogue will then review in summary a number of important current policy questions and will outline the tenor of an educational policy that is inspired by a proper appreciation of the sovereignty of learning.

Market Conceptions of Quality

In a jointly authored book *Total Quality Management and the School* (1993) Stephen Murgatroyd and Colin Morgan recommend to decision makers in education an approach called Total Quality Management ('TQM'). This is an approach which has aroused much interest internationally in the effort to improve quality in manufacturing and service industries. Its educational variant, proposed by Murgatroyd and Morgan, focuses on four themes. Firstly, it conceives of quality as arising from relationships between 'customers and suppliers'. Secondly, it regards relationships as processes to be managed and concentrates on improvements which can be made in these processes. Thirdly, it holds that those best able to make improvements in a process are 'those nearest to the customer for that process'. Fourthly, it maintains that the strategy a school operates from involves choices, and that these must be based in visionary leadership.(pp.x-xii)

The last two of these features identify a commendable combination which the exercise of professional discretion seeks: namely, a visionary leadership which is yet capable of delegating authority and responsibility. In this sense, what are being claimed as features of a new approach with a fashionable label – 'TQM' – are in fact longstanding features of good practice itself. But the first two features are more problematic. Describing pupils and their parents as 'customers' may have a moral and legal point, in reminding us that a culpable failure by teachers or schools in discharging their responsibilities should entitle parents and pupils to formal measures of redress. Acknowledging these entitlements however does not warrant the market image as an appropriate one to describe what quality and accountability involve in education. The designations 'supplier' and 'customer' view the teacher's efforts as a commodity to be 'delivered', and tend to push the cultural core of teachers' work into the background. This calls to mind Michael Apple's critique of the 'commodification' of culture we considered in Chapter Eight. More particularly, the market imagery and vocabulary fail to catch the essential character of the relations between teachers and pupils which we examined in Chapter Seven. They trivialise, and even disfigure the interplay between personal identity and the voices of cultural tradition; an interplay which we explored in that chapter as a kind of courtship of sensibility.

Similarly, describing this relationship (essentially a personal one of trust) as a 'process' to be 'managed', gives priority to the wrong kind of intercourse, namely a manipulative as distinct from a properly communicative form of action. Pursuing this distinction a little further, it must be emphasised that both pupils and their parents are entitled to be convinced by the most honest means possible of the merits that a school, or a particular field of study, has to offer. This convincing must be done from the teacher's convictions; convictions which spring from a defensible *educational* vision, not from a leadership which is visionary mainly because it can discern its customers' tastes and fashion its product range accordingly. In other words, where convincing has to be done, it must be done through the sincere and sustained efforts of teachers, not through crafty advertising or strategies of disinformation. None of this is to suggest that approaches which have been fruitful in the field of industry and commerce have no application in the field of education. It is rather to say that before any such approaches are applied, the integrity of the field in question – what is unique to the benefits and relationships characteristic of that field – must be respected.

Yet the uncritical application of 'industry analysis' to education has been one of the more conspicuous tendencies in educational policy and discourse internationally in recent years.[4] This tendency frequently fails not only to respect the integrity of education, but even to acknowledge it. This is particularly evident in Murgatroyd's and Morgan's book (pp.1-3), which is characteristic of a newly ascendant genre. In this genre, the primary approach to quality is a market-inspired managerialism; a mentality which views practice itself, in any given field, not as the accountable exercise of discretionary judgement, but as *a resource to be managed*. Far from any sovereignty, this mentality envisages a subordinate, even servile role for the enterprise of teaching and learning. For instance, in the opening page of their first chapter Murgatroyd and Morgan review recent international developments in schooling and conclude that 'the underlying dynamic is that schooling is shifting from a public service driven by professionals towards a market-driven service, fuelled by purchasers and consumers'. And of course it must be agreed that this trend has been much in evidence in many Western countries. Unlike the radical critics we considered in Chapter Eight, however, Murgatroyd and Morgan are happy that education should acquiesce in this state of affairs. They dispose of the radical critics' arguments with the following judgement:

> These arguments are ideologically grounded and need to be understood as representing a set of ideological propositions about the nature of schooling, the role of the state in the management of social policy and the relationship between people and capital ... We are not concerned here with such matters; this book is not intended to discuss the ideology of schooling, but to sensitise and help those now leading primary and secondary schools understand and respond to new contexts that governments have legislated. In general, across the world, such legislation has introduced elements of the marketplace so that schools now operate in what might better be termed a modified marketplace. (p.2)

A number of points call for attention here, as they bear directly on how the issue of quality in education is to be understood. Firstly, the attribution of 'ideological' motives to the radical critics carries pejorative connotations. More frankly, is suggests that the accounts of these critics are 'biased'. The disclaimer of ideological intent on their own part which follows this canvasses the reader to the view that what Murgatroyd and Morgan are offering is something more evenhanded or balanced than what they have just dismissed. This impression of non-ideological reasonableness is urged further upon the reader by the apparent modesty of the authors' claim that their aim is to help educational leaders to cope with new challenges in new circumstances. But there is something questionable about the entire thrust of Murgatroyd's and Morgan's arguments here. Consider, for instance, the authors' claim that they are not concerned with ideological matters. While radical critics such as Bowles & Gintis, Apple, Aronowitz & Giroux are prepared to make explicit the propositions which inform their critiques, Murgatroyd and Morgan fail to acknowledge any ideological cast in their own arguments. They seem especially to be ignorant of the point we explored earlier (particularly in the second section of Chapter Seven) that every viewpoint is significantly coloured by presuppositions which have already taken root in our outlooks, and which remain at their most influential when we confidently believe our own insights and arguments to be unencumbered by matters ideological .

Secondly, this failure cannot be counted merely as an omission. Rather it makes Murgatroyd's and Morgan's case a tendentious one. Although it sees itself as a non-ideological document providing schools with fruitful ideas for management, it is clear from the arguments of *Total Quality Management and the School* that its authors are quite happy to promote a conception of education as a customer-supplier relationship, governed primarily by the competitive practices of a market economy. A critical inspection of their comments on 'the quality revolution' reveals this clearly, as does the bright future they seek to map out for 'customer-driven' quality. (pp.50-56)

Thirdly, the priority given to 'customer-driven' conceptions of quality also betrays an attitude which assumes that education as a human undertaking has no *intrinsic* quality; that it lacks anything like a coherent rationale *within itself* – within its own best traditions and practices. This assumption takes it for granted that a system of schools and colleges is first and foremost an enterprise on which the more articulate or powerful interests in society ('stakeholders', 'customers') must stamp their own designs. These designs thus establish the context within which quality in education is to be understood and pursued.

Fourthly, and arising from the previous point, the conception of quality commended in Murgatroyd's and Morgan's book, despite its emphasis on vision, is quite lacking in a vision that is distinctively and defensibly an *educational* one. In defining 'quality', special reference is made to 'quality assurance', 'contract conformance' and 'customer-driven quality' (pp.45ff), as if these encapsulate the concept of quality itself. No reference is made to the setting of high standards for oneself from an *educational* vision, as distinct from a 'customer-driven' one. Similarly absent is any consideration of the discipline of self-evaluation, through which the *quality* which is *intrinsic* to such standards might be articulated and shared, monitored and advanced. More obviously, the preoccupation with 'performance', 'empowerment', 'expectations of stakeholders' and customer-driven quality, bypasses the point that quality in education is essentially a question of the *quality of the pupils' encounters* with the different voices of cultural tradition which seek to address and engage the pupils. Issues which are likewise central to quality in education, such as the recurrent manifestations of emergent identity, the fresh discovery of abilities and limitations, the epiphanies of learning itself, are passed over in silence. Even where 'trust' and 'commitment to shared goals' are recommend (pp.66ff) little is said about the specific character of these goals, or about what would make them worthy candidates for the trust and commitment of teachers.

It is difficult to avoid the conclusion that the logic of the kind of conception of quality we have just been considering is a logic of conquest and colonisation where the purposes of teaching and learning are concerned. The nature and scope of the decisions now allowed to those who have made education their occupational commitment become restricted to the kinds of questions which remain after the more essential questions have already been decided by somebody else. Such essential questions have featured prominently in this book from the opening pages onwards and an attempt has been made in the previous chapters to answer them in universal, if provisional terms. These have included questions such as: What are the central purposes of learning? What distinguishes purposes that are central from ones that are ancillary? How can they be defended from charges of arbitrariness, including cultural arbitrariness? How do these purposes differ from the purposes of fields such as business, law, social welfare? What practices are most conducive to pursuing the purposes of learning? What practices are inimical to this pursuit? Aren't the intrinsic purposes of learning and their pursuit through schooling entitled to public acknowledgement and an accountable measure of sovereignty? The list here is only a partial one but it should be enough to show that if market forces are permitted by legislation to determine the answers to questions like these, then the custodianship of learning assumed in the past by bodies such as church and state yields in effect to a custodianship of a more mercenary kind; a custodianship in which the modern democratic state becomes both author and accomplice.

Without a well-informed and clear commitment on the part of policy-makers to the intrinsic benefits of education and to the integrity of the educational enterprise itself, a competing plurality of voices finds little of substance to agree on and this inconclusiveness tends to yield to something more ominous. The legitimate concern for quality all too easily becomes a preoccupation with a concept of effectiveness which is similar in essentials to the kind of 'performativity' described in Lyotard's 'report' on the contemporary state of knowledge. Recall that Lyotard not only *describes* 'performativity' as the most conspicous criterion of worthiness of human endeavour in contemporary technological societies. While recognising its propensities towards 'brutality and terror' he also *champions* performativity, in a somewhat ambivalent way, as one of the only standards of *justice* in a 'postmodern' world – i.e. a world which he believes to be bereft of anything defensible on either traditional or universal grounds. (*PMC* 63-67) In fact Lyotard's efforts have done a considerable service in identifying something which is the unacknowledged darker side of the new genre of which Murgatroyd and Morgan are optimistic, if not the most circumspect exponents. Lyotard articulates a conception of justice which is the logical outcome of a mentality that denies primacy to moral or substantive considerations, that fails to acknowledge the goods and practices proper to different fields of human endeavour, and that identifies quality more generically with what the verdict of the market judges to be an impressive performance. Recognising moreover the close connection between 'performativity' and motives of power, Lyotard summarises the postmodernist conception of justice as follows:

> a request (that is, a form of prescription) gains nothing in legitimacy by being based on the hardship of an unmet need. Rights do not flow from hardship, but from the fact that the alleviation of hardship improves the system's performance. (*PMC* 62-63)

This conception of justice involves a harnessing of moral energies to cultural norms which have been recast by the imperatives of profit and power. Where the purposes of learning are concerned, it represents more a capitulation of moral agency than a mere loss of sovereignty. That is, it constitutes an effective surrender of the authorship of these purposes themselves. These consequences are rarely made explicit in the writings or the discourse of those who advocate the merits of a market approach to education, or to social policy. If one acknowledges these points, it might still be asked if my own argument against granting primacy to market considerations disregards the place of commercial, economic and vocational considerations in the conduct of teaching and learning. The answer is that it does not, but it raises anew the question of what that place *is* in an educational philosophy which is both practical and defensible. This question is of first importance for the formulation of educational policy and will be addressed in the next section.

Policy, Practice and the Affirmations of Ordinary Life

Although economists, sociologists and planners frequently draw a sharp distinction between private and public purposes in education, it is part of my case that this distinction frequently gives rise to a faulty, or divisive rationale for the consideration of educational policy. The rationale is both incomplete and divisive insofar as it is informed primarily by economic and societal perspectives on educational policy, to the neglect of considerations which are themselves *educational* before they are anything else. To make this criticism is not, however, to discredit the validity of the point that educational policy contains dimensions of economic and social policy. Rather it is to point out that when economic and societal considerations are accorded first priority, as they frequently are in the discourse of educational policy internationally, the cultural and personal purposes of education tend to become an afterthought. On the other hand, a preoccupation with the cultural and personal purposes of learning can neglect the valid concerns of economy and society which must be taken into account when educational policy is being formulated. But when viewed as a practice with its own integrity, education *includes* attention to the social and the economic-vocational aspects of human experience. And these aspects of experience are properly engaged through the learner's curricular and extra-curricular encounters. Where educational policy is concerned, both at national and at school level, it is of first importance then to ensure that what is provided for learners through such encounters is sufficiently high in quality and is sufficiently representative of the traditional and newer fields of knowledge and learning.

But this has rarely enough been satisfactorily the case, primarily because the kind of considerations I have just been referring to here are so often overshadowed by the kind of policy rationale which neglects the integrity of the educational enterprise and views the enterprise itself *primarily* as a strategic instrument of economic and social policy. This kind of faulty rationale has to be ovecome if we are clearly to understand the harmony which should properly be present in educational experience itself between the economic, the social and other purposes of learning. Let us attempt therefore to advance this clarity in the following pages.

The faulty rationale just mentioned has had two main variants, Marxist variants on the one hand and variants inspired by a 'market' mentality on the other. In outline, Marxist variants charge that schooling reproduces the skills, attitudes and dispositions which serve the interests of capitalist society and which maintain hierarchical divisions between social classes. Critiques of this kind, as we have seen in Chapter Eight, frequently employ a concept of 'cultural capital' to explain that those who are in already in possession of substantial gains from learning and its accompaniments are favourably placed to better their own position, but to the systematic detriment of those who are less favourably circumstanced.

The free market rationale is unquestionably the more powerful in Western countries at present and its influences must be examined in any appraisal of contemporary educational policy. This rationale still holds with Adam Smith's view that the best interests of the entrepreneur are also in effect the best interests of society as a whole. To this outlook however it has added some novel features. One of these is that a key responsibility of schooling is to produce as many entrepreneurs as possible and to furnish all students with attitudes which are conducive to entrepreneurship. Another feature it has added is an international dimension. In this perspective the educational enterprise is uged to undertake a central part in producing the kinds of ideas, expertise, technologies, marketing skills and market research, which will give one or other of the major trading blocks of the economically advanced world – America, or Europe, or Japan – the means of outperforming its competitors. The 'market' perspective employs a concept which plays as strategic a part in its designs as the 'cultural capital' concept plays in the Marxist perspective. This is the concept of 'human resource management'. Of course 'human resource management' can be seen as a commiting of resources to the welfare and development of people, in institutions which are too large for staff development to take place in an informal kind of manner. But it can also be seen as one of the more manifest expressions of the managerialism referred to in the previous section. The less benign, but arguably the more influential, significance of this concept for education lies in its conception of human imagination and creativity as a renewable raw-material – to be classified according to its potential, certificated according to its quality, indexed according to its performance, and to be harnessed to the twin imperatives of economic prowess and technological innovation.[5]

In addition to neglecting the integrity of the educational enterprise, both the Marxist and market orientations for educational policy also misconstrue the *educational significance* of that which they push to the fore: namely the claims of productive endeavour, of making and manufacture, of daily work and exchange, and of the human relations and commitments arising from these pursuits. The educational significance of these spheres of action lies not in subordinating them to a political programme, whether Marxist, capitalist, or other in origin. It lies rather in recognising here everyday practices which aim at the achievement of merits that are intrinsic to the practices themselves, just as the practices also admit of shortcomings, or vices, in pursuit of such merits. In other words, we must acknowledge here human goods residing in practices which constitute what Charles Taylor has called 'the affirmations of ordinary life'. (*SoS* Part III) This is particularly so when these practices are considered as learning practices, which must be the case if they are to be counted among the activities proper to schooling. In this way the inclusion in schooling of practices associated with economic, productive, homemaking, and similar features of daily living, strengthens rather than detracts from the case for the sovereignty of learning. To bring out clearly the implications of this for policy-making in education, we need to explore a little more closely 'the affirmations of ordinary life' and to uncover their merits in a way which renders these less vulnerable to mercenary impulses.

In the first chapter we identified a Greek and a Roman contribution to the eclipse of the Socratic. It was the former contribution which played the stronger part in excluding from Western traditions of learning those pursuits which Greek philosophy considered mundane and which Medieval Christendom was later to continue to exclude as 'profane'. Plato's lofty conception of the Good was associated almost exclusively with intellectual contemplation. Aristotle, despite his emphasis on identifying the Good with the goods sought by particular practices, still regarded certain practices – notably crafts and mechanical arts – as unworthy of the dignity a citizen of the *Polis*. Recalling the criticisms by Francis Bacon and Robert Boyle of the intellectual hierarchy maintained by Greek and medieval traditions of learning, Taylor identifies in these criticisms a new appreciation of the work of 'the lowly artisan and artificer' and associates the 'affirmation of ordinary life' evident here with the accomplishments of the emergent scientific temperament of the seventeenth century. Noting that the scope of this affirmation also included criticism of the classical ethic of honour and glory, Taylor concludes as follows:

> an inherent bent towards social levelling is implicit in the affirmation of ordinary life. The centre of the good life lies now in something which everyone can have a part in, rather than in ranges of activity which only the leisured few can do justice to. (*SoS* 214)

Arguing in a somewhat similar vein to Taylor, Hannah Arendt explores in her book, *The Human Condition* (*HC*), how the Greek and Roman influences which came to predominate in Christianity exalted a life of contemplation (*vita contemplativa*) over a life of action (*vita activa*). Arendt discerns influential variants of this hierarchy in the works of Augustine and Aquinas, but also points out that the conviction that the *vita contemplativa* is superior 'can hardly be found in the preachings of Jesus of Nazareth', and that 'it is certainly due to the emphasis of Greek philosophy'. (*HC* 318) Arendt's distinction here parallels in important respects that which we examined in Chapter Two between Christianity and Christendom. She explains moreover that Christianity created no order of merit between different aspects of the *vita activa* itself; that is, between *labour* (e.g. activity such as the toil necessary for survival itself), *work* (e.g. activity which produces an 'artificial world of things and artifacts) and *action* (e.g. activity which has a political dimension, particularly those relationships which arise from human differences - from the fact that 'nobody is ever the same as anybody else who ever lived, lives, or will live'). (*HC* 7-8) The kind of valuing of ordinary life which distinguished Christianity from both classical civilisations and those of Christendom is described by Arendt as follows:

> Christian emphasis on the sacredness of life tended to level out the ancient distinctions and articulations within the *vita activa*; it tended to view labour, work and action as equally subject to the necessity of present life. At the same time it helped to free the labouring activity, that is, whatever is necessary to sustain the biological process itself, from some of the contempt in which antiquity had held it. (*HC* 316)

Of course the Medieval monastic traditions had considered labour a form of prayer, but these traditions were based not on 'ordinary life' but on ascetic renunciation of worldly pursuits, particularly those which involved sexual acts or the exchange of goods and money. With the Reformation, however, a new sense of vocation announced itself. This was based in a Puritan belief in humankind's sinfulness and held that human judgements of the worthiness of different *kinds* of activity were themselves worthless. Instead it placed emphasis on the *spirit* in which an activity was pursued. Taylor quotes Joseph Hall, and other Puritan writers of the seventeenth century, to illustrate how the scientific current in the affirmation of ordinary life was joined by a religious one: 'The homeliest service that we doe in an honest calling, though it be but to plow or digge, if done in obedience, and conscience of God's Commandment, is crowned with ample reward ... God loveth adverbs; and cares not how good, but how well'. (*SoS* 224) Taylor points out that for Puritans, worldly goods could be enjoyed as a result of such efforts but should be used with 'weaned affections'; used, that is, 'as if you used them not'. (*SoS* 223)

But the cultures of work associated with the growth of Protestantism conferred a particular value on one 'calling' of ordinary life more than any other; that of commercial activity. The close connections between Protestantism and the rise of capitalism have been explored in detail by Max Weber (*The Protestant Ethic and the Spirit of Capitalism*) and by R.H. Tawney (*Religion and the Rise of Capitalism*). What I am concernd to emphasise here however are some consequences of the progressive *estrangement* of capitalism from religious sources, a rift which some historians of political science argue was already set under way in Adam Smith's *Wealth of Nations* (1776).[6] The science of economics superseded philosophy in influencing the conduct of public affairs. It supplied a secularising vocabulary which in time came to pervade, and later to dominate, the discourse of politics and public welfare. The decisive momentum given by this discourse to activities associated with the spirit of acquisitiveness, with competitiveness and wealth accumulation as culturally acclaimed goals, contributed massively to technological developments; developments which made life more convenient in many ways but which also had many grim consequences. And the late twentieth century has virtually completed the process of rendering traditional crafts and trades obsolete and their practitioners redundant. If 'the artisan and the artificer' were once regarded as 'lowly' in the social classifications of merit, they have now been *marginalised by the economy* because their performances have been superseded by ever more sophisticated means of mass production.

The 'market' thinking which enjoyed a remarkable renaissance in the nineteen eighties, represents a further unhappy chapter in the historical fortunes of the affirmations of ordinary life. That decade witnessed an unfettering of the more mercenary of impulses which had until then been held in some sort of check by government regulation. Far from affirming the pursuits of ordinary life in either the vocational or religious senses described by Taylor, contemporary (or postmodern) market imperatives exploit the full fruits of de-regulation and have become notoriously unpredictable. Multinational corporations are characteristically footloose rather than faithful; they are frequently more powerful than sovereign nations; they can control and dispose both work and labour in ways which would have been inconceivable in previous centuries. Far from respecting traditions of industry of long-standing, they are restlessly focused on discerning the possibilities of the future, but mainly as a source of increased profits and further acquisition. In addition to pervading the spheres of work and labour, moreover, these imperatives also canvass convictions and political outlooks in the more influential quarters of leadership and decision-making. Allied to this they seek to extend their power through institutionalisation and systematisation. And they do so much more promptly than did a metaphysical conception of Christianity which once sought and achieved supremacy through the institutionalisations which produced Christendom. The manner in which the concept of 'privatisation' has taken over institutions traditionally associated with the provision of public services and utilities is a striking example of how rapidly the institutionalisation of a new creed has pervaded Western cultures in recent decades.[7]

There are of course counter-currents to those we have been just describing. And these seek to influence the mainstream of policy-making in education in most Western countries at present. Alasdair MacIntyre's advocacy of a return to pre-Enlightenment conceptions of learning represents one such current. The radical critiques of authors liks Michael Apple and Henry Giroux represent another. The 'positive politics' and 'moral agentry' recommended by Michael Fullan to professionals in education represent a third.[8] And there are many kinds of 'empowerment' approaches, ranging from those based in the politics of resistance to those, like Murgatroyd's and Morgan's, based in the politics of acquiescence. We have already examined the limitations of some of these orientations and in the next section we will concentrate on a policy approach which seeks to overcome these limitations. This would be an approach which does justice to the affirmations of ordinary life, to the educational promise of modern technologies, to the claims of the economic and the vocational, and not least to the voices of cultural tradition. Far from being 'all things to all men', however, this must first and foremost be a policy approach which safeguards teaching and learning from colonisation by any interests contrary to what we have already put forward as the most defensible purposes of education itself. In sketching this approach, let us take as our theme the practical question of a 'balanced curriculum', because it is here that the consequences of policy become most pertinent to the experience of learners.

Recasting the Balance of Liberal Education

Plato envisaged the kind of learning worthy of his philosopher rulers to be a form of liberal education, as did Aristotle the kind of learning which would benefit those who, as citizens, should be 'at leisure aright'. The higher education of the liberal university envisaged by Humboldt, like that envisaged by Newman for the Christian gentleman, were likewise considered liberal. In each case, however, though in different ways, the refinement of sensibility associated with the liberal character of the education envisaged was a privilige reserved for a small minority of the population. But the nineteenth century witnessed the provision by the state of mass systems of schooling at primary level. And in the case of most countries mass primary schooling remained largely a harsh and custodial regime until well into the twentieth century. The period since the middle of the twentieth century has brought demands, in most Western countries, for universal second-level schooling and for mass access to higher education. So costly have these demands proven that by the end of the nineteen eighties most Governments in OECD countries were allocating between fifteen and twenty percent of public expenditure to education.[9] Moreover, the close connections which are now drawn between a society's state of knowledge and its state of wealth, between a person's level of education and his or her level of employment and remuneration, have made liberal education on any of the patterns mentioned above a thing of the past. The reciprocal dependencies between education and society in the present day also mean that the sovereignty proper to teaching and learning must be a qualified, rather than any absolute one. But 'qualified' here means accountable on defensible educational terms, such as we have explored in earlier chapters, rather than on terms controlled by government, or commercial interests as 'customers' or paymasters.[10]

The constraints we have just been reviewing do not mean however that a liberal education itself is a thing of the past. The commitment to the education of 'the whole person' which has been central to the traditional idea of liberal education is essentially the same as the Socratic commitment we examined in the early pages of the first chapter. It is this commitment moreover which underlies the necessity for education as a public office to enjoy discretionary scope for the making of judicious decisions. These decisions are what determine the question of balance in the curriculum and they affect in a direct way the quality of learning experienced by pupils and students.

In examining the question of balance in the curriculum it is important from the start to understand the curriculum not merely as the contents of one or more syllabi, but as the *experienced quality* of these contents by pupils and teachers, including the *assessment of benefits* which such experiences bring to pupils. Secondly, it is important to realise that what may be a balanced curriculum for one pupil may not be a balanced curriculum for another. Let us take first the question of how assessment affects balance and quality in the curriculum experienced by pupils and then address the issue of balance of elements in the curriculum.

The most legitimate purposes of assessment are those which seek to provide a coherent, valid and adequate picture of the benefits each pupil has received from the educational experiences provided through a particular course of study. Similarly, certification is true to its educational purposes only insofar as it testifies adequately and appropriately to the intrinsic benefits which a particular pupil has actually achieved from his or her educational experiences. In Chapter Seven we took four examples and referred to these experiences as enabling the pupils to discover something of the historian in themselves, or something of linguistic aptitude and appreciation in themselves, or something of the scientist in themselves, or something of their own religious sensibilities. And of course the same goes for any other subject. It would be virtually impossible, and in any case very costly, to devise a system of assessment which was so flexible and so attuned to the different kinds of benefits, and the different nuances within a particular kind of benefit (e.g. kinds of discernment in interpreting a poem), that it achieved fully the purposes outlined at the beginning of this paragraph. On the other hand, some of the inherited forms of assessment which are still with us are so inimical to the intrinsic benefits of education that they disfigure the conduct of teaching and learning; and to such a degree that the practices of teaching are sometimes more an enslavement than an emancipation, more an assault on sensibility than any fruitful courtship in the sense described earlier.

Some of these forms of assessment – such as the major one of placing an almost exclusive emphasis on pupils' performance in unseen questions in an end-of-year three-hour sitting – have given rise not only to a lack of balance in practices of teaching, but also to whole traditions of teaching in which such unbalanced practices have become thoroughly ingrained. Very many teachers are unhappy with this state of affairs, confessing readily that such an education couldn't by any means be called liberal. But most of these would still argue that whatever about liberal education, they are constrained to teach towards what the public examination system rewards. Considerable consolation is also taken from the fact that pupils' performance in the public examinations gives Irish second-level schools an impressive record by international standards. And the force of tradition itself in the cultures of teaching sometimes means that end-of-year examinations are still perceived to reward what they traditionally rewarded, even where some considerable improvements have been made in introducing a variety of approaches, or in giving advance notice of topics to be researched, or in widening the range of benefits the examination is designed to assess. Indeed one of the most vexed problems of the assessment issue in second-level education in Ireland is that the 1878 Education Act established a public examination system rather than an education system. The Act gave the state no legal rights in relation to schools (which were almost exclusively owned and controlled by religious authorities), yet it influenced the daily and yearly quality of teaching and learning in the schools in a manner that was arguably far more intrusive than any compromise of church-state interests at managerial level would have been.

In recent decades a number of curricular innovations in Ireland have included a significant emphasis on a pedagogy of active learning, and on a range of assessment approaches which are consistent with this pedagogy.[11] These initiatives have cultivated among the teachers associated with them an expertise in their own assessment of their pupils' work for certification purposes and have increased the scope for the exercise of professional discretion, both in relation to assessment itself and the whole approach to teaching and learning. It is important to emphasise the point that it is the pupils' work (not their personalities) that was being assessed in these initiatives; namely the objective record (available for external moderation) of the particular benefits the pupils had gained. These points need to be considered in conjunction with the fact that the discourse of educational reform, in Ireland as elsewhere, frequently makes reference to best national and international practice. And it is true that in recent years incremental changes – whether or not prompted by such practice – have been introduced to the assessment system at both the junior and senior cycles of second-level schooling.

Many argue that a decisive shift in the reform of assessment must, however, await a decisive shift in the traditional cultures of teaching, and that this might be slow in coming. The relationship in question is more a reciprocal one however than that of a one-way dependence. The legitimate entitlements of teachers to adequate opportunities for in-service workshops on new modes of assessment and new developments in teaching are far from being adequately met, whether from shortage of funds or shortage of time, or other reasons. Notwithstanding these difficulties, however, if international patterns in educational reform are anything to go by, the constraints on teachers' work are likely to increase, and in ways which are not conducive to any ideals of freedom or sovereignty in learning, or of professional discretion in teaching, unless teachers themselves actively embrace educational reform and influence its tenor. Where reform is actively under way, to play a part that is more reactive than proactive allows leadership to remain in more influential hands. There are more than a few straws in the wind to show that such hands may nowadays make assessment procedures even more bureaucratic than any traditional pattern, and may inaugurate a custodianship of a more crass kind than that traditionally exercised by church authorities.[12]

Turning now to the second issue, namely that of balance among the elements of the curriculum which constitute the learner's experience, an analogy with a balanced diet may illustrate a few important points here, provided the analogy isn't pushed too far. Just as a healthy, balanced, diet should be adjusted to individual constitutional propensities, a balanced curriculum needs to be adjusted in some crucial measure to the pupil's ownmost abilities, aptitudes, sensibilities and potentials. These are the constituents of emergent identity in the pupil, whether as child or youth, and teachers must deal with endless varieties of them. Yet each pupil is entitled to look back on his or her schooling and judge whether or not the school did a good job in unearthing and bringing to fruition such potentials as were most native to him or her (apart, of course, from destructive ones).

But the point of the analogy is not merely to emphasise the connection between balance and individual promise. There is also a less appealing issue to be considered here. A pupil may experience a certain dislike for an element in a curriculum which is perceived as alien, or repugnant; much as, for instance, an individual's sense of taste may recoil from some particular ingredient in an otherwise appetising meal. If we recall here the point that the curriculum is to be regarded not just as the contents, but as the experienced quality of the contents, we are provided with an important insight. There are many fields of study which each of us might find initially alien, or forbidding, or perhaps simply distasteful. Yet some of these fields may still uncover previously unknown abilities and aptitudes in ourselves. The epiphanies of the everyday are invariably a surprise. For this uncovering to happen, however, the field of study in question must be experienced by us in such a way that our sensibility does not altogether recoil. We must experience it as something which is at least tolerable, understandable, and of sufficient significance to us that we are prepared to co-operate in putting some effort into its study. Balance as an aim is defeated from the start if taste becomes the only criterion of choice and commitment, in an analogous way to that in which undisciplined taste can undermine the purposes of a healthy diet.

From here one could extend the analogy further by arguing that just as certain foods are superior to others, so are certain subjects superior to others. Even more particularly, one could claim that within an individual subject, certain topics are superior to others, or that certain topics are central while others are marginal. It is misleading to press the analogy in this area however. These are essentially arguments about disciplines and *canons* and their claims to cultural worthiness; claims which are much more intricate than the claims of certain foods to be more wholesome and nourishing than others. For instance, a committee of the National Council for Curriculum and Assessment (Republic of Ireland) recommended recently that it should not be obligatory to include a Shakespeare play on the Ordinary Level syllabus for Leaving Certificate English. The recommendation caused considerable controversy, received little thoughtful debate, and was turned down by the Minister for Education.[13] Similar recurrent controversies have centered on the status of Irish, religion, science, and other subjects in the curricula of primary and second-level schools in recent years.

But it must be pointed out that claims to cultural worthiness are not the same as claims to educational fruitfulness. A subject or topic of widely acclaimed cultural worth, and in the hands of a competent teacher, may still say little of any significance to pupils who are already deeply prejudiced against it. This emerges clearly enough from the arguments made on the courtship of sensibility in Chapter Seven, as does the necessity to bring inventiveness and resourcefulness to bear in a particular way where this courtship founders. A practical instance was explored there as to how such foundering might be overcome. The chief lesson to be learned from this kind of experience is that canons must in some real sense become flexible and inclusive if they enter the discipline of educational dialogue in a fruitful way. Yet, where a school has clearly exhausted its best ideas and energies in such efforts with its most resistant pupils, but without success, it makes little sense to claim that a particular voice which has widely acclaimed cultural merit has *ipso facto* educational promise, and must therefore be obligatory for all pupils. Balance and quality become the first casualties of such a policy, while persisting with the policy itself may undermine the prospects that the pupils might acknowledge cultural merit in the voice in question even at a later stage.

A balanced curriculum then comprises a school's best efforts – within the constraints of regulation and circumstance – to provide for its pupils what it judges to be the most fruitful experiences in a representative range of the various fields of human endeavour and accomplishment. This remains particularly true of pupils at primary school and in the junior cycle of second-level schools. And judgements concerning the promise or fruitfulness of a particular subject or balance of subjects must involve not only teachers and pupils, but also parents, and, where appropriate, the advice of counsellors. But the argument for balance is still substantially valid as specialisation becomes more pronounced in the senior cycle of second-level and into third level education. Quality is clearly well served if learners are encouraged to play to their personal strengths, but not where the partiality of perspective which is inherent in specialisation (as we saw in Chapter Five) is permitted to dominate the learner's outlooks. In this sense, all applied fields of study remain humanities, because it is in a world of human concerns, anxieties and aspirations that they find their application. Specialised study of any such field therefore becomes insular and tunnel-visioned unless it also includes a study of how the goods aimed at by the subject's application bear on human welfare and the *common* good.[14] This remains true of fields such as engineering and all the information technologies, as it does of medicine, architecture, law, educational studies, business studies, economics, psychology, and the social sciences more generally. Both balance and quality are sacrificed to non-educational concerns if this requirement is not honoured.

The Technological as Liberation and as Tyranny

To understand this 'humanities' requirement itself *in its application*, let us take two examples: firstly traditional 'vocational' and craft subjects and secondly a newcomer to the curriculum, such as technology. We have already argued that the inclusion of 'vocational' subjects rests on their intrinsic merits as practices, particularly when considered as practices of learning. Where the curriculum of second-level schools in Ireland is concerned, such subjects have traditionally included woodwork, metalwork, home economics, technical drawing and art. In a recent essay Joseph Dunne has explored the intrinsic merits of subjects such as these and has pointed out that when properly experienced by pupils, their benefits include the following three main ones:

> release from the tyranny of the ego through a focusing and concentration of energies on goods that trancend themselves (thereby paradoxically enabling them to discover and realise themselves); release from a vacant present through partnership in a tradition that is richly alive in the present, stretches back into the past and, partially through them, can be extended forward into the future; the achievement of competencies which are ones of the whole person and which, just because they are rooted in the body, do not for that reason call any less into play qualities of creative insight, judgement and expression, which only a terribly limited cognitive psychology could fail to recognise as qualities of *intelligence*.[15]

Dunne also points out that participating in practices such as these cultivates qualities like honesty and humility – in admitting the shortcomings of one's own efforts. He shows further that they embody requirements of patience and courage – in persevering with a task. He argues finally that they promote a sense of justice and generosity – in co-operating with others and overcoming individual rivalries to complete a project. In other words, the learning practices involved here are inescapably a form of moral education, in that they involve not only the learning of skills but also of virtues.[16]

There are strong parallels between these arguments of Dunne's and those on the virtues of learning that we explored in Chapter

Seven. And indeed many of the benefits which we have just been considering apply to a wider range of subjects, including our second example, the new subject technology and its further implications. There is however, a crucial difference between the traditional 'vocational' subjects and technology. Unless it is explicitly acknowledged and monitored, moreover, it is a difference which could have unforeseen consequences both for the benefits and the learning ethos illustrated in the previous paragraphs. Because of the increasing importance of technology in education, both as a subject in its own right and as a many-sided cultural force in modern society, it is worth exploring a few of the implications of its newness more closely. To fail to do so might not only allow modern technology's hidden curriculum to remain active behind the backs of teachers and learners, but also behind the backs of policy-makers. Let us briefly examine this hidden curriculum.

The differences between modern technology and the more traditional technologies associated with crafts and trades can initially be stated in the following three-fold way. Modern technology includes a new kind of *attitude to* making, a new *ingenuity in* making and new *cultures of* making. The cultures of making in the past had a strong sense of identity based in tradition. They held in the highest esteem the artistry and reputation of the individual master craftsman. The cultures of making which characterise modern technology are often quite the opposite. Developments in this latter case are frequently swift, impersonal and unpredictable. Preoccupation with the finding of ever more ingenious ways of achieving ends, moreover, makes recurring obsolescence a distinctive feature of a technological culture. In other words, the ethos of design, of making and of communications in a technological culture is different in some essential respects from the ethos of design, of making and of communications in a craft culture.

An education in modern technology, as distinct from one in craftsmanship, not only equips the student with an understanding of some of the most intriguing processes and a facility in employing such processes in some successful degree. More subtly, such an education can cultivate in the student a captivating preference for and commitment to this ever more efficient way of doing things. But with this frequently goes a certain impatience with or disregard for more traditional conceptions of excellence in making. Technology's emphasis is essentially on research and development rather than on cultivating ideals of respect for and emulation of the master craftsman. Its orientation is towards the future and it is likely to view the excellences achieved through apprenticship and traditional practice as an inefficient use of human resources. Recalling then the requirements of balance in the curriculum, it is important that the partiality of one kind of excellence is not sacrificed to that of another. This is not to underestimate the difficulties of promoting an appreciation of and a capacity for *both* kinds of excellence in the experience of the individual pupil. It is however to emphasise the merits of such a combination.

The attitudes resulting from a pupil's sense of progressively identifying with a subject are different in the case of technology from that of virtually all other subjects. This is obviously true when we compare someone who has become enthusiastic about say, German, or geography, with someone who is eager about everything technological. Technology's associations with power are simply much closer than those of most other subjects. This difference also holds between technology and science, though the tendency to refer to technology as 'applied science' obscures it. The difference between technology and science can be better appreciated when we view technology not as some kind of handmaiden of science, but rather – as Heidegger has incisively shown – as an active *attitude*; a mentality which, from the start, has pressing designs not only on science and its fruits, including the social sciences, but on most other spheres of human action as well.[17] That is to say, the kind of *ethos* which a habituation in this mentality builds is one which tends to predispose human sensibility towards a preference for technicity, rational-manipulative capacity, and a preoccupied pressing-ahead.

Learners of all ages are apt to become habituated in certain loyalties and orientations which are prominent within the subjects they are studying. For instance Aristotle's disdain for the technical is even more pronounced in many of the current century's defenders of the traditional kind of liberal education. What I am attempting to highlight here is a similar tendency, but one which installs the aplomb of modern technology in the privileged position which Aristotle gave to the liberal arts. Or to make the comparison in another way, it is illuminating to return for a moment to consider the dominant view throughout Christendom that the different fields of learning pursued their best purposes when informed from the start by spiritual inspirations. John Henry Newman gave this custodial view perhaps its most eloquent expression at a time when Christianity as a cultural force was no longer in an unassailed position of dominance in Western traditions of learning. Newman was explicit however on the degree of freedom which he was keen that these various fields should enjoy. The position is quite otherwise where inspirations originating in a technologised conception of learning and life enjoy a dominance which remains largely unacknowledged; where a latter-day social engineering has already made decision-making itself – in education and elsewhere – largely into a technology. The distortion of a cultural inheritance, including that of its best economic and technological possibilities, extends its sway here through a 'performative' custodianship which fetters the most promising potentials of teachers and pupils alike. In such circumstances the sovereignty of learning suffers its darkest eclipse.

Notes:

1. The reforms in England and Wales have been reviewed by Denis Lawton in the two following works: *Education, Culture and the National Curriculum* (London: Hodder & Stoughton, 1989) and *Education and Politics in the 1990s: Conflict or Consensus?* (London: Falmer Press, 1992). See also Stuart MacLure's book *Education Reformed: A Guide to the Education Reform Act 1988* (Sevenoaks: Hodder & Stoughton, Headway series, 1988). The Report by the Department of Education and Science, *Teaching Quality,* was published by Her Majesty's Stationery Office, 1993.

2. National Commission on Excellence in Education, *A Nation at Risk: The imperative for educational reform* (Washington D.C., 1993). Michael Fullan points out that the publication of *A Nation at Risk* initiated a boom in educational reform at both national level and in the individual States across the United States. See Michael G. Fullan & Suzanne Stiegelbaur, *The New Meaning of Educational Change* (London: Cassell, 1991), pp.4, 6.

3. See *Schools and Quality: An International Report* (Paris: OECD, 1989). See also *Reviews of National Policies for Education – Ireland* (Paris: OECD, 1991), p.69.

4. See for instance the review and defence of this tendency in the opening chapter of a currently popular textbook on management in education, *Effective School Management,* by Bertie Everard and Goeffrey Morris (Second edition, London: Paul Chapman, 1990). Unlike Murgatroyd and Morgan, Everard and Morris acknowledge that there are purposes and 'values' in education which cannot be assimilated to the concerns of business and industry. Everard and Morris have a much more anaemic understanding of the integrity of education, however, than that argued for here.

5. This less benign side of the concept of human resource management has strong parallels with the picture painted by Lyotard. For some contrasting accounts see the special edition of the journal *CRE-Action* devoted to the proceedings of two international conferences on 'Human Resources at a University' held in Maynooth (May) and Barcelona (September) 1993. *CRE-Action* No.102 (Geneva: CRE, 1993). CRE is the Standing Conference of Rectors, Presidents and Vice-Chancellors (of European Universities).

6. See, for instance, Peter Minowitz's *Profits, Priests & Princes: Adam Smith's Emancipation of Economics from Politics and Religion* (Stanford: Stanford

University Press, 1993). I am grateful to Barney O'Reilly for bringing this book to my attention, as I am for helping me to clarify a distinction which I had not made sufficiently clear before now: that between the pursuits of ordinary life (including commercial ones) and the disfigurement of these pursuits by what I have previously called 'the rehabilitation of cupidity' associated with the dominant economic and social politics of the nineteen eighties. See Barney O' Reilly's article, 'Economics, Politics and the Philosophy of Education in Ireland' in *Partnership and the Benefits of Learning* (1995) P. Hogan (ed.), (Maynooth: Educational Studies Association of Ireland) pp. 12-28. In this article O'Reilly expresses the view that I tend to belittle the affirmations of ordinary life in an earlier article of mine titled 'The Sovereignty of Learning, the Fortunes of Schooling and the New Educational Virtuousness', in the *British Journal of Educational Studies,* Vol.XXXX, No. 2, 1992.

7. The verb 'to privatise' and the noun 'privatisation' are now prominent in the vocabulary of current affairs. Yet neither can be found in the Oxford Dictionary prior to 1980.

8. For Fullan's advocacy of what he calls 'moral agentry' among teachers see his book, *Change Forces: Plumbing the Depths of Educational Change* (London: Falmer Press, 1992).

9. See the final page of the Statistical Appendix to *Education for a Changing World* – Green Paper, Ireland 1992.

10. Successive decades of the twentieth century have witnessed an increasing tendency for scientific and social scientific research in universities to be funded by commercial, industrial and military interests. The frequent practice of insisting that the findings become the legal and even confidential property of the funding body represents one of the most striking denials of sovereignty to learning in our own day. Governments and universities in most technologically advanced countries have acquiesed to a greater or lesser degree in this state of affairs.

11. See in particular the contributions on the 'Humanities' project of the City of Dublin Vocational Education Committee and on the 'Senior Certificate' project of the Shannon Curriculum Development Centre in *Achievement and Aspiration: Curricular Initiatives in Irish Post-Primary Education in the 1980s,* edited by Gerry McNamara, Kevin Williams and Don Herron (Dublin: Drumcondra Teachers' Centre, 1990).

12. Kevin Williams has explored in a detailed and illuminating way, the difficult issues which attend assessment as a live concern in Irish second level education at present. See his *Assessment: A Discussion Paper* (Dublin: Association of Secondary Teachers Ireland, 1992).

13. Two thought-provoking and memorable contributions on the Shakespeare question in Irish schooling were presented to the 1995 Annual Conference of the Educational Studies Association of Ireland. These were 'Shakespeare ... To Be or Not to Be', by Tom Mullins and 'Teaching Shakespeare: A Semiotic Approach', by Marian McCarthy. The contrasting claims of the canonical and the educational are highlighted in the first of these and an adventurous solution which has proved fruitful, at least in one school, is examined in the second. Both contributions are due to be published in *Irish Educational Studies*, Vol. 15, 1996.

14. T.G. Gaden has presented a thoughtful and detailed case for specialisation in an unpublished Ph.D. thesis entitled *On the participant's identification with his activity and the value of specialisation in post-primary education* (University College Dublin 1985). Some aspects of my own views on specialisation are indebted to Gaden's work. Others take a contrasting approach.

15. Joseph Dunne's article is called 'What's the Good of Education?' and it appears in *Partnership and the Benefits of Learning*, pp.60-82. The quoted passage is from pp.76-77.

16. ibid., pp.73,77. Dunne points out that where the emphasis is on the external goods of education (e.g. money, jobs), considerations of scarcity and competition come to the fore. This also has implications for balance in teaching. While it is scarcely possible to exclude extrinsic considerations from the experience of teaching and learning, that experience becomes quite imbalanced if such considerations are the ones which gain primacy.

17. See Heidegger's essay, 'The Question Concerning Technology' in *Martin Heidegger - Basic Writings,* Edited with an Introduction by David Farrell Krell (London: Routledge & Kegan Paul, 1978) pp.283-317.

EPILOGUE

Sovereignty, Change and the Tenor of Policy

It requires an alert, committed and energetic educational vision to forestall in the modern arenas of educational policy-making the kind of thraldom discribed in the closing passage of the last chapter. It requires the shared commitment of teachers and educational leaders to a robust, practical and defensible philosophy to forestall it in the daily practices where policy is put to the test. Bearing these two requirements in mind, this epilogue will review briefly a number of central questions of educational policy and suggest lines of action which are consistent with the 'sovereignty' thesis presented in this book. The range of questions selected for this concluding review cannot claim to be exhaustive. The topics included are of particular relevance to the changes which are occurring in the Irish educational system at present, but each of these is also pertinent to the conduct of public education in any country which describes itself as a democracy.

One of the most widely cited studies of reform in education in recent times is Michael Fullan's and Suzanne Stiegelbauer's *The New Meaning of Educational Change* (1991). This book reviews a very extensive range of research studies into policy changes and innovations in education since the nineteen sixties. It traces the causes of success and failure of reform efforts and explores in turn how these are experienced by the major participants in education, including teachers, school principals, students, administrators, consultants, parents and community. Among its most important conclusions for our purposes here are the three following ones:

(a) Reform measures in education are likely to meet with resistance, indifference or otherwise unhappy fortunes, if they spring from political considerations – considerations, that is, that are 'unconnected to the stated purposes of education'. (p.8)

(b) Changes which seek to introduce new structures, goals and roles (i.e. 'second order changes') are much more difficult to implement than changes which are confined to improving the effectiveness of what is done at present (i.e. 'first order changes'). This is particularly so if the impetus for the changes is seen to be associated with those unfamilliar with the classroom as a workplace. (p.29)

(c) Bringing about successful change requires a kind of leadership which combines qualities that seemingly do not go together: having a clear vision *and* being open-minded, taking initiatives *and* enabling others, providing support *and* pressure, starting small *and* thinking big, expecting results *and* being patient, having a plan *and* being flexible, using top-down *and* bottom-up approaches, experiencing uncertainty *and* satisfaction. (p.350)

These conclusions, based on empirical research studies, point to an imperative which coalesces with what I have been arguing for throughout this book. Firstly, they identify the necessity for any effective vision in education to have its sources in the neighbourhood of educational practice itself. Secondly, they underline the importance of allowing those who participate responsibly in organising and conducting this practice to have the authoritative but accountable part in developing this practice in accordance with the most defensible interests of education. Thirdly, they offer good grounds for believing that initiatives pursued along these lines, despite the many setbacks they will inevitably encounter, are clearly worth the effort and worthy of the public's support and resources. With these preliminary remarks let us now proceed to the first of the eight topics in our concluding review.

The Sovereign Purposes of Learning

Emergent identity, the uncovering of its individuality and promise, its search for meaning and acknowledgement, its encounters with the voices of cultural tradition, its epiphanies of achievement and limitation, its contributions to community and economic life; these constitute some of the central concerns of learning as an undertaking worthy of public support. These concerns identify important responsibilities but they also alert us to rights and affirmations which are in a crucial sense inviolable – in particular the right to become what our inherent potentials might enable us to become when these are addressed in a learning climate which is the most conducive to their nourishment and disciplined realisation. So wherever educational authorities presume proprietorial rights on the sensibilities of the young, even from the most altruistic of motives, education as an undertaking is disfigured from the start: the emergent identity of the pupil is cast in an inflexible mould and much of what is most promising and special among each pupil's potentials is obscured or smothered. A mentality which places a primary emphasis on proprietorial rights, moreover, albeit for the most sincere reasons, promotes an ethos of partiality and power-seeking, overlooks the venturesome play of educational experience, and undermines the coherence of teaching and learning as a jointly undertaken quest which builds enduring solidarities.

The Control and Management of Schooling

The control of education is no one's private possession, but is something public, held in trust. This trust involves different parties in a *commitment to partnership*, so that the best benefits of learning are made available, as far as is possible, for pupils and students. Where the management of schooling as an undertaking *committed to education* is concerned then, it matters less what the formal composition of the managing authority is than that this authority should contain a variety of perspectives (e.g. founders, teachers, parents), as distinct from a preponderance of one perspective. It matters less moreover what the precise makeup of the authority is than that this authority should recognise that the responsibilities of partnership summon energies towards dialogue and the mutual education of perspectives than towards factional rivalries. It matters less, finally, what the representative composition of the authority is than that all its members be sufficiently courageous and sufficiently well versed in the basics of a defensible educational philosophy, so as to safeguard against intrusions a responsible exercise of the sovereignty of learning on the part of the school or college and its teachers.

The Conduct of Teaching and Learning

Properly viewed, teachers' efforts with their students represent *overtures* on behalf of one or other of the voices of tradition within the different fields of human accomplishment. These overtures can be appropriately made only by teachers in whom the subject in question speaks with fluency and engaging conviction. Such overtures can rarely or ever be neutral, but they can in defensible measure be honourable and open-minded, just as they can in a defensible way embody strict requirements and demanding expectations. All of this calls for insightful and courageous educational leadership in schools and colleges; the kind of leadership which is capable of building solidarity among teachers, centered on commitment to the pupils, supporting each other as colleagues, and developing their own cultural and pedagogical strengths. Secondly, it calls for systematic co-operation with parents, which enables them to participate in a responsible and structured way in the education of their children. Not least, it calls for discernment and accountability in appointing candidates with the best promise and credentials to leadership positions.

Where teaching and learning in higher education are concerned, the fact that universities are now mass institutions, and that the majority of their teachers see themselves essentially as researchers and have undergone no training as teachers, presents a particular problem. It is now even difficult to maintain the quality of service to graduate students which was available to undergraduates in former times. A type of 'human resource management' and 'quality audit' which emphasises 'performativity' is likely to aggravate rather than address this problem and to increase the alienation and anonymity experienced by very many undergraduates. By contrast, a sustained and adequately resourced commitment to making teaching as important and as fruitful as research in higher education could do much to reduce the dominance of bureaucratised teaching and learning and to enable genuine communities of teachers and learners to emerge and develop at both undergraduate and post-graduate level.

The Education of Teachers

There is still a conception of the teacher – including in educational circles – as one who is schooled and certificated in an approved range of subject knowledge and who is sufficiently competent in its transmission to be licensed by some educational authority to do so. Such a conception may pass muster in maintaining an indifferent status quo, but it does little justice either to the nature of knowledge (i.e. the voices of cultural tradition), to the experience of pupils (their sensibilities, potentials, aptitudes), or to the efforts worthy of teachers. In short, it bypasses from the start the crucial insight that every event of human understanding is an *interplay* of perspectives, whether overt or tacit. Teacher education must set this kind of interplay consciously under way in a three-fold manner among student teachers themselves. Firstly there must be an imaginative interplay between the student teachers and the subjects in which they are striving to achieve an assured fluency. Secondly, there must be an active, regular and reflective interplay between the student teachers and their pupils. Thirdly, the confluences and collisions between both of these kinds of learning must themselves become a major part of the curriculum (agenda if you like) through which student teachers deepen their *self*-understanding in an occupational field which is itself about advancing the understanding of pupils and students, and in circumstances which are ever changing.

Teacher education is therefore the natural nursery (or academy) for those dispositions cultivated by the self-critical discipline of dialogue. But where the initial preparation of teachers is successful in getting this kind of cultural and communicative discipline under way, the discipline itself must be sustained and perfected through the induction and recurrent in-service phases of a teaching career. A statutory authority such as a Teaching Council would have a leading part to play in ensuring and enhancing quality in each of the *phases* of teacher education and indeed within the intermingling *elements* of teacher education. It would play a similarly important part in the articulation and monitoring of a professional code of ethics based on a defensible educational philosophy.

Balance and Equity in the Experience of the Curriculum

The experience of curricula should be sufficiently broad in the primary school and junior cycle of secondary school so as to address the full range of aptitudes and potentials of each pupil. Equity requires moreover that access to such experiences should be equally available to all, and that resources should be judiciously allocated with this criterion in mind. Positive discrimination to offset disadvantage may regularly be a feature of such judiciousness. Specialisation should proceed only when a particular family or cluster of potentials has been identified as a person's most promising ones. Parents and teachers have to co-operate continually with pupils on this. Specialisation should never be such however that a student becomes systematically schooled in one or other exclusive range of perspectives, to the continual neglect of contrasting or contrary ones. Bearing in mind these points, benefit to the pupil, rather than any territorial claims of different subjects for preferential treatment, should be the overriding criterion in ensuring balance in the curriculum.

Assessment and Certification

The legitimate purposes of assessment are concerned not with providing a test of ingenuity in beating an examination system but rather with evaluation of the *quality* of the curricular experiences offered in school: with assessing the benefits of those experiences not just under one main heading such as the strategic recall of and deployment of information, but under headings which would include the following: the pupil's ability to solve problems, to be incisive and consistent in tracing inferences and conclusions, to deal in a fluent way – in writing *and* speech – with concepts, theories, linguistic idioms and images, to discriminate between key issues and minor ones, to identify the focus of a genuine question and to keep that focus continually in view, to carry out a piece of practical work which incorporates an intelligent conception and a high standard of execution, to show the fruits of purposeful co-operation with fellow students, to advance a coherent and consistent case supported by well-chosen evidence, to show that they understand the significance of what they have studied for their own emergent potentialities and inclinations, for their own sustenance and sense of identity. The professional discretion which properly belongs to teachers includes judgements by them on the more inclusive benefits of learning which have been incorporated in the *works* of their own pupils.

The Claims of Economy and Society

If educational effort, governed by the five essentials of dialogue described earlier, concentrates on identifying and cultivating each student's ownmost potentials, and on nurturing a durable sense of identity and community in harmony with those potentials, then it promotes, in a natural and unforced way, a closer match between the natural talents of a population and the kinds of economic activity which are likely to be most fruitful for that population. Of course this is to make an act of faith in the consultative wisdom of teachers, as this is practised with pupils, parents, community and commercial interests. And of course it would call for a greater scope and authority to shape and to make crucial decisions locally. But it would also give priority to the educational talents and aptitudes of persons over the so-called needs of the economy. This order of priority would, moreover, be much more promising, even in terms of economics and the nurturing of resilience and enterprise, than is the utilitarian creed of 'performativity' which is now being internationally urged on schools, often with an urbane plausibility, but yet with an insistence scarcely less forceful than that manifested by a metaphysics of totality during the Middle Ages.

The Integrity of Higher Education

Higher education is vulnerable in a particular way to the mercenary motives of the market. The idea that the first function of the modern university is to fuel the 'economy's' need for advanced expertise, so as to maximise its 'performativity', has made enormous strides in recent years. It warrants – in a manner which is scarcely tacit any longer – the progressive transfer of authorship of research projects to bodies whose first concerns are quite other than the university's traditional commitment to the disinterested search for truth. It also tends to make a cinderella type enterprise of the university's commitments to adult and community education. To make these criticisms however is not to argue that the university should sunder its research efforts from any connection with the commercial world. Campus-industry partnerships have frequently brought credit and distinction on those who have been earnestly engaged in them, and employment to many others, without compromising or sequestering the spirit of research itself. But where such partnerships become asymmetrical, where one party can enforce possessive designs on the other, then the university's purposes have already been violated. This remains true, moreover, even if university authorities acquiesce in, or indeed promote, partnerships which allow research findings to become the confidential property of commercial concerns. And this problem is not contained by the bounds of any nation state. The most promising research teams can be lured by the most enticing of inducements from overseas.

So government declarations to respect the 'autonomy of the university' can at best be counted as well-meaning innocence, or more seriously as culpable negligence, unless governments at *international* level frame and enforce resolutions which allow the university earnestly to pursue 'truth in its infinite variety', as Karl Jaspers put it. But for their part universities have to show that the resources received from governments or through research partnerships are judiciously and fruitfully used. Only by a painstaking and strictly monitored commitment to the highest standards of research and accountability can higher learning be safeguarded from the threat of colonisation which is an ever present reality in most fields of advanced research in our own day.[1] Only thus, moreover, can the university make any significant progress in building an ethos which allows its students and teachers to share in what is possibly the most enduring benefit of higher learning: a well-versed humility in the face of the ventursome infinity of knowledge – even in a single field. Socrates, who has remained a presence throughout our enquiry, would probably put this more simply: the deepening of understanding that comes with an educated sense of our own ignorance.

Notes:

1. For a further exploration of this issue, see John Coolahan's contribution to the CRE conference proceedings mentioned in note No.5 above, titled 'Regional Implications: the Irish university perspective', *CRE-Action No.102*, (Geneva: 1993) pp.21-39.

Bibliography

Abelard, Peter *The Letters of Abelard and Heloise* translated with an Introduction by Betty Radice (Penguin Classics 1974)

Abelard, Peter *Sic et Non* (in Latin) edited by Blanche Boyer and Richard Mc Keon (Chicago: University of Chicago Press in 1977)

Akenson, D.H.*The Irish Education Experiment – The national system of education in the nineteenth century* (London: Routledge and Kegan Paul, 1970)

Allen, R.T. *The Education of Autonomous Man* (Aldershot: Avebury, 1992).

Apple, Michael W. *Education and Power* (Boston: Routledge and Kegan Paul, 1982)

Aquinas, Thomas *Summa Theologiae* translated by the English Dominican Fathers (London: Blackfriars, in association with Eyre & Spottiswoode, 1963-1974)

Arendt, Hannah *The Human Condition* (Chicago: University of Chicago Press, 1958)

Aronowitz, Stanley & Giroux, Henry *Education Under Siege – The Conservative, Liberal and Radical Debate over Schooling* (London: Routledge and Kegan Paul, 1985).

Aristotle, *Nicomachean Ethics* translated by J.A.K. Thompson, revised by H. Trendennick with an Introduction by J. Barnes (London: Penguin, 1976 edition)

Aristotle, *Politics* translated by T.A. Sinclair, revised with an Introduction by T.J. Saunders (London: Penguin, 1981 edition)

Augustine, *Confessions* translated with an Introduction by R.S. Pine-Coffin (New York: Dorset Press, 1986)

Augustine, *De Civitate Dei* (The City of God) Bks. I-XXII, in seven volumes, with various translators. (London UK and Cambridge, Mass: Heinemann and Harvard University Press - Loeb Classical Library: 1957-1972)

Augustine, *De Magistro* (The Teacher) translated by Robert P. Russell, included in Volume 59 of the series *The Fathers of the Church* (Washington: Catholic University of America, 1968)

Bernstein, Richard J. *Beyond Objectivism and Relativism: Science, Hermeneutics and Praxis* (Oxford: Basil Blackwell, 1983)

Bernstein, Richard J. (ed.) *Habermas and Modernity* (Cambridge: Polity Press, in association with Basil Blackwell, Oxford, 1985)

Bernstein, Richard J. *The New Constellation: The Ethical-Political Horizons of Modernity / Postmodernity* (Cambridge: Polity Press, in association with Basil Blackwell, Oxford 1991)

Blake, Nigel 'Modernity and Cultural Pluralism' in *Journal of Philosophy of Education* Vol.26, No.1, 1992, pp.39-50)

Bourdieu, P. & Passeron, J.C. *Reproduction in Education, Society and Culture* translated by Richard Nice, with Foreword by Tom Bottomore (London: Sage, 1977)

Boyd, William *The History of Western Education* revised by E.J. King. (London: Adam & Charles Black, 1966 edition)

Bronowski, J.& Mazlish, B. *The Western Intellectual Tradition* (Harmondsworth: Pelican, 1963)

Buchmann, Margret & Floden, Robert E. *Detachment and Concern — Conversations in the Philosophy of Teaching and Teacher Education* (New York: Teachers' College Press, Columbia University, 1993)

Carr, Wilfred & Kemmis, Stephen *Becoming Critical – Education, Knowledge and Action Research* (Lewes: Falmer Press, 1986)

Caputo, John D. *Radical Hermeneutics: Repetition, Deconstruction and the Hermeneutic Project* (Bloomington & Indianapolis: Indiana University Press, 1987)

Cicero, *On the Good Life: Selected Writings of Cicero* translated by M.Grant (London: Penguin, 1971)

Coolahan, John *Irish Education – History and Structure* (Dublin: Institute of Public Administration, 1981)

Coolahan, John 'Fact and Imagination in the Battle for the Books' in *Studies in Education* Vol. 4, No. 2, 1986. (Dublin: School of Education, Trinity College)

Conference of Rectors Europe (CRE) *CRE-Action* No.102 (Geneva: CRE,1993)

Curtis, S.J & Boultwood, M.E.A. *A Short History of Educational Ideas* (Slough: University Tutorial Press 1953/1977)

Department of Education and Science (UK)*Teaching Quality*, Her Majesty's Stationery Office, 1993

Derrida, Jacques *Margins of Philosophy* translated by Alan Bass (Chicago: University of Chicago Press, 1972)

Derrida, Jacques *Writing and Difference* translated by Alan Bass (London: Routledge & Kegan Paul, 1978)

Derrida, Jacques 'The Principle of Reason: The University in the Eyes of its Pupils', in *Diacritics*, Vol.XIX, 1984, pp.3-20

Descartes, René *Discourse on Method* and *Meditations on First Philosophy* translated and edited with an Introduction by F.E. Sutcliffe (London: Penguin, 1968)

Dewey, John *Democracy and Education* (New York: Macmillan, 1916, 1944).

Dewey, John *Experience and Education* (New York: Macmillan, 1938, 1963)

Dewey, John 'Experience, knowledge and value - a rejoinder', in *The Philosophy of John Dewey* P.A. Schilpp (ed.) (New York, Tudor Publishing Company, 1951), p.530

Dunne, Joseph *Back to the Rough Ground – 'Phronesis' and 'Techne' in Modern Philosophy and in Aristotle* (Notre Dame: University of Notre Dame Press, 1993)

Dunne, Joseph 'What's the Good of Education?' in *Partnership and the Benefits of Learning – Symposium* edited by Pádraig Hogan (Maynooth: Educational Studies Association of Ireland, 1995) pp.60-82

Elliott, John *Action Research for Educational Change* (Milton Keynes: Open University Press, 1991)

Ellman, Richard *James Joyce* (Oxford: Oxford University Press, revised edition 1983)

Everard, B. & Morris, G, *Effective School Management* Second Edition (London: Paul Chapman, 1990)

Everhart, Robert *The In-Between Years: Student Life in a Junior High School* (Santa Barbara: Graduate School of Education, University of California, 1979)

Freire, Paulo *Cultural Action for Freedom* (Harmondsworth: Penguin, 1972)

Freire, Paulo *Pedagogy of the Oppressed* (Harmondsworth: Penguin, 1972)

Fullan, Michael G. & Stiegelbaur, Suzanne *The New Meaning of Educational Change* (London: Cassell, 1991)

Fullan, Michael *Change Forces: Probing the Depths of Educational Change* (London: Falmer Press, 1992)

Gadamer, Hans-Georg *Truth and Method* (*Wahrheit und Methode* 1960) translated by Garrett Barden and John Cumming (London: Sheed and Ward, 1975)

Gadamer, Hans-Georg *Philosophical Hermeneutics* translated by David E. Linge (Berkeley: University of California Press, 1977)

Gadamer, Hans-Georg *Philosophical Apprenticeships* translated by Robert R. Sullivan (Cambridge Mass.: MIT Press, 1985)

Gadamer, Hans-Georg *The Idea of the Good in Platonic-Aristotelian Philosophy* translated with an Introduction by P. Christopher Smith (New Haven: Yale University Press, 1986)

Gadamer, Hans-Georg *The Relevance of the Beautiful and Other Essays* translated by Nicholas Walker; edited with an introduction by Robert Bernasconi (Cambridge: Cambridge University Press, 1986)

Gaden, T.G. *On the participant's identification with his activity and the value of specialisation in post-primary education* (unpublished Ph.D. thesis, University College Dublin 1985)

Gardner, Howard *Frames of Mind – The Theory of Multiple Intelligences* (London: Paladin, 1983)

Gardner, Peter 'Religious Upbringing and the liberal ideal of religious autonomy' in *Journal of Philosophy of Education*, Vol.22, No. 1, 1988, pp.89-105

Gardner, Peter 'Personal Autonomy and Religious Upbringing: the "problem"' in *Journal of Philosophy of Education*, Vol. 25, No.1, 1991, pp.69-81

Government of Ireland *Education for a Changing World* Green Paper 1992 (Dublin: Stationery Office)

Goverment of Ireland *Charting our Education Future* White Paper 1995 (Dublin: Stationery Office)

Habermas, Jürgen *Knowledge and Human Interests* translated by Jeremy J. Shapiro (London: Heinemann 1972)

Habermas, Jürgen 'What is Universal Pragmatics' in his*Communication and the Evolution of Society* translated by Thomas McCarthy (Boston: Beacon Press, 1979).

Habermas, Jürgen'*The Theory of Communicative Action* Volume One, translated by Thomas McCarthy (Boston: Beacon Press, Vol.1, 1984; Vol 2, 1987)

Habermas, Jürgen *The Philosophical Discourse of Modernity* translated by F.Lawrence, (Cambridge: Polity Press, in association with Basil Blackwell, Oxford,1987)

Habermas, Jürgen *Moral Consciousness and Communicative Action* translated by Christian Lenhardt and Shierry Weber Nicholson (Cambridge: Polity Press, in association with Basil Blackwell, Oxford, 1990)

Heidegger, Martin *Being and Time*, translated by John Macquarrie and Edward Robinson (Oxford: Blackwell, 1973)

Heidegger, Martin 'The Thinker as Poet' in *Poetry, Language, Thought* trans. and intro. by Albert Hofstadter (New York: Harper and Row, 1971)

Heidegger, Martin 'The Origin of the Work of Art' in *Poetry, Language, Thought* translated and introduced by Albert Hofstadter (New York: Harper and Row, 1975)

Heidegger, Martin 'The Question Concerning Technology' in *Martin Heidegger - Basic Writings* edited with an Introduction by David Farrell Krell (London: Routledge & Kegan Paul, 1978)

Hogan, Pádraig 'The Sovereignty of Learning, the Fortunes of Schooling and the New Educational Virtuousness', in the *British Journal of Educational Studies*, Vol.XXXX, No. 2, 1992

Hogan, Pádraig (ed.) *Partnership and the Benefits of Learning - Symposium on Philosophical Issues in Educational Policy* (Maynooth: Educational Studies Association of Ireland, 1995)

Hollinger, Robert (ed.) *Hermeneutics and Praxis* (Notre Dame: University of Notre Dame Press, 1985)

Huizinga, Johan *Erasmus of Rotterdam - with a selection of the Letters of Erasmus* translated by F. Hopman and Barbara Flower (London: Phaidon Press, 1952)

Jaspers, Karl *The Idea of the University* (1945) translated by H.A.T. Reiche & H. F. Vanderschmit, and edited by K.W. Deutsche (London: Peter Owen, undated)

Kant, Immanuel, *The Critique of Practical Reason and Other Writings in Moral Philosophy* translated and edited with an Introduction by Lewis White Beck (Chicago: University of Chicago Press, 1949)

Kearney, Richard *Dialogues with Contemporary Continental Thinkers* (Manchester: Manchester University Press, 1984)

Ker, Ian *John Henry Newman - A Biography* (Oxford: Clarendon Press, 1988)

Kierkegaard, Soren *The Concept of Irony - with constant reference to Socrates* (Bloomington: Indiana University Press, 1982)

Lawton, Denis *Education, Culture and the National Curriculum* (London: Hodder & Stoughton, 1989)

Lawton, Denis *Education and Politics in the 1990s: Conflict or Consensus?* (London: Falmer Press, 1992)

Locke, John *Some Thoughts Concerning Education* (1693) edited by Peter Gay (New York: Teachers College Press, 1971 edition)

Lynch, Kathleen, *The Hidden Curriculum: Reproduction in Education, A Reappraisal* (London: Falmer Press, 1989)

Lyotard, Jean François *The Postmodern Condition: A Report on Knowledge* translated by G. Bennington & B. Massumi, with a Foreword by F. Jameson (Manchester: Manchester University Press, 1992 edition)

McGrath, Fergal *The Consecration of Learning* (Dublin: Gill & Son, 1962)

MacIntyre, Alasdair *After Virtue: a study in moral theory* (London: Duckworth, second edition 1985)

MacIntyre, Alasdair *Whose Justice? Which Rationality?* (London: Duckworth, 1988)

MacIntyre, Alasdair 'The Idea of an Educated Public' in *Education and Values* Graham Haydon (ed.) (London: University of London Institute of Education, 1987)

McLaughlin, T.H. 'Peter Gardner on Religious Upbringing and the Liberal Ideal of Religious Autonomy' in *Journal of Philosophy of Education*, Vol. 24, No.1, 1990, pp.107-125

MacLure, Stuart *Education Reformed: A Guide to the Education Reform Act 1988* (Sevenoaks: Hodder & Stoughton, Headway series, 1988).

McCarthy, Thomas *Ideals and Illusions: On Reconstruction and*

Deconstruction in Contemporary Critical Theory (Cambridge, Mass: MIT Press, 1993)

McNamara, Gerry, Williams, Kevin & Herron, Don (eds) *Achievement and Aspiration: Curricular Initiatives in Irish Post-Primary Education in the 1980s* (Dublin: Drumcondra Teachers' Centre, 1990)

McRobbie, Angela 'Working Class Girls and the Culture of Femininity' in *Women Take Issue*, Women's Studies group (ed.) (London: Hutchinson, 1978) pp.96-108

Matthews, Michael R., *The Marxist Theory of Schooling: A study of epistemology and education* (Brighton: Harvester, 1980)

Mill, John Stuart & Bentham, Jeremy *Utilitatianism and other Essays*, (London: Penguin, 1987 edition)

Minowitz, Peter *Profits, Priests & Princes: Adam Smith's Emancipation of Economics from Politics and Religion* (Stanford: Stanford University Press, 1993).

Montaigne, Michel de *Essays* translated with an Introduction by J.M. Cohen (London: Penguin, 1958)

Murphy, Daniel *Comenius – A Critical Reassessment of his Life and Work* (Dublin: Irish Academic Press, 1995)

National Commission on Excellence in Education, *A Nation at Risk: The imperative for educational reform* (Washington D.C.: 1993)

Newman, John Henry *Apologia Pro Vita Sua* (1865) 1891 edition (London: Longman's Green & Co.); 1973 edition, with an Introduction by Maisie Ward (London: Sheed and Ward).

Newman, John Henry *The Idea of a University* (1852, 1873, 1889), edited with an Introduction by Ian Ker, (Oxford: Clarendon Press, 1976)

Nietzsche, Friedrich *Thus Spoke Zarathustra*, translated with an Introduction by R.J. Hollingdale (London: Penguin, 1986 edition)

Nietzsche, Friedrich *Beyond Good and Evil* translated by R.J. Hollingdale, with an Introduction by Michael Tanner (London: Penguin, 1990 edition)

Nietzsche, Friedrich *On the Genealogy of Morals* translated by Walter Kaufmann and R.J. Hollingdale (New York: Vintage Press, 1968)

Nussbaum, Martha *The Fragility of Goodness: Luck and ethics in Greek tragedy and Philosophy* (Cambridge: Cambridge University Press, 1986)

Oakeshott, Michael 'The Idea of a University' in Timothy Fuller, (ed.) *The Voice of Liberal Learning - Michael Oakeshott on Education* (New Haven: Yale University Press, 1989)

Oakeshott, Michael *Rationalism in Politics and Other Essays* (London: Methuen, 1962)

OECD,*Schools and Quality: An International Report* (Paris: OECD, 1989)

OECD, *Reviews of National Policies for Education: Ireland* (Paris: OECD, 1991)

O' Reilly, Barney 'Economics, Politics and the Philosophy of Education in Ireland' in *Partnership and the Benefits of Learning* edited by Pádaig Hogan, (Maynooth: Educational Studies Association of Ireland, 1995)

Piltz, Anders *The World of Medieval Learning* translated by David Jones (Oxford: Basil Blackwell, 1981)

Plato: *The Dialogues of Plato*, translated by B.Jowett (New York: Random House, 1937 edition, two volumes)

Plato, *The Last Days of Socrates*, (including the Dialogues *Euthyphro, Apology, Crito, Phaedo*) translated with an Introduction by Hugh Trendennick (London: Penguin, 1969 edition)

Plato, *Gorgias*, translated with an Introduction by Walter Hamilton (London: Penguin, 1976 edition)

Plato, *Protagoras* and *Meno*, translated by W.K.C.Guthrie (London: Penguin, 1980 edition)

Popper, Karl *The Open Society and its Enemies: Volume 1 – The Spell of Plato* (London: Routledge and Kegan Paul 1950, 1980)

Popper, Karl *Objective Knowledge: An Evolutionary Approach* (Oxford: Clarendon Press, 1972, 1979)

Popper, Karl *Conjectures and Refutations –The Growth of Scientific Knowledge* (London: Routledge & Kegan Paul, 1963, 1972)

Prigogine, Ilya & Stenger, Isabelle *Order out of Chaos – Man's New Dialogue with Nature* (English edition, London: Fontana, 1985)

Quintillian, *Institutio Oratoria* translated by H.E. Butler (London: Heinemann, Loeb Classical Library, 1969 edition)

Rorty, Richard *Philosophy and the Mirror of Nature* (Oxford: Basil Blackwell, 1980)

Rousseau, Jean Jacques *Émile* translated by Barbara Foxley (London: Dent/Everyman 1974)

Rusk, Robert R. *Doctrines of the Great Educators* (fifth edition, edited by J.Scotland; London: Macmillan 1979)

Sarup, Madan *Marxism and Education* (London: Routledge and Kegan Paul, 1978)

Screech, M.A, *Erasmus: Ecstacy and The Praise of Folly* (London Penguin/Peregrine 1988)

Steiner, George, *Real Presences: Is there anything **in** what we say?* (London: Faber and Faber, 1989)

Tawney, R.H. *Religion and the Rise of Capitalism* (London: Murray, 1943)

Taylor, Charles *Sources of the Self: The Making of the Modern Identity* (Cambridge: Cambridge University Press, 1989)

Vlastos, Gregory *Socrates – Ironist and Moral Philosopher* (Cambridge: Cambridge University Press, 1991)

Walsh, Paddy *Education and Meaning – Philosophy in Practice* (London: Cassell, 1993)

Watson, Gerard *Greek Philosophy and the Christian Notion of God* (Dublin: Columba Press, 1994)

Weber, MaxThe Protestant Ethic and the Spirit of Capitalism translatedby Talcott Parsons (London: Allen and Unwin 1976 edition)

Williams, Kevin 'Usefulness and Liberal Learning' in *Religion, Education and the Constitution* edited by Dermot A. Lane (Dublin: The Columba Press, 1992) pp.34-59

Williams, Kevin *Assessment: A Discussion Paper* (Dublin: Association of Secondary Teachers Ireland, 1992)

Willis, Paul *Learning to Labour - How working clas kids get working class jobs* (Aldershot: Gower Publishing Company, 1977, 1980)

Woodward, W.H. *Desiderius Erasmus - Concerning the the Aim and Method of Education* (Cambridge: Cambridge University Press 1904)

Index